AF650492

KABDWAL BOOK INTERNATIONAL (KBI Publishers) was established on 28th February' 2003 by Naveen Chand Kabdwal. Our journey began by marketing traditional technical and management books. In 7 years of working, we realized the need for International Standards. Result of this need, KABDWAL BOOK INTERNATIONAL entered in the field of foreign standards.

With our continuous efforts of pursuing the needs of International Standards, fair and smooth dealing, most of the international agencies gave us the opportunity to deal directly for their published standards.

In 2014 we published our first book and after a hiatus of 8 years we resumed our journey in publishing.

HISTORY OF HRD IN INDIA

Thank you for choosing a KBI Publishers product!
If you have any comment, observation or feedback,
I would like to personally hear from you.

Please write to me at **kbipublishers@kabdwalbook.com**

Rajesh Raheja, Publishing Head at KBI Publishers.

Bulk Sales

KBI Publishers offers special discounts.
We also make available special imprints
and excerpts from our books on demand
for purchase of books in bulk

For Orders and enquiries, write to us at:

Marketing Department
KBI Publishers (A unit of Kabdwal Book International)
TEX Centre Premises, Unit No. L – 3, 4, 5 & 6
4th Floor, Narayan Plaza
26-A, Chandivali Road, Near Boomerang Building,
Andheri East, Mumbai 400 072
Tel: 022 4802 5368

E-mail us at **order@kabdwalbook.com**

HISTORY OF HRD IN INDIA

A Tale of Two Institutions

Compiled by Dr. T.V. Rao
Chairman, T. V. Rao Learning Systems (TVRLS)

Project Associate
Shachi Kotecha
Summer Intern, T. V. Rao Learning Systems (TVRLS)

INTERNATIONAL

First published by **Naveen Chand Kabdwal for Kabdwal Book International (KBI Publishers) in 2025.**

INTERNATIONAL

Kabdwal Book International
TEX Centre Premises, Unit No. L – 3, 4, 5 & 6
4th Floor, Narayan Plaza
26-A, Chandivali Road, Near Boomerang Building,
Andheri East, Mumbai 400 072, Maharashtra, India
www.kabdwalbook.com / www.kbipublishers.com

Name: Rao T.V.
Title: History of HRD in India / T.V. Rao
Printed by SAP Print Solutions Pvt. Ltd, Mumbai 400013 India

ISBN: 978-81-985-2319-8 (PB)

KBI Team: Rajesh Raheja, Syed Husain Mendhdi Naqvi

Contents

Dedicated to the memory of

Dr. Udai Pareek
Mr. M R R Nair
Fr. E. Abraham
and
Countless others who spent countless hours of their time and worked with dedication for NHRDN and AHRD

Preface

This is about the relevance of this book today. The history of the HRD movement was well described in an earlier article by Udai Pareek and TV Rao. The history is incomplete without reference to starting of the first HRD department in L&T in 1975 and the HR Function in 1977. Since then XLRI Center for HRD, National HRD Network and Academy of HRD have been started. The famous Indian Soicety for Training and Development started in 1970 and the National Institute of Personnel Management started in 1982 have made their own contributions as professional bodies that promote HRD and Personnel functions. Mr. Baburaj Nair documented well the first 10 years of the National HRD Network in his book "Growth of a Professional Association: National HRD Network" in 1996.

TVRLS appointed a summer trainee SHACHI KOTECHA to work on the history of the HRD movement. I have handed over all my files to her and she scanned through them and prepared a good report. Ever since that report was made available, I wanted to publish the report. It is only now I felt that there is a need to communicate to the outside world what went behind the building of the National HRD Network (NHRDN) and the Academy of HRD (AHRD). Both are registered societies and trusts registered in Ahmedabad. The document prepared by the summer trainee stops at the year 2003. This covers almost the first 20 years of NHRDN and the first 12 years of AHRD.

After the year 2003, NHRDN got stabilized with excellent leadership starting with Dr. Arvind Agrawal. Subsequent presidents of NHRDN and their teams have done a marvelous job in stabilizing expanding and growing NHRDN. The current president Prem Singh has extended NHRDN to universities and is doing a great job. The previous president S V Nathan extended NHRDN to other countries and established chapters. The President before him Krish Shankar stabilised the less stable NHRDN, which was in a low key in those years and brought it back to life. The previous presidents like Ram

Kumar, Mr. Roy, NS Rajan, SY Siddiqui, Aquil Busrai, Dwarakanath and Santrupt Mishra have done a marvelous job in giving Credibility to HRD network and also offering qualitative services to the HR fraternity. I would say the last decade and a half has been golden years of NHRD, despite the pandemic. NHRDN has proved itself and established itself as a number one professional body in the country. It has established a solid secretariat with a Director General and a number of staff offering various services. These services include periodic publication of a newsletter, journal, which is now published by Sage publications, many podcasts, webinars, a number of programmes and other social media-based services. Conferences continue to be at the same pace as before. There are more conferences, seminars, and other events offered by various chapters. The decentralization move started by Dr. Udai Pareek has yielded lot of positive results and today the chapters function on their own. There have been several accomplishments by the NHRDN. They collaborate with other bodies, government, and various other institutions. However, across the last few years, the divide between the NHRDN and AHRD that started as an extension and academic center of NHRDN has widened rather than getting narrow. Each of them operate on their own and or perusing the same goals with different instruments. The AHRD has its own board. Though the NHRDN president is a member of the AHRD board, he rarely attends their meetings. AHRD also does not go out of way to ensure that the network office is informed in advance of its meetings, AHRD Director used to be on the NHRDN Board which was discontinued for lack of formalization. AHRD has successfully pursued its mission of contributing to the knowledge generation and dissemination through its program. By now there are about 50 who got their Doctorate or fellowship title and another 70 are enrolled in various batches of the academy. Financially AHRD runs with a hand-to-mouth existence and largely runs with sleek staff- a director and four staff. On the other hand, NHRDN has a strong secretariat, and good number of staff besides unpaid volunteers and office bearers and various Boards, chapters and leaders across the country. If the same funding that is available to NHRDN is available to AHRD and they work together, the history of HRD could have been altogether different in India. The contributions would have been on a large scale and more.

I do not blame anyone for this widening gap and lack of integration. In fact, this is one of the purposes of this book to demonstrate how NHRDN and AHRD leverage each other in earlier years. One of the points of both these organizations is that they share the same objectives. AHRD was started as an academic wing of NHRD. The need to maintain itself as an academic institution required it to have its own board and membership like any other institution. The last 30 years have demonstrated that institutions started for the same purpose grow in their own ways and synergy does get affected. This is not only true with NHRDN and AHRD, but also true with IIMs and IITs which compete with each other more than they collaborate. They do collaborate at faculty level. They collaborate through common agenda. They collaborate through appointments of faculty who are graduates from each other's Institute. Many processes in the nation help IIMs and IITs to grow. The same way it is okay if an NHRDN and AHRD to grow in their own ways, it is for both these bodies to think of how they can leverage each other. The President of NHRDN as well as the board of AHRD are independent. The Founders of both these bodies are common and are well-established leaders in their own fields. They donate their time to both these bodies. The secretariat of both these bodies have a wide gap in terms of the number, activities, compensation patterns, and so on. The AHRD has perhaps the largest space and a promise of land donated by some industries which are in dispute. NHRD also has a building at Hyderabad, which is under construction for over a decade. It looks that Buildings don't matter but activities matter. Both of them are doing activities as per their capacity and are doing a good job. Both of them are trying to have collaborations with other agencies like AHRD is trying to have collaboration with universities for granting degrees and NHRDN is collaboration with government agencies, consulting companies and other organizations to promote its knowledge and skill base. As a common co-founder of both these bodies, I wish they leverage each other. This is perhaps my and Dr. Pareek's dream.

One of the purposes of this book is to demonstrate and make available to the larger world. How both these organisations functioned at one time and the crucible experiences these bodies experienced in the process of their building and their outcomes.

This book will demonstrate how institutions are built, not by one person, but by many people. This book will also demonstrate the number of people that are involved behind the scenes in institution building. My estimate is that at least 1000 HR professionals and over a hundred of scholars have contributed to the building of both these institutions across 30 to 40 years.

In addition to the people, what matters in the institutional building is the mission, the purpose and the programs. All these have been enormous in the last 30 to 40 years. This book focuses only on the first 20 years to make this point. I hope you will enjoy reading this book and find it of some use and providing insights into institution, building process, collaborative work, comparisons and conflicts on both sides of growth of these two institutions. I have made no attempt in this book to document the accomplishments of NHRDN or AHRD. Both of them have accomplished a lot. For example, both of them have brought out a large number of publications like books and reports and PhD thesis. They are all available in the library of the Academy of HRD. Interested people may write to them and get access to the same. I hope you will find this document of some relevance and use. To enhance the use of this document and to demonstrate the bundle of data that is produced by NHRDN and available at AHRD have been given at the end of this book. A list of abstracts of papers published in the in the early years of NHRDN are provided as an illustration of the fund of knowledge generated by NHRDN and stored at AHRD. All the books and publications of NHRDN may not be available at NHRD head office, despite my personal effort to consolidate and share the same but may be available at AHRD. This symbolizes the intended synergy between these two institutions. If this book service the purpose of one day, both these organizations working together, I am sure it's founders, Dr. Udai Pareek, Fr. E. Abraham, and Mr. M R.R. Nair, who are in heaven will rejoice. All the best for well-integrated NHRDN and AHRD

TV Rao

Cofounder NHRDN and AHRD

This book is dedicated to the Memory of Dr. Udai Pareek, Fr. E. Abraham and Mr. M. R. R. Nair

Past office bearers, Co-founders of NHRDN and AHRD.

Introduction

Institutions like people, in their life journey go through some defining experiences that build institutions and make them what they eventually turn out to be. Some of these could be exhilarating or traumatic to various degrees and are foundations to institutional identity. Good Institutions literally get baked through these intense experiences and emerge stronger and transformed. Bennis & Thomas called such transformative events, 'crucibles', after the vessels medieval alchemists used in their attempts to turn base metal into gold. Crucibles could be violent and sometimes even life-threatening. They could also be positive yet profoundly challenging by the demanding world. Institution builders learn from both of these experiences and share for making others seasoned Institution Builders. Pareek, Udai & Rao, Talam. (2008) in their article "From a sapling to the forest: the saga of the development of HRD in India" have narrated some of the events. This chapter heavily borrows from "My Institution Building Experiences at IIMA, NHRDN and AHRD (A reflective essay in honor of Prof. Ishwar Dayal) by T V Rao and the paper by Pareek and Rao to narrate a brief history of HRD in India. Part 1 of this book is devoted to presentation of some historical facts and events. This also presents some dilemmas and events which can qualify both as points in the life of an institution outlined by the author in his book on Effective People (Rao, 2014 and 2024). They may also qualify to be called as Crucible events outlined by Bennis and Thomas (2002). Bennis and Thomas outlined crucible events in the life of a leader. I would like to hypothesize that what is true of leaders is also true of institutions. The crucible events are faced mostly by institutional leaders, founders, heads of Institutions, Chairmen, Boards, faculty, staff, Students or learners, community, policy makes and also society at large. Some crucible event are faced by many stakeholders at the same time. For example, when an institution goes through financial crisis or when campus disturbances occur, cyclones, earth quakes and other natural calamities strike. Some of the crucibles are faced by one or more of the stake holders. For example, student protests will be faced differently by different stake holders. In the initial stages of crucible experiences are they are faced by Founders and later by those appointed to lead. Ethical issues create testing times for leaders and also affect institutional brand or image in community. Professional bodies have different issues. Specially if the profession is being built and most people are voluntary workers and are there by their choice and not for any pecuniary benefits, the issues faced are different. Most professional besides are managed and led by a professionals from academics and the world of practice. This creates its own dynamics.

In the first part of this book, an attempt is made to trace the history of HRD in India in the context of two bodies that tried to create history: The National HRD Network and the Academy of HRD. This is largely based on accounts shared by the author earlier in papers. In the second part of this book, we present many events that have led to the formation and stabilization as growth of these two bodies NHRDN and AHRD. The crucible experiences covered are not exhaustive but anecdotal. They are presented here as evidence or incidents from minutes of meetings, HRD Newsletter, Personal emails from the files of Dr. T. V. Rao, brochures and announcements etc.

Part 1 is an account of the growth and development of HRD function in India. What started in the mid-seventies as a conceptualization of an Integrated HRD system to change the performance appraisal systems in a large engineering company, resulted in the establishment of HRD departments in many firms. Further dissemination and perseverance resulted in the establishment of a Center for HRD, and subsequently the birth of a Professional body and later an Academic Institution. The authors describe the growth in eight stages and conclude the path for the future is in moving towards National HR policies and other social sectors.

PART 1

The Saga of HRD in India from Sapling to Forest

This part is largely from Pareek and Rao (2008) paper of the same topic. Some additional information has been added in parts.

The notion of integrated HRD systems in India is perhaps the oldest among all countries in terms of both conceptualization and implementation. At a time when the term HRD has not yet achieved its full meaning, in early seventies the authors of this article conceptualized this as an integrated system to drive organizational change. It was first implemented successfully in one organization, and then spread to other organizations as a mission by the authors at the Indian Institute of Management, Ahmedabad (IIMA), with the support of other CEOs and several other academicians who joined them later. What started as a system designed for one company found its way to other companies, resulted in the creation of a Chair, the establishment of a Center for HRD at an Academic institute and subsequently the formation of a large professional body of the stature of SHRM and ASTD in the USA. This essay is a personal account of this saga of introducing a new HRD function in the mid-seventies, and its diffusion and institutionalization at the national level. Both singly, and together, the authors have been contributing to the development of HRD in India[1]. The evolution and institutionalization of HRD in India is described in eight stages.

[1] Udai will be used for Udai Pareek and TV for T V Rao throughout this article.

Stage I: The Beginnings (1974–1975)

In 1973 after joining the Indian Institute of Management, Ahmedabad as the Faculty, Udai worked on the problems of reorganization in Larsen and Toubro (L&T), an engineering company. While conducting role clarification and role negotiation exercises, Udai realized the need of working on the larger issues of development of people. With TV Rao, later joining the Faculty of IIM, Ahmedabad, Udai shared this concern, and both TV and Udai decided to work on designing a new way of developing people in an organization. They presented a proposal to the Chairman. Shri N.M. Desai, Chairman L & T, arranged the discussion with the top group and accepted the proposal to try out the new system of developing people. Performance appraisal became a core system around which HRD systems were woven. Performance planning, analysis, review, coaching, development etc. became systems linked to role clarity, role efficacy, individual growth, integration, training, career development, and OD activities. A number of subsystems were developed and grouped into HRD. Around this time in the USA the new term HRD was being propagated enlarging the scope of Training.

Two main features of the proposed concept of HRD were that HRD dealt with all the human units of the organization (from persons to the total organization), and It was value-based. The following 14 principles were shared with the organization as the guiding principles for designing the HR function. The HRD systems should:

1. Help the company to increase enabling capabilities
2. Help individuals to recognize their potential and help them to contribute their best towards the various organizational roles they are expected to perform
3. Help maximize individual autonomy through increased responsibility
4. Facilitate decentralization through delegation and shared responsibility
5. Facilitate participative decision making
6. Attempt to balance the current organizational culture with changing culture

7. Balance between differentiation and integration
8. Balance between specialization of the function with its diffusion into the others
9. Ensure responsibility for the function
10. Build upon feedback and reinforcement mechanisms
11. Maintain a balance between quantification and qualitative decisions
12. Balance between external and internal help
13. Planed as an evolution of the function, and
14. Promote continuous review and renewal of the function

In sum the Integrated HRD systems approach designed by us had the following elements: (i) a separate and differentiated HRD department with full-time HRD staff. (ii) Six HRD subsystems including performance appraisal, Feedback and coaching, Potential identification and development, career development, Training and OD, (iii) Interlinkages between the various subsystems, (IV) designed with 14 principles in mind, and (v) linked to other subsystems of Human Resource Function.

The Factors of its Success

The implementation of the Integrated HRD systems approach in L&T was one of the most successful change management experiences in the organization. Several factors contributed to the success of change. Some of these are briefly mentioned below.

1. *Committed top:* The top management of L&T including its Chairman Mr. N. M. Desai, and founder Mr. Holk Larsen showed deep interest in re-designing the personnel system. L & T was a very successful company, and there was no apparent reason for it to think of a new system.
2. *Appointment of High level implementation task Force*: They promptly appointed a high level Task force headed by a General Manager along with some of the top management team as members. The task force functioned for nearly three years in introducing and monitoring the implementation of the system.

3. *Placement of the system at high level in the organization*: One of the conditions the authors stated for the success of the new function was its strategic placement. Generally at that time the personnel function was given low priority and was generally placed at the lower level in the organizations. This was the first company to assign a top level position to HRD in those years.
4. *The competent Head of the function*: While selecting a person to head the new function, it was strongly recommended that a very competent person should be given the responsibility. The CEO agreed to request a highly respected and competent Engineer (Mr. S. R. Subramaniam), to head the function. Mr. Subramaniam ensured thoroughness and effective implementation of the various parts of the new system. Subsequently Mr. Subramaniam became the CEO of the company. The success of the new function very much depended on the competent leadership provided in the organization. Since then L&T is a story of internal successions to lead the company. The current Chairman Mr. A. M. Naik was one of the input providers to the HRD system in the mid-seventies.
5. *The strong internal resource*: No change can succeed unless there is strong and competent internal resource to implement and monitor the change. Dr. Pereira, the first to head the HRD, combined his insightful experience in the organization with his academic competence and drive to search new ways of solving problems.
6. *Involvement of all levels of the organization*: The authors emphasized that the systems and processes being introduced must be discussed in various forms of employees, helping them to raise questions for any modification in the system as required. Workshops and seminars were held on the new systems and procedures. This facilitated the success of the system.
7. *Developing internal competence*: The Company needed several people to help in implementing the new system. It was necessary that the system and process were adopted with the help of key line managers. Therefore, an extensive training programme was organized to develop relevant competencies for implementing the systems. Over a hundred internal managers were developed to communicate the system all through the company. The term

L&T University was used informally by these members to represent the new education and learning they were facilitating through the HRD system.

Stage II: Spread to Other Strategic Organizations (1975–1978)

The State Bank of India (SBI) is the largest bank in India with around 0.2 million employees at that time. The new HRD system was also developed for the bank immediately after its reorganization by the Indian Institute of Management, Ahmedabad (IIMA) team. The Chairman of SBI took personal interest. Then the system was recommended for SBI and its associates, and their CEOs were so excited by the new concept that they suggested taking responsibility for introducing the system themselves! They promptly appointed HRD managers who were given the task of conducting organizational diagnosis studies and also revamping the performance appraisals make them HRD oriented. The implementation of HRD systems in SBI is the second most significant step. The authors of this article, as IIMA professors, facilitated the training of the HRD managers to conduct OD interventions and revamp their performance appraisal systems.

Stage III: Action Research in Implementing HRD Systems (1978–1979)

It is at this time that IIMA's former Director, Ravi Matthai on the Board of a public sector company Bharat Earth Movers Ltd. (BEML), suggested the company should think big and expand. They were making rail coaches and earth moving equipment with a turnover of Rupees 700 million. Prof. S. K. Bhattacharya another professor from IIMA worked with them and gave them a long-term plan which required developing human resources for making it happen. Udai gave them the conceptualization for the integrated HRD systems to move into the future. As BEML was debating about where to get the resource to head HRD, TV volunteered to join as General Manager and implement the systems recommended. Though a Defense Ministry undertaking, BEML Chairman showed the boldness to appoint a young professor in his early thirties to be general manager and pay him the highest salaries.

This is the most significant period of experimentation in a highly structured and public organization. The experiences were both successful and frustrating. The systems lasted as long as TV was associated but declined a few years after he returned back to IIMA. The experiences became most enriching and laid the foundation for a lot of insights into the implementation of HRD systems.

Stage IV: Dissemination Begins (1979–82)

Capitalizing on this experience both the authors offered the first workshop on HRD systems at the IIMA in 1979. A draft of their proposed book on Designing and Managing HR systems was circulated in this workshop. Later a course and a series of executive development programs were started by the authors at IIMA to popularize and promote HRD. Crompton Greaves, State Bank of India and its associates and a few other organizations followed this initiative and the authors worked as their consultants in introducing and implementing the HRD systems and starting new HRD departments separated from personnel. The spread of change to these strategic organizations has been well documented (Rao, 2004). IIMA played a significant role in this dissemination process.

Stage V: Institutionalization of Diffusion of Change (1982–1985)

At that time Udai went on a long consulting assignment, as USAID OD Advisor to the Health Department of the Government of Indonesia, TV continued the work of diffusing HRD-based change in India. Larsen & Toubro created a Chair Professorship in HRD at XLRI Institute Jamshedpur, which was taken up by T V in 1983. Included in the conditions of his appointment as the L&T Chair Professor, TV got approval to start a Center for HRD at XLRI and also to give an annual public seminar on his work. T V used this to get L&T to host the 4-day seminar at Mumbai, where more people could attend. The seminar focused on the recent experiences in

HRD. About 40 persons participated in the seminar. TV presented the integrated HRD model developed at L&T. The HR Head of L&T spoke about how it was being implemented. The seminar explored what was happening and not happening in HRD, how many organizations were not able to understand the right spirit of HRD, and the helplessness of HRD managers in convincing some CEOs etc. A number of success stories were also shared and there was new enthusiasm in all the members. In response to a suggestion from TV who was leaving XLRI to return to IIMA, the members proposed the continuation of the Initiative under a new banner. Several suggestions were given. The discussions were steered by TV towards setting up a professional body outside the Institutional framework of Management schools (IIMA or XLRI etc.) to facilitate learning of practitioners on a continuing basis from each other. This lead to the conceptualizing of the National HRD Network. It was also agreed that different cities should have such Networks. A newsletter was initiated to disseminate the new knowledge about HRD. It was agreed to have one intellectual article by an academician, one essay profiling in details the practices of accompany, a few case lets of problems and issues, which may be posed to the reader, some references and bibliography and news items. In the initial years of the newsletter, the HRD center coordinators Fr. E Abraham and TV Rao managed to get every number sponsored by a company committed to HRD and having done some good work worthy of sharing. It would meet the cost of printing 2000 copies of the newsletter and also mailing it free to all HRD chiefs and CEOs in the country. L&T was the natural choice as everyone was talking about L&T in relation to HRD. L & T readily agreed. The seminar proceedings were published as a book "Recent Experiences in HRD" and the formation of the Network was announced in 1985 through this book and the HRD Newsletter.

Stage VI: The Spread of HRD Network (1985–1990)

In the first newsletter edited by Fr. Abraham the idea of forming the HRD Network was announced. The authors worked with: State Bank of Patiala, Indian oil, Sundram Clayton, Hindustan Petroleum,

MMTC etc. and got the Newsletters sponsored and distributed free of cost to all potential members of the new body. While Fr. Abraham continued to coordinate the HRD Newsletter from XLRI, TV helped in setting up the National HRD Network (NHRDN) from IIMA. The South Indian chapter of NHRDN was launched at Madras with the help of the Madras Management Association which launched the first meeting of the chapter. Subsequently, the National HRD Network was Registered as a not for profit Society and a Charitable Trust in Ahmedabad.

The journey from then for the next five years has been that of hard work and perseverance. No one knew NHRDN and many did not see the reason for NHRDN when ISTD was serving the same purpose. Only those who saw the distinction between HRD and training appreciated the need. The First National Conference is a record of sorts. It had a full day devoted to CEO presentations.

While the preparations for the second conference began almost two years in advance the preparations of the election for the next President also began. The Director Personnel (Mr. M R R Nair) of Steel Authority of India showed a lot of support to HRD activities. Mr. MRR Nair was requested to take charge as the next President. Heading the NHRDN as a practitioner and an influential person who is committed to the cause of HRD ensured the growth and stabilization of the NHRDN. The next conference at Delhi was managed by a team lead by Mr. Nair and the focus was on HRD for workmen- a hitherto neglected theme. The theme attracted the attention of most academics and practitioners as well as union leaders. It became a landmark conference. Udai Pareek took over as president of NHRDN after Mr. Nair and ensured both intellectual implementation and dissemination continuity.

Some initiatives in governance practices helped NHRD to evolve as a vibrant democratic organization. During the tenure of Udai Pareek as President of NHRD, two provisions were built into the constitution, one that each person would be a President only for one term and would not be re-elected. The other provision except was to avoid election, and search the next President by a team appointed by the Governing Board. Elections introduce politics in the process, and therefore, it was thought important to have some other modes for searching for the President.

Subsequent presidents of the NHRDN were carefully chosen for their commitment and organizational support. Prior to their appointment the support of their organizations was ensured. They came from large and well-respected organizations like the RPG group, Aditya Birla Group etc. Mr. Arvind Agarwal and Dr. Santrupt Mishra, during their tenure as Presidents, introduced another useful tradition that the search committee, after identifying the potential President, would interview the CEO of the company to negotiate release of time and energy for the candidate to be appointed as President. The provisions have made NHRD a democratic body.

Today NHRDN has over forty chapters, nearly twenty publications to its credit, collaborating with Confederation of Indian Industry (CII) to develop HRD models and assess HR professionals and is collaborating with International bodies. By any means it has done a great service to young HR professionals. It has given opportunities to many young managers to test out their leadership potential and has helped a number of young professionals to acquire HR knowledge and set their careers in the right direction.

Phase VII: Strengthening the Academic Base: The Academy of HRD (1990–1995)

Origins: The National HRD Network (NHRDN) in a Mission-Vision workshop held in 1990 conceived a Center for Research and Education in NHRD to further the objectives of NHRDN. The office bearers of NHRDN decided to name it as the Academy of Human Resources Development (India).

Vision, Scope and Activities: AHRD was conceived as a place that facilitates scholarly work in HRD; A place where scholars from all over the country come for short periods of time to do research, reflection, writing, experience sharing and dissemination of knowledge; A place where Seminars, workshops, Round Tables, Doctoral and other professional development programs are conducted covering contemporary issues; A place that should have a residential center to accommodate about 40 participants at a time with faculties for families to stay; An institution that brings out HRD Journals.

Achievements: In the last fifteen years the following are the accomplishments: Round Tables, sponsored by one or a few companies were planned as mini-conferences around a theme of contemporary significance. It was intended to share issues and come up with implementable solutions and models for use by all participating companies. Participation was limited and by invitation and sponsors were required to finance the publication and also share experiences. Each Round Table (RTC) would result in recommendations, widely circulated all through the country for the impact of the AHRD. The following RTCs were held:

1) Career Planning and Promotion policies
2) Redesigning Performance Appraisal systems
3) Role of HRD in Restructuring Organizations jointly with Delhi Management Association
4) Role of Unions and Associations in HRD
5) HRD For workers and Empowering Workers.
6) Leadership for Organizational Excellence in Global Economy

The recommendations of each of these were widely circulated and also published.

Research Fellowships: AHRD had in the initial years research fellowships sponsored by organizations. Each organization would choose a research theme of interest to them and sponsor a study which should include the salaries for six months to a year for a Research Fellow to join AHRD and work on them, AHRD developed a list of Research themes. Fellows worked on this research theme and developed monograph for dissemination.

Diploma Programmes: A large number of HRD professionals were designated as HRD Managers, but did not have adequate professional preparation in HRD. They needed to be developed. This was done through distance education programs. NHRDN Chapters facilitated mobilizing students and offering contact programs.

AHRD also decided to extend this to other Management Schools like TA PAI Institute Manipal, SCM HRD Pune, and IIPS Indore and offer joint diplomas to promote specialization in HRD. The design was to admit students wanting to specialize in HRD who should take a minimum of six specialization courses from among the list supplied by AHRD. The design was to offer technical collaboration, supply the curriculum, examine the students and certify them. One of the Management schools SCMHRD subsequently started a one year program in HRD and continued till 2001 to focus more on the full-time two-year program.

Doctoral Program: There is a need for research in HRD. HRD Managers like other managers are sitting on huge amounts of data. If they learn research methods and research writing they may be able to do research and contribute to the field. In the process, they can also get a Doctoral Degree. An agreement was signed between AHRD and XLRI to start a Doctoral level program.

The arrangements were as follows:

1) AHRD conducted all the courses and provided all inputs and administered the program both academically and financially managed it
2) XLRI played a role in admissions and standards and approval of proposals and thesis examination to ensure standards.
3) AHRD to admit students, organize the Guides, conduct the contact programs (two programs of six weeks duration covering six courses each), organize thesis proposal presentations, guide students
4) Fellowship to be awarded jointly by AHRD and XLRI and they will be called as XLRI-AHRD Fellows

In all, 75 Candidates were admitted, and about 25 completed their Fellow program by the time the arrangement with XLRI ended in 2006 When XLRI preferred to focus its attention on its own programs. Some of the graduated candidates are working as Faculty at IIM Indore, XIM Bhubaneshwar, and ASCI etc. The Quality of thesis work of the candidates was appreciated by the Professionals.

Work in Social Sector: AHRD decided to extend its work with not for profit sector. The objective was to develop the Non-Governmental Organizations' (NGOs) capabilities through self -renewal methodologies. The objective was to develop an NGO network and develop self-renewal capabilities for the development agencies.

AHRD started a journal, *Renewal*, supported by EZE Germany. The first issue was brought out from Ahmedabad. The second issue from Hyderabad and subsequently it was stopped for want of committed editors.

Learning Resources Center (Knowledge Management Center): During the earlier years of AHRD many associates donated their collection of books, material and data of practices. The applications received by NHRD for annual HRD Awards used to be compiled and included in the best practices data base of AHRD. A lot of Instruments were collected and a data bank of HRD tools was instituted. A Data Bank of HRD Practices of companies was also instituted. All theses from Indian Universities dealing with HRD were collected. The library was built as a unique collection of all books and monographs in HRD. Several students from various colleges and institutions of Hyderabad used the center.

An Individual and Organizational Assessment Center: IOAC, as a new concept of AHRD, was initiated. The concept was to provide an opportunity to HRD Managers to renew their roles by focusing on development through Assessment. The concept was developed in Ahmedabad and Dr Sethumadhavan was recruited to take charge of this in 1995. He provided leadership and direction to this center for 3 years.

IOAC was defined as a center set up by an organization for continuous assessment of the competencies of Individuals, Dyads, Teams or Groups and Organization. The IOAC was designed to focus on organizational and team assessments besides the individual assessment done in the traditional assessment centers.

A Conference taking stock of the experiences of organizations conducting Assessment centers was organized in Mumbai in 1999. A book on Assessment Centers was planned and a manuscript was sent to Sage. It never saw the light of the day due to internal coordination issues. A number of in-basket exercises were developed. Consultancy services in Assessment Centers were offered to various organizations.

AHRD contributed a great deal so far to Human Capital Formation among HRD Professionals in India. However, there was much more scope. AHRD could have been a globally recognised institution and would have been considered the only place to go or main place to go for scholars across the world. The great dream still remains a dream – the great dream was to have its own campus, data-bank, and library, residential accommodation furnished for scholars to visit, write, renew and disseminate their work. The relevance and need for such an institution still exists today. Its doctoral programme could have become a flagship programme and would have contributed a great deal to HRD Knowledge.

Stage VIII: The Future: Globalization and Nationalization (2008-2014)

In the last 20 years, NHRDN has grown vastly. The seeds for its growth were sown and the foundation was laid in the first three years. The agenda of learning from each other continues. The annual or biannual conferences and the chapter meetings for learning from each other and networking continued. The chapters have grown in number. The culture of publishing papers to be distributed during conference continues.

However, a few more things could be done by NHRD:

1. Setting standards for HRD profession and creating curricula and accreditation methodologies
2. Creating assessment tools and rating methods in HRD for individuals and corporations
3. Building AHRD as a much stronger research institution as there is no other institution in India devoted exclusively to HRD research.
4. The future of the HRD movement in India is in realizing that we have not even touched the most important sectors like education, health, infrastructure, government etc. where HR interventions are most needed. We need to pay attention to these strategic sectors. The spirit of HRD lies in learning from each other's: teachers, managers, doctors, nurses, in fact all citizens involved in the pursuit of change and development.
5. The future focus also should be on globalization and learning from experiences from other countries. Participating in the world

events and sharing and disseminating a lot of knowledge being generated in India is the next natural step.

This account of the success story of the HRD Movement in India indicates how a few committed individuals with sustained effort and perseverance can create a concept and turn it into a movement. The conceptualization of HRD as an enabling function and an essential part of organizational growth and human development on the part of a few individuals lead to the establishment of HRD in India. However, the profession and the body have a long way to go. Those involved in the HRD movement in India need to step out to know how HRD is a national policy issue and how they have not touched even a small part of humanity and that the HRD movement is so incomplete if it is confined to the corporate sector. It cannot ignore the billions of people who need to improve their longevity, skills base, income, health and quality of life. The authors continue to work on these issues but unless a body like the NHRDN takes up these issues Integrated HRD may remain beneficial only to the industry and to the humanity at large.

PART 2

The Crucible Experiences

This section is devoted to present various experiences as reflected in correspondence, e-mails, brochures, minutes of meetings, announcements etc. as evidence of crucible experiences. All events mentioned are significant and are points in the life of an institution. Among the significant events which can be considered as crucible experiences include the following:

1. Organizing conferences, seminars and symposia; This included a number of activities including preparing the ground, designing inputs, involving and writing to speakers, publication, printing of books, souvenir, mobilizing funds, organizing Board and AGM meetings etc.
2. HRD Newsletter occupied a significant role in disseminating the HRD and NHRDN
3. Selecting office bearers, clarifying their roles, dealing with non-performance, structuring the institution, and ensuring right processes are followed and people get committed and the body adds value to members.
4. Awards in appreciation of good work, setting criteria, appointing committees and writing citations, designing the award formats etc.
5. Resolving conflicts and ensuring good governance
6. Creating a culture and dealing with deviations
7. Collaborations and MOUs and dealing with dissatisfaction of other n0n-actors of collaborating agencies.
8. Land or property acquisition and dynamics of dealing with preferences.

9. Dealing with unexpected departures of office bearers like resignations and other forms of separations
10. Setting priorities and developing the profession versus time on administration
11. Mobilizing and managing motivation of volunteers as against salaried employees

There are several crucible experiences we faced during the process of building the Institution NHRDN. Some of these are sketched in the form of experiences. No solutions and what went on in our mind is not given here.

1. For the First NHRDN Conference we wanted all the papers to be printed and distributed beforehand. We wanted everyone to have the copy of the book in their hand as they register for the Conference. We also wanted the papers to be bench marking and path breaking because the credibility of the new body is in the new knowledge it can offer. Rawat Publications agreed to print and make the conference papers book available. One of the papers was on Successful conduct of the Assessment centers in one company that has done path breaking work. All the papers were ready and proofs were received from the book and program schedule was announced. We received a request from one of the paper presenters that he would like to withdraw his paper on assessment centers. We were hoping this paper to be path breaking. Apparently the author who heads HR in his company and a top level highly respected leader circulated the paper he wrote on Assessment Centers in his own company. One of the top level candidates who was a part of the assessment felt that his identity is being revealed and he has serious objections about what is written in the paper and wanted the author to withdraw. The author of the paper called me up and announced he was withdrawing the paper. When I mentioned to him that the paper is printed and books are getting ready for all the participants the HR leader requested that all copies be destroyed and new book printed without his paper. He has withdrawn the paper and he would meet the costs of reprinting etc.

2. One well known professor from one of the Institutes of Management who has a fan following wanted to be invited to the conference and given space to speak. Somme of us knew that he did not believe in the concept of HRD and he has been going round criticizing the same. We were sure if he comes to the conference, we will run the risk of creating unwanted debate. We're just building the credibility of HR function. The professor was known in his filed but we were not sure of our ability to contain him.
3. On the positive side a great event that has happened was the Economic Times editor agreed to being out a special issue of Economic Times a day before the conference to create right background for the HRD Conference
4. Another crucible experience was to have most CEOs we invited on the first day to stick to their time and over shoot or not say things contrary to HR philosophy and values. We had to keep our fingers crossed but fortunately we had great speakers from industry who spoke well.
5. A very interesting crucible experiences at the end of the program in the AGM on the last day of the conference someone made an important observations that all these three days the discussions were on HRD for managers. Is HRD an elitist concept? What happens to the poor workers who are the main contributors to organizations? She said she is walking away with the impression that HRD is an elitist concept and NHRDN is an elitist in organizations
6. In the second conference held at Delhi, there was a huge registration. It was on workmen. There were union leaders and many CEOs and prominent personalities called for the Conference. The conference was to begin at 9.00 am with a prayer and Chinmaya Mission has organized with Anil Sachdeva's help and all arrangements were ready. Shri Abid Hussein, Member Planning Commission was to inaugurate the program. Mr. M R R Nair President went to receive him but Abid Hussain got delayed. To wait for him and start late or to start the program without the Chief Guest was an issue. We started the program and on arrival Ag bid Hussain complimented us for what we had

done. Staring on time became a part of the culture of NHRDN conferences

7. Thanks to the contacts of S. Chandrasekhar program organizer from L&T, we had all lunches and dinners hosted by local companies and thus we saved all the registration fee collection. Hotel expenses and conference hall etc. were all hosted by Chennai based industry. NHRDN did not pay for any speakers travel or stay. Every speaker arranged their own travel and some of us were put up in guest houses courtesy EID Parry and other bodies
8. Handing over the book of papers Alternative Strategies and Approaches to HRD co-edited by Abraham, Khandelwal, KK Verma and T V Rao was the most exciting highlight other program
9. Every CEO we invited participated in the first day and some of them stayed across all the three days.
10. S. Chandrasekhar also organized a great cultural program of dances and music by Krishnaswamy associates.
11. The interestingly designed conference souvenir brought out by H N Arora of Reliance group is another highlight of the program
12. During the process of NHRDN functioning we had questions raised by some members from one of the IIMs about representation of minorities in the NHRDN executive Board. This was a difficult issue to resolve.
13. The NHRDN was registered in Ahmedabad. Soon after the first conference Fr. Abraham was appointed dean of XIMB at Bhubaneswar. He was maintaining accounts and we had to work out mechanisms to submit the accounts. We also had to apply for 80 G and other tax concessions. We had some issues in finalising the accounts and submitting our fist accounts in Bhubaneswar versus Ahmedabad. Finally it had to be done at Ahmedabad as the registered office was in wing No 15 of IIMA.
14. By 1989 we were getting a feel of a growing organization run by volunteers. There was no full time secretary. Rakesh Kumar who was working in SAIL was appointed as Joint Secretary and MRR agreed to lend his services. That was the time both Suresh Krishna, Mr. Munjal Founder Chairman of Hero Cycles and also Chairman of CII offered to give space for NHRDN in CII

building in Delhi. Tarun Das also agreed. However we did not take this offer as at that time as we were trying to negotiate a place in Ahmedabad itself as registered office. Finally we bought 40, Cosmoville Row Houses in Ahmedabad for ₹5 lakhs. It was bought from Prof. Vyas Former Director of IIMA.

15. The land matters of NHRDN as well as AHRD remain painful experiences till date. A full book can be written on it on the efforts made and blocks we faced. In fact Arvind Agarwal booked a land with Haryana Government but withdrew later to buy the property in Ahmedabad. The Delhi (Gurgaon) office was bought essentially to use the fund allocated for the building by a particular date without which the tax liability of NHRDN would have gone up. The Hyderabad property is another series of stories for NHRDN and AHRD some of which are briefly mentioned in the description of AHRD at the end.
16. The Mission vision workshop held in Chennai is another path breaking event and a crucible experience that remained in the psyche of NHRDN and AHRD. The outcomes of this workshop were never internalized by NHRDN except by those who were a part of the workshop. AHRD was born out of this workshop but subsequent office bearers of NHRDN were too much engrossed in governance of NHRDN. Structural arrangements of AHRD increased the distance between the two. Many efforts made to integrate them and help them work collaboratively did not yield fruits.
17. In early years all accounts were centralized. They had to be consolidated and submitted to audit and returns filed in Ahmedabad. Some of the chapters opened accounts but failed to submit them on time for consolidation, this created major issues in NHRDN. This is one of the reasons for restructuring NHRDN with decentralized set up. Another important reasons was to let chapters grow independently by being autonomous. Creativity was to be promoted. NHRDN tried to live by the values of its promoters: OCTAPACE values
18. Performance of office bearers has always been an issue. It created major issues for Presidents. NHRDN is professional body

with volunteers. People take up roles out of their interest. They lose interest midway sometimes for different reasons. They find it embarrassing to resign and make way for others. The central NHRDN has no option but to carry them along. This has been major sour point. In the case of one chapter the President refused to resign even after two terms and when an attempt was made to get another candidate ready to take up the job, he threatened the candidate stating that he would be sending union leaders to his home.

19. Presidents leaving mid-way was not expected. V. S. Mahesh who took over as fourth President from Udai Pareek decided to shift to UK. As a result of this NHRDN was thrown into uncertainty. I took over as Interim President for six months and got Rajesh Vidya Sagar elected and take over as Fifth President.
20. After Rajesh Vidyasagar we had to get someone who was not socialized into NHRDN Debashish Mitra as Rajesh felt he would do justice to the role. Rajesh was not there to guide. Debashish' term as President was more an obligatory term by Debashish. During this period AHRD took charge of the NHRDN and the secretariat operated from AHRD. Baburraj Nair was appointed as full time Executive Secretary. He did a good job of documenting the first ten years of NHRDN
21. Another significant crucible experience NHRDN faced was the pressure on President. If the President was unable to tour and connect with various chapters the chapters slowly die. That is what happened from 1998- to 1999 after Debashish and Arvind Pande's time. There were organizational al challenges faced by SAIL and Pande had his limits in travelling. No other person could fulfil this. Chapters like Delhi were doing well. But as a National body the morale became low. It is a this time the Board took a decision to appoint Interim Rejuvenation committee with T V Rao as Coordinator and Aquil PVR, Udai, Rupa etc. as members. This committee too six months to put NHRDN on the track. Once Arvind Agrawal was appointed everything after the year 2000 came into one stream. Rejuvenation has begun. During this period AHRD was also going through its pain points. These

points were very painful and are not discussed with the intention not to hurt anyone.

22. For Academy of HRD the pleasure and pain points were many. These are presented in the below description of AHRD in a short PowerPoint format.
23. A lot has been accomplished in building the National HRD Network. A detailed description of people involved and various events in the first decade were presented in a separate book by Baburaj Nair (Growth of a Professional Association: National HRD Network 1985–1995) Baburaj was the First Executive Secretary of the NHRDN. The paid secretariat concept started with Baburaj. Baburaj was at that time in Bangalore but lived earlier in Ahmedabad. Prof. Keith D'Souza as Director of AHRD and Rajesh Vidya Sagar as the President of HRD felt the need for full time secretary of NHRDN to make sure that all correspondence is handled and memberships are served. He was offered to be placed in Ahmedabad and was asked to develop N0. 40 Cosmoville row houses as the secretariat of NHRDN. Many crucible experiences between 2003 and 2025 are not mentioned here and are left for respective generations of Office bearers to pen them in course of time.

Academy of HRD: Some Crucible Experiences from 1990–2002

Origins:

National HRD Network (NHRDN) in a Mission-Vision workshop held at Chennai in on September 11, 1990 conceives a Center for Research and education in NHRD to set up to further the objectives of NHRDN; This Workshop facilitated by Anil Sachdeva and V S Mahesh. *(While AHRD is a brain child of NHRDN and it started with active involvement of the first Three Presidents of NHRDN (TV Rao, MRR Nair and Udai Pareek) and XLRI support (Fr. Abraham and Keith D'Souza) and institution building support from IIMA (Prof. N. R. Sheth and P N Khandwalla in subsequent years). NHRDN in later years did not leverage this institution. What should one do to leverage is always an issue.)*

Christening the Academy: October 1990

MRR Nair (MD Bokaro Steel and Second President NHRDN), Udai Pareek (President), T V Rao (Founder President), Fr. E. Abraham (Founder Secretary), Keith D'Souza (XLRI, Secretary and Editor Newsletter) and Rakesh Kumar Associate Secretary, NHRDN) Office bearers of NHRDN meet at Bokaro and decide to name it as the Academy of Human Resources Development.

The Beginnings: A Power Point Presentation

MRR Nair writes to Director IIMA requesting Prof. Rao's involvement as Honorary Director of AHRD

Dr. N. R. Sheth approves Dr. Rao's involvement on behalf of the Ravi Matthai Center

Dr. Rao starts working as First Honorary Director to take the concept forward - October 1990 and Initiates discussions with a number of CEOs to join the Board;

First Board

Mr. M R Nair, Chairman; Mr. Subodh Bhargava (Eicher); Dr B. K. Modi (Modi Xerox); Mr. K. K. Nohria; Shri A K Jain (Chairman SAIL); Dr. P. P. Gupta from Industry; Mr. N. Vittal (Secretary), Mr. J. Veeraraghavan (Secretary HRD), from Government; Prof. Udai Pareek, Prof. Ishwar Dayal, Prof. Dharani Sinha from Academics

AMA

Dr. Rao w discusses with AMA President for their support in establishing the Academy. Prof. Kalro, President AMA agrees to support. Mr. K. K. Nair Executive Secretary AMA recruits the first full time Secretary Mr. Raghu for AHRD. AHRD is given office space in AMA.

First Programmes: 1991

The First program on Competency Mapping for HR Professionals held facilitated by Mr. Rob Nelson and Carol Nelson (Canadian

Consultants: Courtesy NDDB), Prof. S. Ramnarayan (IIMA) and Prof. T V Rao at IIMA Campus. Diploma Program launched on Distance Education mode preparing HRD professionals. HRD Facilitators Program being held at Jaipur taken over by AHRD from NHRDN and the two phased program launched by AHRD. Bob Nelson's Program at IIMA.

Doctoral Program

Prof. Rao starts Negotiations with Indira Gandhi National Open University for the Doctoral Program in HRD and submits the design. Dr. Rao writes to various leading academics from all over the country (IIMs, IITs and reputed Universities etc.) For their involvement as guides in Ph. D. Program.

List submitted to IGNOU.

Land

Search for land begins in Ahmedabad. Mr. Arora from Reliance helps in the search. Ministers and Government officials met. Explorations with CEE (Kartik Sarabhai), next to the land taken by Mudra for MICA. The land prices go up exorbitantly due to MICA buying land. Negotiations stopped. Sterling city explored for two acres of land, Abandoned for want of money. Cosmo Ville:

12 Cosmo Ville row houses purchased out of the savings from various programs (Rs four and half lakhs). Academy shifts from AMA to 12 Cosmo ville. Function attended by various dignitaries from AMA, IIMA, AHRD and Udai Pareek President NHRDN.

Vision, Scope and Activities

AHRD should be a place that facilitates scholarly work in HRD. Will have an excellent and exclusive library and resources in HRD. It should be place where scholars from all over the country come for short periods of time to do research, reflection, writing, experience sharing and dissemination of knowledge. A place where Seminars, workshops, Round Tables, Doctoral and other professional development programs are conducted covering contemporary issues. Should have a residential center to accommodate about 40 participants at a time with faculties for families to stay. Bring out HRD Journals.

Round Tables

Concept: Sponsored by one or a few companies a Round Table is a mini-conference round a theme of contemporary significance. It is intended to share issues and come up with implement able solutions and models for use by all participating companies. Round Tables- Design: Participation is limited and by invitation. Sponsors to finance the publication and also share experiences. Each Round Table should result in recommendations which should be widely circulated all through the country for impact of the AHRD. **Round Tables: Accomplishments:** First Round Table on Career Planning and Promotion policies sponsored by SAIL resulted in the publication by T V Rao and Jerome Joseph on the theme. Second Round Table on Redesigning Performance Appraisal systems (a number of organizations) resulted in a book published by Tata McGraw-Hill. Third Round Table on Role of HRD in Restructuring Organizations jointly with DMA Papers distributed book not come out. Fourth Round Table on the Role of Unions and Associations in HRD attended by number of companies. Recommendations widely circulated. Fifth Round Table on HRD For workers sponsored by Samtel. Coordinated by Uma Jain Resulted in a book on Empowering Workers. The recommendations of each of these were widely circulated and also published in the HRD Newsletter.

Research Fellowships: Rationale

AHRD to have research fellowships sponsored by organizations. Each organization may choose a research theme of interest to them and sponsor a study which should include the salaries for six months to a year for a Research Fellow to join AHRD and work on them. AHRD developed a list of Research themes. The Fellow will work on this research theme and develop monograph for dissemination. AHRD thus contributes to the development of research.

Research Fellowships in the first five years

SAIL sponsored study on reorienting Personnel Departments to HRD (Oleti Jagannath worked on this and developed manuals). NDDB sponsored Research Fellowship on HRD for Unions and Cooperatives (Nihar Ghosh worked on this). OD in L&T ECC (Prof. N. Dixit from IIML joined AHRD and worked on this). Value Development through Training (AHRD itself sponsored this. J. Sampath worked on this and latter pursued in the form of his Ph.D. work). A Follow-up study of the Managers from PSUs joining Private Sector and MNCs (Archana and Sripathy worked on this). A study of the Tasks and Developmental needs of NGO Staff sponsored by Excel Industries (Liza Thomas worked on this and prepared a monograph).

Diploma Programs

Rationale: There are a large number of HRD professionals who carry the designation of HRD Managers but did not have adequate professional preparation in HRD. They need to be developed. These will be done in Distance Education mode. **Course structure innovative**: Eight papers. Each paper has assignments. Contact sessions in various chapters. NHRDN Chapters to facilitate mobilizing students and offering contact programs.

Diploma Program: experience

Prof. S. Ramnarayan of IIMA worked as Chairman of the Program. Three batches were prepared. First batch 113 candidates, second batch about 50 candidates and the third batch about 20 candidates.

Several contact programs were held. First Convocation was held in the NHRDN Conference held at Taj

Second Convocation was held at Calcutta. Diploma in HRD: Experience; IGNOU acknowledged the innovative design of the diploma and published it in one of their Newsletters. AHRD found the administration difficult to handle as it required lot of correspondence and promptness. Hence it was decided to join hands with AIMA who can conduct it jointly with AHRD. The collaboration continued and AHRD contributed very nominally to this subsequently.

Joint Diplomas with Management Schools

AHRD also decided to extend this to Management Schools and offer joint diplomas to promote specialization in HRD. TAPAI Institute Manipal, SCM HRD Pune, and IIPS Indore participated in this.

Students wanting to specialize in HRD should take a minimum of six specialization courses from among the list supplied by AHRD. The design is to offer technical collaboration, supply the curriculum, examine the students and certify. SCMHRD subsequently started a one year program in HRD with SCMHRD.

Doctoral Program

Rationale: There is a need for research in HRD. HRD Managers like other managers are sitting on huge amount of data. If they learn research methods and research writing they may be able to do research and contribute to the field. In the process they can also get a Doctoral Degree. **Doctoral Program: Efforts:** IGNOU bought this concept and decided to extend this to all Management disciplines. Unfortunately it did not take off due to other internal priorities of IGNOU. AHRD decided to approach XLRI. XLRI indicates its interest and discusses in the Board. AHRD discusses in its Board. Director XLRI invited for a special meeting at Delhi with the AHRD Board. Mr. MRR Nair flies to XLRI to discuss this in the Board of XLRI. He was also a member of the Board of XLRI and Chairman of AHRD Board

Both the Boards approve. MOU signed between AHRD and XLRI. Fr. Abraham's term as Director XLRI gets over.

Doctoral Program in HRD with XLRI

Arrangements: AHRD to conduct all the courses and provide all inputs and administer the program both academically and financially manage it. XLRI to play a role in admissions criteria and standards and approval of proposals and thesis examination to ensure standards. XLRI to get AICTE recognition for this. AHRD to admit students,

Awards used to be compiled. A lot of Instruments were collected and a data bank of HRD tools instituted. A Data Bank of HRD Practices of companies also instituted. All Theses from Indian Universities dealing with HRD were collected. The library was built as a unique collection of all books and monographs in HRD. A number of students from various colleges and institutions of Hyderabad used the center. The library is located in 40 Cosmo Ville and should be made available for use by larger number and the collection needs to be updated.

IOAC:

Rationale: Individual and Organizational Assessment Center as a new concept of AHRD was initiated. The concept is to give a new handle to HRD Managers to renew their role by focusing on Development through Assessment. Concept developed in Ahmedabad and Dr Sethumadhavan was recruited to take charge of this in 1995. IOAC: definition- IOAC is a center set up by an organization for continuous assessment of the competencies of Individuals, Dyads, Teams or Groups and Organization. The IOAC is managed internally by HRD manager and uses multiple methods of assessment and development and is an improvement over the traditional Assessment centers started in the US. First IOAC at Goa: Dr. Sethumadhavan. **IOAC: Experience;** IOAC had an advisory committee including Prof. Udai Pareek, J. S. Chokkar, S. Ramnarayan, Sasi Misra, Keith D'Souza and T V Rao. First IOAC Facilitators program was conducted in Goa in 1995. Since then over 300 candidates have gone through IOAC and 14 IOACs were conducted. The 14th IOAC was held in 2001 at Ahmedabdad. IOAC: Experiences- All the members became members of the forum as an IOAC Forum was constituted and a Conference taking stock of the experiences of organizations conducting Assessment centers was organized in Mumbai in 1999.

A book on Assessment Centers was planned. A number of in-basket exercises were developed

Consultancy services in Assessment centers were offered to various organizations. IOAC: Opportunities: AHRD has not adequately cashed on this. AHRD needs to register this as an IPR of AHRD (original idea conceived by Dr. T. V. Rao and AHRD promoted it and Dr. Rao is ready to give the IPR to AHRD and has always been promoting this as AHRD concept). Needs to revive the IOAC Forum

Needs to publish the book (parts of the manuscript with Balaji and in various program materials)

Needs to promote this and become a center for learning about assessment and development.

Organizational Structure of the AHRD

The following are the main Constitutional bodies of the Academy: The AHRD Society consisting of all the paid members and Donors (SAIL, Voltas, Crompton Greaves, TISCO, IL&FS, Gati, Satyam, Dr. Reddy's, Visakhapatnam Steel, etc.); Board of Governors consisting of the Patron members of the Society, representatives of Academic institutions, Government and NGOS, President NHRDN and Director XLRI, and Director of AHRD. The following are the other bodies constituted by AHRD Board:

Executive Committee which is subcommittee of the Board to oversee and guide the activities of the AHRD, its Director and Faculty and take financial and administrative decisions delegated to it. Academic Council to formulate policies and guidelines for academic programs and activities of the AHRD and keep reviewing the same and to link its work with the practitioners. Diploma Committee to design and implement the PG Diploma (discontinued after the diploma was given to AIMA). FPHRD Committee to look after the affairs of the joint Fellow program of AHRD and XLRI.

Academic Council

Was set up from the first year of the AHRD. Consisted of all Chapter Presidents and Board of the NHRDN. Representatives of the other professional bodies like NIPM, ISTD, AIMA, and other professional bodies. Representative of the collaborating institutions with AHRD. Eminent scholars and Institutional Heads. All Guides of the Doctoral program, Faculty of AHRD. Also connected and disseminated the work of the AHRD with the external environment. Used to meet once a year during the Conference of the NHRDN to save travel expenses of AHRD.

Academic Council: Current Status in 2003

Served as linkage between NHRDN and AHRD. Took decisions in the past like starting the Diploma program, Doctoral program, approved the content and design and approved in 2000 the new PG Diploma to be started in HRD and collaborations with George Washington University (GWU), USA

Size was brought down from about 100 members to 25 in the year 1999–2000. The last meeting held was in Hyderabad in 2000 January and latter correspondence was by email and the last approval was for a PG Program in HRD to be started at Ahmedabad and explorations jointly with GWU.

Academic Council: Future -Dr. T. V. Rao was Chairman since the inception till 2002. Director used to work as Vice-Chairman. Twice recommendations were made to the Board to dissolve the Academic Council and both the times the Board rejected the same. It is useful body. Financial considerations do not allow AHRD to have meetings and get the best. A decision needs to be taken by the Board to continue, discontinue or re-constitute the Academic Council. **Board:** Earlier years the Board consisted of CEOs, Government Representatives, NGO representatives, Scholars and Institution Builders. These were carefully chosen for their experience and guidance. After the AHRD got registered Members became nominated from the Society who have paid the fee but representation from Government, social sector and Academics continued. Members of the Board: **Past CEOS** -

Dr. Anji Reddy, M R R Nair, Dr P P Gupta, KK Nohria, Subodh Bhargava, Dr B K Modi, Dr H A Dave, Mr. C R Ramakrishna, Mr. Mahendra Agarwal, Mr. Ravi Parthasarathy, Mr. V H Munshi, Ramesh Gelli, A G Krishnamurthy, Arvind Pande, Ramalinga Raju, B K Singh. **Government representatives:** Mr. J. Veeraraghavan (secretary, HRD); Mr. N. Vittal (Secretary, Electronics); Mr. Yugandhar (Retd. Secretary to PM); Mr. Inderjit Khanna (Chief Secretary Rajasthan and Secretary UGC), T L Shankar. **Institution Builders and HRD Scholars:** Udai Pareek, Ishwar Dayal, Dharni Sinha, Y R K Reddy, T V Rao. **Social Sector;** Dr N C B Nath, Ex-Officio: Director, Director XLRI and President NHRDN.

Current members of the Board- 2003

Society Members (KK Nohria, S Chandrasekhar, Saumen Chakravarthy, M K Agrawal, and other representatives of ILFS, Voltas, Satyam, SAIL, TISCO etc.); Ex-officio: Santrupt Misra (NHRDN), P D Thomas (XLRI), Arvind Agrawal; Invited members; Mallika Sarabhai, Gita Piramal, Ashok Chatterjee, Pradip Khandwalla, Udai Pareek, T V Rao, S P Agarwal. **Chairman of the Board;** M R R Nair (1990–1995) Two terms; Dr Anji Reddy (1995–2001) Two terms; Dr. Udai Pareek (2001–2007)

Directors of AHRD; Dr. T V Rao (Honorary October 1990–June 1992); Prof. Keith D'Souza (1992 June – Jan 1994); T V Rao (Honorary Jan 1994 – April 1996); Fr. E. Abraham, Joint Director (1995–96); Dr P Sethumadhavan (April 1996 – May 1997); Prof. C Balaji (May 1997 – August 2000); Dr. T. V. Rao (Honorary August 2000 – January 2001); Mr. Tapash Sengupta (Jan 2001 – June 2001); Prof. Uma Jain (July 2001–2003).

Professors Emeritus

To honor and to utilize the scholarship and availability of eminent retired professionals AHRD started the concept of Professors Emeritus. It was designed to give them grants to help them do work in areas relating to HRD. The following Professors were appointed: Prof. Udai Pareek, Prof. Gaurango Chattopadhyaya, Prof. Dharni Sinha, Prof. E. G. Parameswaran (SAIL Professor), Prof. Prayag Mehta, Prof. Rolf Lynton. The Professors Emeritus concept needs to be appropriately promoted and their help taken to promote research and training in HRD. Rolf Lynton visits every year but he is not well networked by AHRD.

Executive Committee

Rationale: The Personnel & Finance committee of the Board used to take all major personnel decisions and give approvals in early years. Subsequently it was converted into Executive Committee. **Structure:**

A subcommittee of the Board to make finance, personnel and other Institutional related major decisions of the Board and monitor the implementation of the same. **Executive Committee: Role;** To Guide the Director and the Faculty from time to time and ensure the financial health of the AHRD; To approve all the consultancy projects and tours and travel etc.. Of the Director and periodical review the performance of the Director and faculty and ensure fulfillment of organizational objectives;

To act as mini Board and take all decisions needed to facilitate effective and efficient functioning of AHRD; Executive Committee Earlier Years at Ahmedabad: M R R Nair, T V Rao and Udai Pareek

Since 1996: Dr Y R K Reddy (Chairman), Mr. T L Shanakar, Mr. M. K. Agarwal, and Director AHRD

Ahmedabad after it shifted: Mr. Arvind Agarwal, Udai Pareek, T V Rao (Chairman), Ashok Chatterjee, S P Agarwal and Director AHRD. More active involvement by the EC in reviewing and guiding the Directors could have helped a great deal.

FPHRD Committee

As a part of the MOU with XLRI A fellow program Committee was constituted to manage the FPHRD Program. Role: Formulate policies, approve thesis proposals, and manage the program.

This is a joint committee of AHRD and XLRI. **Members as on 2002:** E G Parameswaran (Chairman); Prof. E S Srinivas, Prof. Madhukar Shukla, Prof. ISF Irudayaraj; Prof Ravi Kumar, Prof. Mathew Manimala, Prof. Udai Pareek, Fr PD Thomas and Prof. J B P Sinha. **FPHRD Chairman :**

Prof. E. G. Parameswaran did a commendable job of managing the program last few years. The credit for ensuring that 23 of the candidates submit their thesis is largely attributable him. AHRD needs to thank him for his contributions.

Ravi Matthai Lectures: Rationale: AHRD was set up with collaboration from Ravi Matthai center of IIMA. As a mark of respect for the Institution Builder AHRD decided to institute annual lecture series in honor of Ravi Matthai. Four lectures were held. Those who delivered these include: Dr C Rangarajan Governor, RBI; Dr. Prakash Tandon; Dr. Udai Pareek and Mr Narayana Murthy (Infosys). Fund needs to be collected for this purpose and the tradition needs to be continued

Campus: Efforts

Efforts were made from earlier on to have campus. Dr Rao spent almost six months searching for the campus in 1990 at Ahmedabad. 1991 An industrialist from Hyderabad who visited IIMA promised 15 acres of land near the Film city. He was taken on to the Board and the promised land was visited thrice by Dr Pareek, T V Rao, PVR Murthy and others. Campus: Aborted early efforts as demands by donors were not acceptable for the Board of AHRD. The AHRD was registered as a separate to enable it to receive the land. The industrialist put strict conditions almost amounting to deny the land. For example if the buildings are not constructed within one year all the property will be taken back by the donor etc. AHRD abandoned this idea. Campus: Dr Reddy Donates land. Dr Anji Reddy took lot of interest on AHRD after Dr Rao met Mr. Satish Reddy and was introduced to Dr Anji Reddy. Dr Anji Reddy helped acquire about ten acres of land and gave financial support to AHRD to buy this land adjacent to Dr Reddy's laboratories. and plans were made to build the AHRD. The campus could not be constructed due to accessibility problems of this land and AHRD fenced this land and spent some money for this. Aborted plans for campus at Hyderabad

Land and Fixed assets

After it moved to Hyderabad with the intention of construction of its campus AHRD also thought of a Social development Center located at another place. Due to this and uncertainties associated with the land from DRL, AHRD purchased another acre of land near Hussein Sagar Kismatpur, about 15 kms away from Hyderabad. In addition AHRD had flat in Srikrishna Society. It was taken up to accommodate visiting scholars and research staff. This is in addition to 12 Cosmo Ville row houses.

Publications

1. D'Souza, Keith, Upadhyaya, G & Rakesh Kumar; (1997) Empowering Workers through Human Resources development, New Delhi: Allied
2. Singh, Kuldeep. Rao, T. V., & Nair, Baburaj. (1998) Selected readings in HRD. Tata McGraw Hill, 1996
3. Joseph, Jerome & Rao, T. V. (1992) Career Planning and Promotion Policies: The Indian Experience, Headband: Academy of HRD; & New Delhi, Oxford & IBH,
4. Jain Uma & Rao, T. V. (editors) (1995) Organizational Renewal in NGOs: Experiences and Case Studies, Hyderabad: Academy of HRD, 1995
5. Rao, T. V., Abraham, E & Nair, Baburaj V. (eds) (1994) HRD Philosophies and Concepts: The Indian Perspective, Headband: Academy of HRD, 1994
6. Jain, Uma. Pareek, Udai & Jomon, M. G. (1996) Road to Empowerment: HRD Experiences with Workers and support staff, New Delhi: Oxford & IBH, 1996
7. Sarupriya, D. S., Rao, T. V. & Sethumadhavan, P. (editors) (1996) Measuring Organizational Climate, Headband: Academy of HRD, 1996
8. Pareek, Udai & Rao, T. V. Pioneering Human Resources Development: The L&T System, Headband: Academy of HRD1998
9. Srinivas, Kandula & Hari Bapuji, B (editors) (2000) Perspectives in HRD & OD in Indian Organizations, Hyderabad: Academy of HRD
10. Rao, T. V. Developing and Managing Managerial Performance, Headband: Academy of Human Resources development, 1994.
11. Pareek, U. and Rao, T. V. Redesigning Performance Appraisal Systems, New Delhi: Tata McGraw Hill, 1994

Publications: Monographs and Working Papers

1. AHRD also has a number of monographs by its Research Fellows
2. OD in L&T (N Dixit)

3. Reorienting Personnel to HRD (O Jagannath)
4. HRD for Cooperatives (Nihar Ghosh)
5. Task Analysis of NGOs (Liza Thomas)
6. Study of Managers from PSUs joining MNCs (Sripathy)
7. There were three working papers published under the working paper series

Doctoral Dissertation Topics: AHRD-XLRI Program

1. Study of work motivation among Indian managers (Mohan Parameswaran)
2. Study of Individual Values and Organizational Values and Its Impact on Organizational Commitment (S. Ramachandran)
3. Professional values, value conflict and coping mechanisms of HRD professionals in India (Madhavi Mehta)
4. Study of gender differences in ethical behavior of middle level managers in their interpersonal relationships (Geeta Kaza Prabhakar)
5. Study of the relationship between empowerment focus and the empowering process among women in managerial positions in business organizations (Jacob Thomas)
6. Measurement, antecedents and outcomes of organizational citizenship behavior in high technology software organizations (Hari Iyer)
7. Status and Outcomes of self-managing teams Implementation in India (S. Nirmala)
8. The dynamics of designing, nurturing and determining organizational transformation (A C Augustine)
9. Individual factors associated with career success and growth in an Insurance organization (G Buhril)
10. Transfer of learning of management Education program in IOC (M K Suri)
11. Study of factors enabling and hindering effectiveness of a knowledge management initiative in an IT organization (Roshan Joseph)
12. Study of organizational role stress and burn out as function of perceived overload. Ethico-moral climate, organizational structure

and self-efficacy among middle managers of Indian organizations (H C Taneja)

13. Study of managerial leadership styles, locus of control and behavioral preference in relation to role efficacy and HRD climate (P V Bhide)
14. Management style and its impact on organizational learning process (M R Surendra)
15. Relationship between management style and organizational culture on the performance of ICSE schools (Uma C Sampathy)
16. Mentoring as a HRD intervention in Indian Organizations (Salman Kureshi)
17. Relationship between strategic response of firms to changing environment and scope and degree of involvement of worker development initiatives (S R Kandula)
18. Transcendental Meditation program and development of Individual potential (Arindam Banerjee)
19. A study of the relationship between the level of IT and employee alienation and its impact on HRD processes (Sunitha Mishra)
20. Knowledge Management and its impact on organizational performance and the HRD implications (Devakamal Datta)
21. Impact of advanced manufacturing technologies on shop-floor personnel in Indian engineering industry- a HRD perspective (A Vittaleswar)
22. An assessment of the role of HR in Indian corporate sector (Anuradha Challu)
23. Impact of the changed business environment on the role of HR professionals (Ann Anderson)
24. Career-anchor-based congruence in HR practices and its relation with job satisfaction, organizational commitment, and turn over intention; a study of software professionals (Pallav Bandhopadhyay)
25. Role and pattern of HR interventions in managing strategic processes in Indian firms (Ranjan Das)
26. Study of impact of sensitivity training on the behavior and performance of bank officers (R N Saxena)
27. A study of the competency based HR practices in Indian organizations (Archana Arcot)

28. A study of socio-cultural context of the credit needs of rural women and the response gaps in alternative institutional credit delivery process: implications for HRD (Liza Thomas)
29. Evolution of the role of HR professionals in Indian Organizations (Harismita Trivedi)

Faculty and Research Staff

Faculty who worked with AHRD at different points of time include: C Balaji; Kuldeep Singh; M G Jomon; Paturi Ravi; ISF Irudayaraj; Himank Priyadarshi; Baburaj Nair; Gautam Jain; Sripathy; Archana Sripathy; Sridhar; Madhavi Mehta; Liza Thomas; Monica Sawhney Programs with International Scholars

1. Program on LSIP with Kathy Dane Miller jointly organized with Eicher Consultancy services
2. Train the Trainer in Future Search Methodology organized by Marwin Weisboard and Sandra Janoff jointly organized with TV Rao Learning Systems
3. Mapping HRD Competencies with Rob Nelson and Carol Nelson
4. Program on Human Capital Accounting by Keith Bradley from London School of Economics
5. Keith Bradleys workshops

International Exhibition

In 1995 AHRD has put up an exhibition of its products at Singapore to publicize and go international.

The exhibition was a great success and some local ministers also visited the AHRD. AHRD did not cash on the contacts established at that time.

International Conference

From the beginning the dream of AHRD has been to put the HRD work done in India on the international map. Accordingly the AHRD

International was contacted and Dr Rao indicated his interest in hosting a Asian HRD Conference in India. Accordingly the First Asian HRD Conference was conducted at IIM Bangalore in 2002 October. Attended by 37 delegates from all over the world

100 papers were presented and discussed. The International community is now aware of the work going on in India. More scholarship needs to be developed and research skills of Indian Scholars need to be strengthened.

NHRDN and AHRD Linkages

AHRD was set up by NHRDN to further the objectives of NHRDN. NHRDN gave a small financial assistance to AHRD at the time of setting it. AHRD was made autonomous institutions from the beginning to enable it to have high power Board and to mobilize its own finances. This has happened as desired. AHRD actively presents NHRDN Conferences. **Structural Linkages;** AHRD was to write on its letterhead that it is an Institution of NHRDN. President of NHRDN is a member of the Board of AHRD. Highlights of AHRD annual reports and activities to be reported in HRD Newsletter of NHRDN.

AHRD to serve as a Secretariat of NHRDN. Baburaj Nair was recruited by AHRD and housed in AHRD Ahmedabad. This discontinued after ED was appointed to manage NHRDN and AHRD was shifted back to Ahmedabad. Director AHRD to be on the Board of NHRDN (informal). **NHRD and AHRD Linkages: Experience:** Chapters helped in mobilizing participants for AHRD programs like the diploma and conducting diploma programs. Doctoral fellow candidates were to present their thesis proposals and findings in chapters (informal. Never implemented). Academic Council meetings to be held in NHRDN conferences and NHRDN used to facilitate this (up to Delhi Conference 1999 this used to happen). Newsletter to devote a special section to AHRD news and publish. Faculty of AHRD and scholars to publish articles in NHRDN. AHRD assisted NHRDN in organizing the Conferences (T V Rao, Balaji, Keith helped NHRDN in editing various volumes. Rajesh Vidyasagar visited and spent two full days at Ahmedabad editing the Conference papers of Bombay Conference. Subsequent conference papers (Except the recently held

Bombay Conference had AHRD associated with it).AHRD served as the secretariat of the Awards Committee in the first few years. NHRDN papers were compiled by AHRD for wider use (Kuldeep's book, Baburaj Nair's book etc.). AHRD Contributed a great deal so far to Human Capital Formation among HRD Professionals in India as summarized below.

AHRD Accomplishments by 2003: Summary

Education: 23 Doctorates and many other helped; About 1000 diploma holders (First three years, AIMA, SCMHRD, IIPS, TAPMI etc.); Several students benefited from AHRD; Professional Development:

About 200 trained through HRD Facilitators program; About 300 trained in IOAC who can conduct Assessment centers; Accomplishments: Research and Publications: 12 books, 4 working papers, five monographs and several articles written by AHRD staff. Publications in Organizational climate and Round Tables etc. available for HRD professionals. **Social Sector:** New methodologies of LSIP and Future Search made available for several NGOs and Facilitators. Most of them are using

Over 200 NGOs exposed to Renewal methodologies. Over a 100 NGO facilitators developed in HRD

By no means these are small contributions. NHRDN should be proud of these. Yet the dream we started with remains unfulfilled.

Note: This is a biography of AHRD prepared by Dr Rao from his memory. If he has left out anything please indicate the same and pass on. Please pass this on to the Board and all others as a socialization process and to take forward and fulfill the unfulfilled dreams of our HRD professionals.

Thanks

Some Crucible Experiences in Integrating NHRDN and AHRD: A Missed Opportunity:

There are many other crucible experiences in terms of the efforts made to integrate both these bodies NHRDN and AHRD.

1. At one time it was felt that the President of NHRDN should also be the chairman of the board of governors of the Academy of HRD. The President of NHRD was sounded. However,

later discussions in the committee set up to find the chairman of AHRD felt that NHRDN itself required a lot of attention of the president of NHRDN, and he may not be able to justice to both the roles. However, as this was already communicated by Dr. Udai Pareek informally to the president concerned, it became difficult and embarrassing to change the chairman of NHRDN and appoint somebody else. This has resulted I am sure in some amount of uncomfortableness on the part of NHRDN president.

2. Professor Keith Bradley from London School of Economics was invited to offer a series of programs in India by the Academy of HRD. These workshops were organized in different cities like Bombay, Hyderabad, and Bangalore. They had to be marketed by the respective chapters of National HRD Network. Keith Bradley was from London, taking care of his stay, travel and local travel cost enormous amounts of money for AHRD. However, the NHRD chapters had put in quite some work in mobilizing participants for the programs. After the programs ended AHRD could not compensate the respective chapters as there was no surplus that was made available. AHRD felt that NHRD chapters will understand this. However, differences already started showing up in the minds of some of the chapters that they had worked for mobilizing participants, but AHRD did not compensate them. On the other hand, AHRD felt That NHRDN should be the big brother of AHRD and should have itself funded AHRD rather than raising these questions. This had led to some differences in perceptions and expectations from each other.
3. There were some good success experiences too. For example, whenever NHRD conference took place, AHRD used to hold its meetings along with the conference. The academic council, which consisted of all the chapter presidents of NHRD and a large number of academics used it to meet. This was a high integrating experience. Structurally it was felt that the chapter presidents being members of academic Council integration would take place. Unfortunately, in later years this practice was discontinued. Neither the conferences became venues for academic council nor kept the academic council meeting. If this happened, post-pandemic life would have been different. Because after the

pandemic, there was no need for physical get together of the academic council members and zoom and other Media could have been used. Unfortunately, in the early part of this century that is between 2000 and 2010. The practice of academic Council meeting was discontinued this further widen the gap between the two bodies.

4. Another crucible experience happened with corporatization of NHRDN. Every NHRDN president wanted to leave his mark and streamline many activities with all good intentions. A high-level director general (DG) was appointed to look after the administrative matters of NHRDN. This director, general and staff were put on high salaries comparable to that of the corporate sector. They were also told that they should be helping NHRDN to generate enough income so that their salary could be met. In addition, NHRDN was told that the director general and the staff salaries will get incentivize if the income exceeds the expenditure. This has introduced budget drive and profit driven corporate mindset and approach. When the director of the Academy of HRD was appointed from academics, the director was given salaries which are comparable to academic institutions. The director often felt that he/she was not treated properly by the NHRDN as AHRD is a part of NHRDN. There were times when the director compared the salaries of director of AHRD and felt that the director general of NHRDN who does not have the kind of qualifications that the director of AHRD has gets many times the salary of the director. They introduce a feeling of being look down upon and a feeling of competitiveness on the part of AHRD. This was a major issue, which was neither recognized nor could be handled well. In later years, when directors of AHRD came from corporate sector, they were either retired or were willing to come for academic salaries. Since then, the salaries of the director of AHRD have always been low as it had a lot of hand to mouth existence. This has continuously been a crucible experience.
5. XLRI's withdrawal from the Fellow program has been another crucible experience. After Fr. Abraham's term as Director of XLRI was over Fr. P. D. Thomas took over as Director. For

some reasons he had his biases or was influenced by some faculty who were not in favor of XLRI's collaboration with AHRD. He wanted an exit clause to be incorporated in the MOU for which AHRD did not agree as one batch has already been admitted and classes begun. In fact the classes were held at IIMA campus and Fr. Thomas himself came to inaugurate the program. Sometime after four batches were completed admission XLRI wrote to AHRD withdrawing their collaboration for the program. The Fellow Program at that time was being Chaired by Dr. E. G. Parameswaran who suggested that AHRD could run it independently and if XLRI is keen to withdraw let them withdraw. This decision went by default unlike the decision to start the program taken by the Boards of XLRI and AHRD. In later years AHRD had to explore collaboration with other Universities for recognition as Ph. D. program but continued to offer it as a Fellow of AHRD. Many candidates when contacted said that they are interested in being designated as fellow of AHRD rather than a Ph. D. with a Doctor of Philosophy title. This continued to be a difficult point in the minds of all those who promoted this program.

PART 3

Institution Building of NHRDN

1985: Recent Experiences in HRD: Birth of NHRDN: A National seminar by L&T on "Recent Experiences in HRD" was conducted from 27th Feb 27–2nd Mar, 1985.

- In 1983, while joining as L&T Professor of HRD at XLRI, Dr. Rao got approval to start a Center for HRD at XLRI and to give an annual public seminar on his work. Dr. Rao used this opportunity to get L&T to host the 4-day seminar at Mumbai, where more people could attend. The seminar focused on the recent experiences in HRD. About 40 persons participated in the seminar. Dr. Rao presented the integrated HRD model developed at L&T. The HR Head of L&T spoke about how it was being implemented. The seminar explored what was happening and not happening in HRD, how many organizations were not able to understand the right spirit of HRD, and the helplessness of HRD managers in convincing some CEOs etc. A number of success stories were also shared and there was new enthusiasm in all the members. In response to a suggestion from Dr. T. V. Rao who was leaving XLRI to return to IIMA, the members proposed the continuation of the Initiative under a new banner. Several suggestions were given. The discussions were steered by Dr. T. V. Rao towards setting up a professional body outside the Institutional framework of Management schools (IIMA or XLRI etc.) to facilitate learning of practitioners on a continuing basis from each other. This lead to the conceptualizing of the National HRD Network. It was also agreed that different cities should have such Networks. A newsletter was initiated to disseminate the new knowledge about HRD. It was agreed to have one intellectual article by an academician, one essay profiling in details the practices of a company, a few caselets of problems and issues, which may be posed to the reader, some references and bibliography and news items. In the initial years of the newsletter the HRD center coordinators Fr. E Abraham and Dr. T.V. Rao managed to get every number sponsored by a company committed to HRD and having done some good work worthy of sharing. It would meet the cost of printing 2000 copies of the newsletter and also mailing it free to all HRD chiefs and CEOs in the country. L&T was the natural choice as everyone was talking about L&T in relation to HRD. L&T readily agreed. The seminar proceedings were published as a book "Recent Experiences in HRD" and the formation of the Network was announced in 1985 through this book and the HRD Newsletter.

- **March 2, 1985 Proposing National HRD Network**
  - Seeds of the idea to start NHRDN was conceptualized at the "National Programme in HRD" held at Bombay to form a network of HR professionals and to learn from each other's experiences. Many participants volunteered to become the contact persons in various cities where the chapter wise NHRDN were supposed to start.

CITY	NAME	COMPANY
Madras	Mr. S. Chandrashekar	Manager (P&OD) E.C.C. (L&T)
	Dr. P. V. R. Murthy	Dy. Manager (HRD) Sundaram Clayton
Delhi	Mr. S. Raghavan	Sr. Manager (P) Maruti Udhyog Ltd.
	Mr. P.K. Sarangi	Sr. Manager (HRD) I O C
Bangalore	Mr. K. Prasannan	Sr. Manager (P) Ind Suzuki Motor Cycles Ltd.
	Mr. K. S. Rao	Manager (P&A) Madhura Coats
Baroda	Dr. Rajan Gupta	Manager (HRD) Jyoti Ltd.
	Mr. S. A. Dixit	Manager (HRD) Petrofils Corporation
Bombay	Mr. T.P. Raman	Chief Officer (HRD) SBI
	Dr. D.F. Pereira	Dy. G. M. (HRD) L&T

Not all of them have paid an active role. TVR used to keep in touch with all of them and use others whenever some of them could not become active or changed their place of work. The brochure given in Box below presents the initial thoughts. Once they have agreed the biggest challenge was to keep their interest alive and demonstrate that networking is essential to learning and leadership action.

After this seminar I returned to IIMA in March 1985.. Before I left Fr. Abraham and I made sure that the first Newsletter of the Center for HRD "HRD Newsletter ís printed and mailed. Fr. Abraham stayed back in Mumbai to get Dr Pereira to complete his article of HRD in L&T which was published in the first issue. This was a crucible experience. I still remember Abe and I going on my two wheeler to the press to read proofs and get the newsletter out. This Newsletter provided a model for subsequent Newsletters.

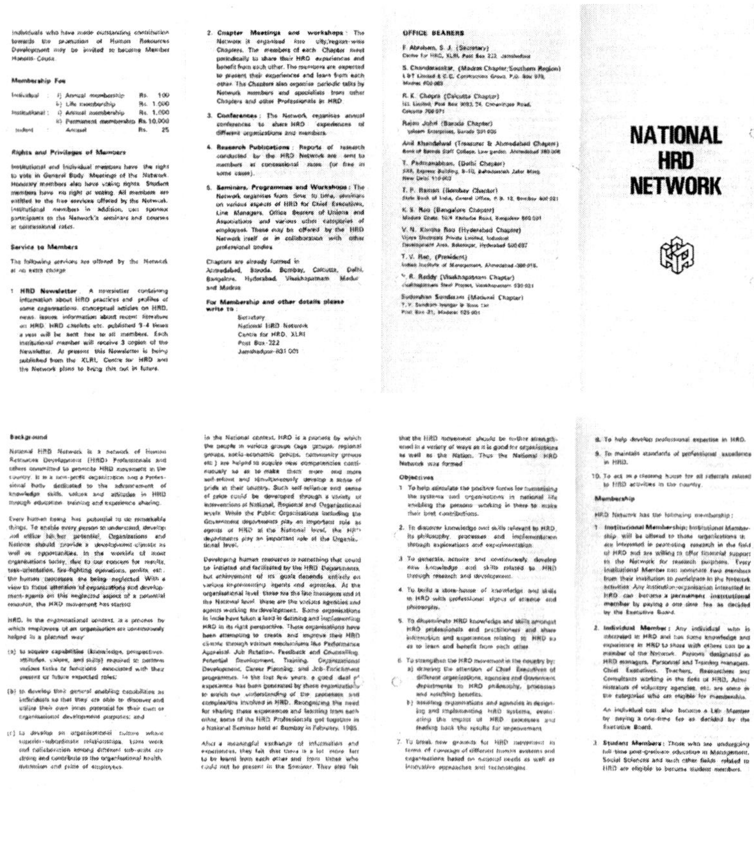

- Initially the membership was kept open without charging any membership fees. Anyone who filled in the form in b Box was admitted.

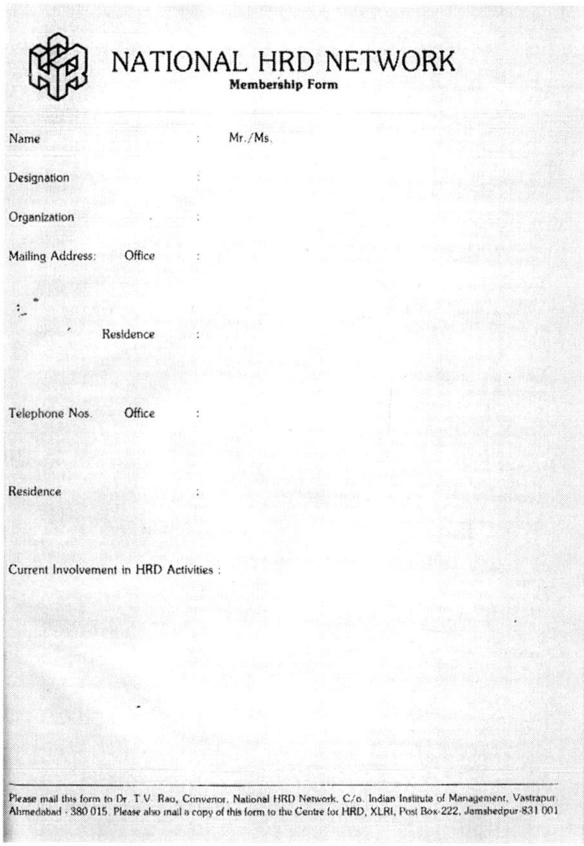

NATIONAL HRD NETWORK

Membership Form

Name : Mr./Ms.

Designation :

Organization :

Mailing Address: Office :

Residence :

Telephone Nos. Office :

Residence :

Current Involvement in HRD Activities :

Please mail this form to Dr. T.V. Rao, Convenor, National HRD Network, C/o. Indian Institute of Management, Vastrapur Ahmedabad - 380 015. Please also mail a copy of this form to the Centre for HRD, XLRI, Post Box-222, Jamshedpur-831 001

- Once the National HRD Network became established and started functioning full-fledged across the country through various city wise chapters, HRD Newsletters were published every year by National HRD Network and XLRI jointly to keep all the members of National HRD Network aware of the events and important happenings in the area of HRD as well as it served as medium of mass communication to all the members of National HRD Network across India.

- The document below shows how National HRD Network and XLRI jointly produced the HRD Newsletters and how the people were invited to contribute articles for the same.
- This newsletter was initiated to disseminate the new knowledge about HRD. It was agreed to have one intellectual article by an academician, one essay profiling in details the practices of accompany, a few caselets of problems and issues, which may be posed to the reader, some references and bibliography and news items. In the initial years of the newsletter the HRD center coordinators Fr. E Abraham and TV Rao managed to get every number sponsored by a company committed to HRD and having done some good work worthy of sharing. It would meet the cost of printing 2000 copies of the newsletter and also mailing it free to all HRD chiefs and CEOs in the country. L&T was the natural choice as everyone was talking about L&T in relation to HRD. L & T readily agreed. The seminar proceedings were published as a book "Recent Experiences in HRD" and the formation of the Network was announced in 1985 through this book and the HRD Newsletter.

This is how the articles were invited for the newsletter.

Prof. T.V. Rao
Organizational Behaviour Area

August 3, 1992

Mr. P. Jeevan Joshi
Editor, Sapphire
Men's Hostel
XLRI
Post Box 222, CH Area East
Jamshedpur - 831 001

Dear Mr. Joshi:

I am happy to know that you have a newsletter for promotion of Personnel Management, Industrial Relations and HRD and that you are interested in having some outsiders write for it. I would very much encourage you to pursue this effort. As some of you might know, I have always considered myself as a part of the XLRI family since the time I was at XLRI between 1983 and 1985 to set up the Centre for HRD. I would like to share with you a small experience we had during 1984 Summer. The Centre for HRD took seven PMIR students as summer trainees and gave a one week training in HRD during the summer vacation. After the training they were sent to different cities (Madras, Delhi, Bombay, Baroda and Calcutta). They were attached to HRD managers in one of the companies. Their task was to study the HRD practices of a small group of companies on that city and prepare case studies. They did an excellent job. Ofcourse they also had some frustrating time. Later the case studies they collected were published in the HRD Newsletter. I understand that this experience became quite handy for a number of them in handling HRD jobs.

As some of you are aware, the HRD Newsletter which is currently published by the National HRD Network and XLRI jointly was started at XLRI. In fact the HRD Network itself was born out of a seminar organised by XLRI (HRD Centre) and L&T. If some of you want to keep in touch with what is happening in the outside world, the HRD Newsletter is a good way. Atleast four times a year you will receive it if you become a student member. Although HRD Network was promoted by XLRI till today there is no HRD Network Chapter at Jamshedpur. The students of IIM, Lucknow formed a student chapter last year and Management students in Pune also take active part but XLRI students have not yet taken any initiative. You can both contribute and learn if you start a chapter of the HRD Network. You could write to Prof. Keith D'Souza or Dr. Udai Pareek for details. Once you start a chapter you may even be able to get some executives to come over and address you. You could write caselets or share your summer assignment experiences. HRD Newsletter reaches over 1000 HRD/Personnel managers and is read by a larger number including line managers. It is a good way to keep in touch with outside world. It only needs about ten of you to get together and become student members by contributing Rs.50/- each

The newsletter contained caselets, NHRDN News, Books and articles published etc. This kind of articles were published in newsletter to facilitate collaborative learning.

nalisation of HRD processes and culture is a slow process and may take some years

In view of these, the HRD managers have a complex role to perform. In order to make an impact the HRD manager should:

1. be a person with a high degree of commitment to HRD and HRD philosophy,
2. have a high degree of perseverance;
3. be closer to the chief executive and be able to get and communicate the top management's commitment to employees.
4. be given enough time (a minimum of 5 years) to work as HRD manager without being transferred.

In addition, the top management should be sensitive to the organizational processes and be able to perceive the incremental changes occuring in the development climate of the organization.

HRD ISSUES

The following letter has been received from the HRD Manager of a Bank. We request our readers to give their views on the issues raised. Please send your views to **Prof. T.V. Rao, Indian Institute of Management, Vastrapur, Ahmedabad-380 015** for publication in the next Newsletter.

PRO-HRD or ANTI-HRD

Dear Sir,

Our bank has launched an Operational Plan for the year 1985-87, with a view to bring about substantial qualitative improvement in bank's operation through specific programmes drawn up for overcoming identified short-comings. One of the aspects in this effort, requiring attention of HRD department, is of morale and motivation of staff at all levels.

During the discussions amongst my colleagues a point came up that we must ensure right type of jobs for right type of personnel. A group of my colleagues is of the opinion that the concept of "right job for the right man" is anti-HRD. They are of the view that if an individual is found very effective in a particular area, according to the concept mentioned above, he cannot be assigned other job as he may not be right man for that particular job. In this process, he cannot change or develop. The concept, thus, is exploitation of the employee than H.R.D. orientation.

Another thought pattern also cropped up according to which the concept is not anti-HRD from broader perspective. They argue that as per the concept, right man is to be trained and developed for an existing particular job. HRD is also involved in identifying right man for a particular job in a large organisation like banking.

Kindly let me have your views.

Sincerely yours
Mahesh Kaul

KRITIKA ENTERPRISES: Some Responses

Response No. 1

Newly established H R Depts. often fail because there has been little analysis of the problems that face the organisation, and virtually no setting of long and medium term business goals for the organisation. In such companies, HRD work is over generalised and represents more a sort of "philosophic stand" on the issue of employee development. Characteristically, such a "formula approach" centres around the introduction of new appraisal systems and extensive training efforts. It is not surprising that managers in such organisations find it difficult to see the connection between the work of the H R Dept. and the immediate "real life" problems facing the company.

The failure to make such an analysis is equally the fault of top management as of the H R function. Top Management often excludes the H R function from the process of strategic business planning, and the Human Resource function often draws up policies without due consideration of top management's business plans and the organisation's immediate business conditions.

This is what appears to have happened in Kritika Enterprises also.

In Kritika Enterprises the problem is compounded by the MD's unclear concept of the role of the H R Dept. and the reluctance of senior managers to accept the work of Mr Appa Rao and his H R dept. This reluctance has probably been caused by non-involvement of senior line managers in the decision to start an H R dept., the carving out of a role for H R dept. by taking away an area originally handled by the Personnel Dept., the over-use of outside consultants for OD work, and the drawing out of line people from their normal work to attend OD exercises.

However, closing down the H R dept. to effect a saving of Rs. 2 lakhs is no answer. This crisis provides the

9

organisation and Mr Appa Rao's dept, with an opportunity to do some really vital and relevant OD work.

The H R Dept. must recognise that the immediate concern of senior managers and the MD is the financial viability of the company and improvement in its profitability. The thrust of OD activity should be in helping the MD & line managers to identify areas where priority action needs to be taken for improving the company's overall performance. Providing assistance in drawing up and executing such action plans will make the H R dept's work really relevant to the organisation.

Mr Appa Rao could suggest that the MD meets his senior executives to go into the role that the H R dept. can play at the present time. Mr Appa Rao could at such a session make the group aware of the contribution his department could make in addressing the problems the organisation faces.

Once senior managers in Kritika Enterprises see the short-term relevance of HRD & OD work, they would be better able to appreciate and accept the long-term perspective that such a function, and indeed the whole business demands.

Mr Appa Rao must go slow on the appraisal system. It is certainly not the most critical thing for the organisation at this time.

Sarosh J. Ghandy, Resident Director, TELCO, Jamshedpur, Chairman Board of Governors, XLRI

Response No. 2

From the work done in the area of HRD so far I find it difficult to believe there is a threat of a closure move. If the threat is real then I strongly suggest a Boss Confrontation Meeting with the MD. HRD Manager should bring up the following issues in confrontation:

1) The absurdity of initiating HRD and withdrawing the effort, leading to ambiguity in the perception of employees of organisation's value system; and values one does not change at will.

As it is with the experience of one HRD Manager having initiated a Performance Appraisal System and abandoned, move to close HRD would seriously damage the image of top management in the eyes of the employees.

2) Correlation of HRD, organisation culture and improved performance as narrated in "In Search of Excellence", "Change Masters" and "Leaders".

3) MD to draft a circular stating HRD achievement in the organisation so far and plans for future to put the rumours to rest.

Experience Sharing of Other Companies

4) Experience of other Companies e.g. CGL continued its HRD effort right through its economy drive. HRD was used positively to build/improve performance at critical periods of company's performance. Such experiences would help MD look at HRD as an instrument to accelerate performance rather than decelerate.

5) Budgetory cut is not a major constraint. In HRD, in the last 3 years, CG has spent a negligible amount as professional charges. HRD System work therefore should not suffer at all in the light of the budgetory cut.

6) HRD Department must change its outlook with changed circumstances of organisation. Its training emphasis should be on areas like optimisation and cost effectiveness (Value Engineering and other Operations Research techniques) building the morale of employees etc. Those areas which do not have a direct impact on performance and external programmes, unless of a specialised nature, can be curtailed. In case of redundant persons, at HRD they can be redeployed.

7) HRD must come out with a HRD Newsletter on a regular basis to inform all line Managers about what HRD has done and the impact of its performance.

I strongly believe this threat that HRD Manager senses should be made an opportunity to hasten the approval of performance appraisal system build linkages with line functions and synthesise the HRD work done so far.

Susan Varughese, Senior HRD Executive, Crompton Greaves Ltd., Bombay.

Response No. 3

In the organization Kritika Enterprises, the issue seem to be that of relationship between the Manager—Human Resource Development and Managing Director on the one side and old managerial staff on the other. One needs to understand the present relationship in the perspective of last 5 years. At the time of entry of young Managing Director, organization can be described as under:

1. The management staff had worked with old Managing Director for decades and therefore might have developed the informal culture of personal loyalty.
2. The company has gone adding more and more divisions without modernising the existing divisions resulting into overstaffing, incompetitive products, and high cost of maintaining the infrastructure etc.
3. May be concentrating on low margin profit products for quick cashflow resulting into lose at time due to slippages.
4. Maintaining R&D infrastructure without really getting any commercially viable product due to lack of funds.

The two groups seem to be working on two different premise. The old timers have the conviction that whatever growth is achieved, it is because of their efforts and functioning style, while the young Managing Director have the belief that the survival and further growth call for certain changes. Thus, two groups (1) old timers discrediting the approach of the youngster as theoretical and 2) youngsters making efforts to introduce new systems based on the recent advancement in management theory and practice and lamenting old timers not responding to their ideas.

The success of an organization can be attributed to two types of decisions:

(1) Entrepreneurial

By entrepreneurial decision, it is meant the strategic conceptual decision, like location of a plant, selection of a new product, discontinuation of a particular division or department etc.

(2) Managerial Decision

By managerial decision, it is meant, in terms of the implementation of entrepreneurial decision, i.e. giving real shape of ideas of the entrepreneur.

In this case of Kritika Enterprises, two things are of great importance in the present crisis:

1. The preception of the managerial team about the young Managing Director's ability to take strategic conceptual decision:

   Since the company seem to be passing through financial crisis, the Managing Director might be exercising stringent budgetary control and seem to be cutting the dead-wood. He may treat this to be the realistic and normal course of action in bad time. But the managerial staff may take it as a punishment for the bad decision in which the company has been loosing more than a crore of rupees per annum and for which they may not own any sort of responsibility.

2. Perception of Managing Director about the affect of his decision on the functioning of the company, i.e. effect on the morale of the employees:

   This action of Managing Director will have negative impact on their initiative, and will develop mis-trust and the old timers will depend on each and every decision on the Managing Director. This will call for pre-occupations of Managing Director with the day-to-day working.

Role HRD can play

Apparently the focus of HRD department had been on the evaluation of managerial staff rather than on the organizational needs/problems that can be sorted out through HRD intervention.

It is said, people have the objective not the organizations. Since the HRD function itself is being debated, the HRD Manager needs to re-examine his own approach and think strategies to improve the acceptability of HRD as a function. In addition, there are some suggestions:

1. Needs to get real commitment of Managing Director in specific tasks related to HRD.
2. Accept the need of existing staff's cooperation as a reality for the survival of the organization.
3. Should spell out the organizational issues quickly and there should not be much gap between thinking, deciding and implementation of a course of action.
4. The OD intervention should be on the issues where the results can be seen quantitatively.

R.C. Wadhwa,
Asst. Manager, Trg & Dev.
Reliance Industries Ltd.
Ahmedabad.

Response No. 4

You would appreciate that the role of the HRD Department has become more important and challenging during the period of crisis rather than the period of prosperity only. When everything is going good the morale of the people is high and at that time, role of the HRD is often at low level. The need of HRD department becomes very intense when profits start shrinking, there are allround set-backs and the morale of the people start going down. At this particular point HRD Department has to ensure the following.

(a) to hold a workshop of the concerned people, find out the problems, root cause, analyse them and with the help of PEOPLE try to find out the solution. At that stage HRD department shall provide solace to the line People.

(b) HRD Department should help in reorganising the total structure of the company, redefining the responsibility and goal settings and work out with the help of others the solutions, new high technologies & methodology. HRD Department should have '*vision*' and with the help of PEOPLE rework out the '*values*' and priority in each area and THRUST should be given in those areas wherever required;

HRD in such circumstances, no doubt, should discourage the unproductive programmes but should concentrate more on productive and quite result - oriented programmes and wherever required additional faculty must be hired & tempo of the *people* must be maintained and rebuilt. In this particular case the company may save Rs. 2 lacs but in reality if HRD does not work the company may go into liquidation. It is only HRD Departm. through whose good efforts, the company can revive and Rs. 2 lacs, as a matter of fact, is negligible for the cause for which the HRD Department would be working. It shall be a drop in the ocean.

Problems do come in the organisation and it is this particular department which helps in finding solutions, rebuilding structures and finally see a ray of hope in the organisation.

V P. Duggal
Chief Personnel Manager
Modipon Limited
Modinagar

- National HRD Network in collaboration with Indian Society for Behavioral Sciences (ISABS) had started offering HRD & OD Facilitators Lab.

HRD AND OD FACILITATORS DEVELOPMENT PROGRAMME

Need

Many organizations today are looking for HRD professionals to initiate and strengthen the HRD systems and processes. There is a realisation in most organizations that HRD is more than training and many other mechanisms like performance appraisal and development systems, potential development exercises, counselling and OD interventions can go a long way in creating a healthy and development oriented culture. While there is a need for HRD professionals organizations are also finding it difficult to locate trained HRD professionals who can handle most of the HRD subsystems simultaneously. The dearth for competent HRD professionalsis because there are no indepth long term programmes to develop HRD professionals. The existing training programmes do not extend beyond a week which is very insufficient time to develop HRD professionals. Recognizing this need the National HRD Network in collaboration with the Indian Society for Applied Behavioural Sciences (ISABS) have designed this three phased programme to develop HRD professionals.

Target Group

This programme is meant for middle or senior level executives who are interested in developing their competencies as HRD professionals. While this programme is ideally suited for those in Personnel + Training and HRD Departments, other line managers who are interested in developing their competencies in HRD. Theparticipant should have some scope in his/her organization to initiate or facilitate HRD mechanisms or processes.

Objectives

This programme is expected to help the participant to gain an in-depth knowledge and understanding of HRD and OD interventions possible and practiced in Indian organizations. The participant will also be helped to examine and develop process, facilitation skills (e.g. listening, empathy, organizational diagnosis, problem-solving, counselling positive and helpful attitude etc.) required for HRD facilitators.

Design

The programme is designed in 3 phases. The first phase is a laboratory based learning, the second phase is reading and action-interventions, and the third phase is review and reinforcement of skill development.

Phase - I : Two Week HRD and OD Facilitator's Laboratory (June 6-18, 1988)

The two week laboratory will have the following inputs:

- 3 days of Group Learning based on T-Group technology
- 3 days HRD Interventions Lab including conceptual inputs, experience sharing and experimentation centering round performance appraisals, counselling, potential development, career development, training etc.
- 2 days conceptual and experiential inputs on Organizational Diagnosis and OD interventions
- 2 days OD skill development labs dealing with (i) team-building interventions; (ii) Role Analysis exercises; (iii) Survey Feedback; (iv) Stress Audit or (v) any others. The participant will choose any two interventions from these that suits his role and his organizational requirements.
- One day of action planning.

Each participant is required to prepare an plan of action outlining the HRD/OD facilitation he wishes to undertake in his organization and is expected to share with the rest of the participants.

Phase - II : Facilitation - Action Phase

This phase deals with what the participant does in the next one year on his job in the farm of HRD and OD facilitation i.e. the implementation phase of action plans. The participant is expected to do the following during this phase: (i) present his action plans on return from Phase-I to his reporting officer/department, seek support needed and implement the action plans; (ii) Read the prescribed readings (about 10 books and articles on HRD and OD);

(iii) Be in touch with one of the Senior HRD Facilitators and keep reviewing progress and keep maintaining diary of significant events in facilitation process, and (iv) Prepare a review paper at the end of the year.

Phase - III : Review and Reinforcement Phase

This phase consists of a one-week Review Workshop in 1989 Summer. In this workshop the participants will share their experiences, identify personal/ environmental facilitators and inhibitors in HRD facilitation, review their work and further strengthen their facilitation skills through experimentation.

Certification

On successful completion of the third phase the participants will be certified.

Fees

Rs.7,500/- for Phases I & II. Mainly to cover the living expenses of the participants and faculty travel and living and overheads. No fee will be charged for Phase II. Fee for Phase III will be announced next year and is mostly on the basics of actuals. As ISABS and National HRD Network are professional bodies, faculty work on honorary capacity by donating their time due to their commitment to the profession. No faculty fee is charged and marginal surplus if any from the programme fee is utilised for the advancement of the Applied Behavioural Science and HRD professions.

Nominations

Please send nominations giving the following details of the candidate: Candidate's Name; designation; address for correspondence; age; qualifications; nature of experience in HRD; current and future likely HRD responsibilities; HRD related training programmes attended in the past. Please send the nominations to: ____________________

Venue

Hotel Clarks Amer, Jaipur.

Honorary Faculty

Mr. S. Chandarasekar

Mr. Anil Sachdev

Dr. Dharni P. Sinha

Dr. D.M.Pestonjee

Dr. T.V. Rao

Dr. S.N. Chattopadhyay

Mr. Deepankar Roy

Dr. Abad Ahmed

Dr. Rajen Gupta

Dr. M. Athreya

Mr. A.S. Vasudevan

- - - -

1986

- Inception of NHRDN
  - Inviting nominations
  - Dr. Rao becomes the first convener of NHRDN

NATIONAL HRD NETWORK
INTRODUCTION

Background

National HRD Network is a network of Human Resources Development (HRD) Professionals and others committed to promote HRD movement in the country. It is a non-profit organization and a Professional body dedicated to the advancement of knowledge, skills, values and attitudes in HRD through education, training and experience sharing.

Every human being has potential to do remarkable things. To enable every person to understand, develop and utilize his/her potential, Organizations and Nations should provide a development-climate as well as opportunities. In the worklife of most organisations today, due to our concern for results, task-orientation, fire-fighting operations, profits, etc., the human processes are being neglected. With a view to focus attention of organizations and development-agents on this neglected aspect of a potential resource, the HRD movement has started.

HRD, in the organisational context, is a process by which employees of an organisation are continuously helped in a planned way :

(a) to acquire capabilities (knowledge, perspectives, attitudes, values, and skills) required to perform various tasks or functions associated with their present or future expected roles;

(b) to develop their general enabling capabilities as individuals so that they are able to discover and utilize their own inner potential for their own or organisational development purposes; and

(c) to develop an organisational culture where superior-subordinate relationships, team work and collaboration among different sub-units are strong and contribute to the organisational health, dynamism and pride of employees.

In the National context, HRD is a process by which the people in various groups (age groups, regional groups, socio-economic groups, community groups etc.) are helped to acquire new competencies continuously so as to make them more and more self-reliant and simultaneously develop a sense of pride in their country. Such self-reliance and sense of pride could be developed through a variety of interventions at National, Regional and Organizational levels. While the Public Organisations including the Government departments play an important role as agents of HRD at the National level, the HRD departments play an important role at the Organizational level.

Developing human resources is something that could be initiated and facilitated by the HRD Departments, but achievement of its goals depends entirely on various implementing agents and agencies. At the organisational level, these are the line managers and at the National level, these are the various agencies and agents working for development. Some organisations in India have taken a lead in defining and implementing HRD in its right perspective. These organisations have been attempting to create and improve their HRD climate through various mechanism like Performance Appraisal, Job Rotation, Feedback and Counselling, Potential Development, Training, Organizational Development, Career Planning, and Job-Enrichment programmes. In the last few years, a good deal of experience has been generated by these organizations to enrich our understanding of the processes and complexities involved in HRD. Recognizing the need for sharing these experiences and learning from each other, some of the HRD Professionals got together in a National Seminar held at Bombay in February, 1985.

After a meaningful exchange of information and experiences, they felt that there is a lot more left to be learnt from each other and from those who could not be present in the Seminar. They also felt that the HRD movement should be further strengthened in a variety of ways as it is good for organisations as well as the Nation. Thus the National HRD Network was formed

Objectives

1. To help stimulate the positive forces for humanising the systems and organisations in nationl life enabling the persons working there to make their best contributions.

2. To discover knowledge and skills relevant to HRD, its philosophy, processes and implementation through explorations and experimentation. ...

3. To generate, acquire and continuously develop new knowledge and skills related to HRD through research and development.

4. To build a store-house of knowledge and skills in HRD with professional rigour of science and philosophy.

5. To disseminate HRD knowledge and skills amongst HRD professionals and practitioners and share information and experiences relating to HRD so as to learn and benefit from each other.
6. To strengthen the HRD movement in the country by :

   a) drawing the attention of Chief Executives of different organizations, agencies and Government departments to HRD philosophy, processes and resulting benefits;

   b) assisting organisations and agencies in designing and implementing HRD systems, evaluating the impact of HRD processes and feeding back the results for improvement.

7. To break new grounds for HRD movement in terms of coverage of different human systems and organisations based on national needs as well as innovative approaches and technologies.

8. To help develop professional expertise in HRD.

9. To maintain standards of professional excellence in HRD.

10. To act as a clearing house for all referrals related to HRD activities in the country.

Membership

HRD Network has the following membership :

1. **Institutional Membership** : Institutional Membership will be offered to those organizations that are interested in promoting research in the field of HRD and are willing to offer financial support to the Network for research purposes. Every Institutional Member can nominate two members from their institution to participate in the Network activities. Any institution/organisation interested in HRD can become a **permanent institutional member** by paying a one-time fee as decided by the Executive Board.

2. **Individual Member** : Any individual who is interested in HRD and has some knowledge and experience in HRD to share with others can be a member of the Network. Persons designated as HRD managers, Personnel and Training managers, Chief Executives, Teachers-Researchers and Consultants working in the field of HRD, Administrators of voluntary agencies, etc. are some of the categories who are eligible for membership.

An individual can also become a life Member by paying a one-time fee as decided by the Executive Board.

3. **Student Members** : Those who are undergoing full-time post-graduate education in Management, Social Sciences and such other fields related to HRD are eligible to become student members.

Individuals who have made outstanding contribution towards the promotion of Human Resources Development may be invited to become Member Honoris-Causa.

Membership Fee

Individual :	(i) Annual membership	Rs. 100
	(ii) Life membership	Rs. 1,000
Institutional :	(i) Annual membership	Rs. 1,000
	(ii) Permanent membership	Rs. 10,000
Student :	Annual	Rs. 25

Rights and Privileges of Members

Institutional and Individual members have the right to vote in General Body Meetings of the Network. Honorary members also have voting rights. Student members have no right of voting. All members are entitled to the free services offered by the Network. Institutional members in addition, can sponsor participants to the Network's seminars and courses at concessional rates.

Service to Members

The following services are offered by the Network at no extra charge.

1. **HRD Newsletter** : A newsletter containing information about HRD practice and profiles of some organisations, conceptual articles on HRD, news, issues, information about recent literature on HRD, HRD caselets etc. published 3-4 times a year will be sent free to all members. Each institutional members will receive 3 copies of the Newsletter.

2. **Chapter Meetings and workshops** : The Network is organised into city/region-wise Chapters. The members of each Chapter meet periodically

to share their HRD experiences and benefit from each other. The members are expected to present their experiences and learn from each other. The Chapters also organise periodic talks by Network members and specialists from other Chapters and other Professionals in HRD.

3. **Conferences** : The Network organises annual conferences to share HRD experiences of different organizations and members.

4. **Research Publications** : Reports of research conducted by the HRD Network are sent to members at concessional rates (or free in some cases).

5. **Seminars, Programmes and Workshops** : The Network organises from time to time, seminars on various aspects of HRD for Chief Executives, Line Managers, Office Bearers of Unions and Associations and various other categories of employees. These may be offered by the HRD Network itself or in collaboration with other professional bodies.

For Membership and other details please write to :

Secretary
National HRD Network
Centre for HRD, XLRI
Post Box-222
Jamshedpur-831 001

MESSAGE FROM THE PRESIDENT, NATIONAL HRD NETWORK

One of the objectives of HRD is competency development. The second important objective is the creation of a healthy climate in the organisation so that employees are able to enjoy work and contribute their best to the organisation. Both these are fairly complex objectives to be achieved and there is no single way of achieving these objectives. The last decade has seen a good deal of experimentation by a few organisations to achieve these objectives of HRD. Some have used performance appraisals as instruments to achieve these. A few others have used OD exercises including team building, survey feedback, training, role analysis and such other mechanisms. Training as a direct mechanism of competency development also continues with some improvements in the training methodologies and strategies.

This conference aims at bringing together a group of those organisations that have used such new and non-traditional strategies of HRD and making available their experiences to a larger group. What is non-traditional today may become soon traditional as experience is growing at a fast rate. For example nearly twelve years ago when L&T started using "performance appraisal" and "feedback and counselling" as mechanism of HRD it was very new to the corporate world. Today many organisations have begun to redesign their appraisal systems to focus on developmental objectives and knowledge, and experience in this field is getting enriched every day. Soon performance appraisals may become traditional instruments of HRD.

Most of the papers that will be presented and discussed in the conference are specially invited papers. The programme committee has discussed with a number of individuals in this field to identify organisations that are using relatively new strategies of HRD. On the basis of these they have selected a few organisations. The turn-around in SAIL through major HRD initiatives like "priorities for action", "new performance appraisal system", "new training strategy" etc.; the HRD experience of BHEL primarily through OD interventions in the beginning and later through other mechanisms; new experience in L&T (particularly the ECC group) through OD with top management's involvement as well as their new performance analysis and development system; the use of role analysis and other mechanisms by IOC and their integrated HRD strategies; the role analysis, performance appraisal and potential development experiences of Crompton Greaves, the re-definition of personnel role and the Task-Force approach of BILT; the experiences and difficulties in implementing integrated HRD systems in large organisations like the SBI and the BOB; the

11

turn-around through OD and team development and culture building experiences of RHL; the HRD experience of fast expanding and highly employee welfare oriented organisations like Sundram Fasteners and Sundaram Clayton are some of the themes selected for sharing in this conference.

In addition discussion on some of the important, emerging and neglected aspects of HRD is also attempted to be focussed through academic and conceptual papers and presentations. The themes chosen for this purpose include : Integrated HRD Systems, HRD for workers, Role of Unions in HRD, HRD approach to IR, Structuring of HRD departments, Stress Audit and HRD etc. The expositions given by the Chief Executives of a number of leading organisations in the country about their philosophy and values of HRD is likely to highlight further the different approaches and strategies used by organisations as perceived by their top management. ...

We hope that the participants will enjoy this conference and in the true spirit of the HRD Network they will come forward in future to share their own experiences of developing and implementing HRD approaches and strategies in their own organisations. Such sharing of experiences is welcome through the HRD Newsletter or through the future conferences. Most of the papers are being brought out as a special volume of the conference papers which will be available during the conference itself. Papers received during the conference and the proceedings of the conference including the highlights of the Chief Executive speeches will be bought out as a second volume or as special issue of the Newsletter.

WITH BEST WISHES
T. V. Rao

- **HRD spreads to colleges**
    - In order to examine its adequacies/inadequacies of its own structures and processes and for the purpose of developing its Human Resources, several colleges in Karnataka like St. Joseph group of colleges and Mount Carmel College in Bangalore and Teresian College, Mysore approached HRD Center, XLRI.
- **Residential and non-residential Conference on Designing and Implementing Performance Appraisal Systems for Development. (NHRDN) in April, 1986 in Madras.**

Performance Appraisal for Development

A four-day workshop on "Designing and implementing Performance Appraisal systems for Development" organised by the Madras Chapter of the National HRD Network and the Centre for HRD at XLRI, was held at the Adayar park hotel in Madras from 23-26 April, 1986. 27 participants from 24 organisations participated in the workshop. The Faculty members included Dr. T.V. Rao, (IIMA) Dr. Udai Pareek (ISABS), Keith D'Souza) (XLRI), E. Abraham (CHRD), M.S.S. varadan (Om Consultants), V. V. Mohan (SBI) S. Chandrasekar (L&T, ECC) and C. M. Srivastava (L&T). There was a good deal of sharing among the participants and exchange of views. They found the programme very useful and recommended to the organisers of the workshop to conduct similar ones in the future.

14

- Books Launched
  - A Book- "Recent Experiences in HRD" by Dr. T.V Rao and Dr. Pereira was launched. It is a compilation of all the papers presented at the conference "National Programme in HRD" at Bombay.
- **Activities in National HRD Network**
  - HRD Network in South-Southern Regional HRD Network was inaugurated by Dr. Udai Pareek in Madras on 26th April, 1986 at a meeting jointly organized by Madras Management Association and National HRD N. Mr. S. Chandrasekhar becomes the first South Region HRD Network convener.
  - Ahmedabad and Baroda Chapter had a joint Meeting which was hosted by Mr. Anil Khandelwal and it was held at BOB Staff College, Ahmedabad on 5th April 1986.
  - 24 members attended this meeting.
  - Ahmedabad Chapter organized its 2nd meeting on 13th May, 1986 at BOB Staff College.
  - Bombay chapter had organized its first meeting on 15th March, 1986 in State Bank of India Central Office hosted by Mr. T.P. Raman.

1987

- **Dr. T.V. Rao became the president of Indian Society of Applied Behavioural Sciences (ISABS) in Jan 1987.**
  - He took the charge in the Annual Body Meeting held on 7th June, 1987 at Jaipur.
- **Mr. D.N.B. Singh (HRD Manager, Indian Oil Corporation) nominated for the HRD Facilitators Lab, organized by ISABS at Jaipur in June 1987.**
- **National HRD Network had organized a National Conference on "Alternative Approaches and Strategies of HRD" from 10th-13th Sept, 1987 in Madras.**

NATIONAL HRD NETWORK

ANNOUNCES

A Four Day

NATIONAL CONFERENCE ON

HUMAN RESOURCES DEVELOPMENT

Theme

"Alternative Approaches and Strategies of HRD"

10-13, September, 1987

Venue : Madras, Taj Coromandel Hotel

Last date for nominations: August 20, 1987

Please send your nominations to:

Mr. S. Chandarasekar, Dy. General Manager (HRD & P)
E.C.C. Construction Group, Larsen and Toubro Limited
Post Box 979, Manappakkam, Madras-660 089
Phone: 432741 Grams: CIVION Telex: 041-7157

Registration: Fees Rs. 1,500 for non-members of HRD Network and Rs. 1,200 for members

---

On the occasion of this national conference it is proposed to bring out a souvenir which would consist of abstracts of articles being presented and information of high calibre. The souvenir would be widely circulated among all the participants in the conference. The size of the souvenir is expected to be 26 cm × 19 cm and the tariff rates are as follows :

Back Cover Page	: Rs. 5000/-
Inside Cover Pages	: Rs. 4000/-
Donating space for the abstracts of the articles	: Rs. 3000/-
Art Paper Colour Page	: Rs. 3000/-
Ordinary Full Page	: Rs. 2500/-

For further details
Please contact:

(H. N. Arora)
Chairman, Souvenir Committee
C/o. Reliance Industries Ltd.
Naroda Industrial Estate
Ahmedabad-382 330

NATIONAL HRD NETWORK

SOUVENIR

National Conference on

Alternative Approaches and Strategies of HRD

September 10-13, 1987

Madras

NATIONAL CONFERENCE

ON

ALTERNATIVE APPROACHES AND STRATEGIES OF HRD

10-13 September, 1987

COMMITTEE OF PATRONS :

Coehlo S. J., Chief Executive, Ahmedabad Electricity Co. Limited.
Daga Ramesh K. Executive Vice-President, Hindustan Motors Limited, Madras.
Dayal Ishwar, Director, IIM Lucknow.
Deenadayalu V. R. Chairman & Managing Director, Madras Refineries Ltd. Madras.
Desai N. M. Chairman & President, Larsen & Toubro Limited, Bombay.
Gupta P. P. Chairman & Managing Director, CMC Ltd., New Delhi.
Kalyanasundaram. C. S. Managing Director, State Bank of India, Bombay.
Khosla S. L. Chairman, Indian Oil Corporation, New Delhi.
Krishnamurthy V. Chairman, SAIL, New Delhi.
Nohria K. K. Managing Director & President, Crompton Greaves, Bombay.
Pareek Udai, HRD Consultant, Jakarta, Indonesia.
Philip Joe, Director IIM Bangalore.
Premjit Singh, Chairman & Managing Director, Bank of Baroda, Bombay.
Raghavan, SVS, Chairman, MMTC, New Delhi.
Ramkrishnan, C. R. Vice-President Larsen & Toubro Limited, Madras.
R. D'Souza, s. j. Director XLRI, Jamshedpur.
Sharma, R. N. Vice-President, TISCO Jamshedpur.
Subbiah, M. V. Vice-Chairman & Managing Director E.I.D. Parry (India) Limited, Madras.
Sinha Dharni P. Principal, Administrative Staff College of India, Hyderabad.
Sheth N. R. Director, IIM-Ahmedabad.
Suresh Krishna, Chairman & Managing Director, Sundram Fasteners Limited, Madras.
Tarneja R. S. Director, Bennett Coleman & Company, Bombay.
Vaghul N. Chairman & Managing Director, ICICI Bombay.
Venu Srinivasan, Managing Director, Sundaram Clayton Limited, Madras.
Wahi S. P. Chairman, ONGC, Dehra Dun.

15

ALTERNATIVE APPROACHES AND STRATEGIES OF HRD

CONFERENCE COMMITTEES

Programme Committee

(1) K. K. Verma (Chairman)
Principal, Bank of Baroda Staff College, Ahmedabad
(2) E. Abraham, SJ
Coordinator, Centre for HRD, XLRI, Jamshedpur
(3) T. V. Rao
Professor, Indian Institute of Management, Ahmedabad
(4) D. M. Pestonjee
Professor, Indian Institute of Management, Ahmedabad
(5) Anil Khandelwal
Senior Faculty, Bank of Baroda Staff College, Ahmedabad

Public Relations Committee

(1) Rajan Johri (Chairman)
Manager, Human Resources, NIIT, New Delhi
(2) T. Padmanabhan
Manager, HRD Shriram Fibres Ltd., New Delhi
(3) R. M. Rajagopal
General Manager, (Personnel) Shri Ram Fibres, New Delhi
(4) Anil Sachdev
General Manager, Eicher Goodearth Ltd., New Delhi

Souvenir Committee

(1) H. N. Arora (Chairman)
General Manager (Personnel & Adm.)
M/s Reliance Industries, Ahmedabad
(2) Rakesh Kumar
R.A., Organizational Behaviour Area,
Indian Institute of Management, Ahmedabad
(3) N. Mirchandani
Manager, HRD, Crompton Greaves Ltd., Bombay
(4) J. K. Parikh
Manager, HRD, State Bank of India, Ahmedabad.

(1) ORGANISING SUB-COMMITTEE

S Chandarasekar
DGM (P & HRD)
Engineering Construction Corporation
Mount Poonamallee High Road,
Madras 600 089

19

P V R Murthy
Manager (HRD)
Sundaram Clayton Limited
8 Haddows Road
Madras 600 006

N C Sridharan
Personnel Manager
Durametallic (India) Limited
147 Karapakkam Village
Madras 600 096

D Harish
Senior Officer (HRD)
Sundaram Fasteners Ltd.
Padi, Madras 600 050

(2) REGISTRATION SUB-COMMITTEE

J X Gregory
Sr. Personnel Executive (HRD)
Sundaram Clayton Limited
8 Haddows Road
Madras 600 006

B Nambiar
Indian Oil Corporation Ltd
Indian Oil Bhavan, N. H. Road
Madras 600 034

E Sethuraman
Manager (HRD)
Indian Oil Corporation Ltd
Indian Oil Bhavan, N. H. Road
Madras 600 034

(3) HRD INFORMATION SUB-COMMITTEE

N C Vasudevan
Asst Personnel Officer
Sundaram Clayton Ltd
8 Haddows Road
Madras 600 006.

A O Joseph
Asst Manager - Mgt Development
Ashok Leyland Limited
Rajaji Salai
MADRAS 600 001

K S Venkiteswaran
Personnel Manager
Chemicals & Plastics India Limited
8 Cathedral Road
MADRAS 600 086

R N Dravid
Sr Consultant
Tata Consultancy Srevices
MADRAS

V Ramnarayan
Project Co-ordinator
Sundaram Industries Ltd
Mount Road
Madras 600 002

(4) CATERING SUB-COMMITTEE

R Mukundan
Asst. Manager - Recruitment,
Manpower Plg. & Traning,
Larsen & Toubro Ltd
ECC Group, Madras 600 089

(5) AUDITORIUM SUB-COMMITTEE

S K Mukherjee
General Manager (HRD)
Indchem Electronics Ltd
102 Velachery Road, Madras 600 032

P Nathan
Officer (HRD)
Indchem Electronics Ltd
102 Valachery Road, Madras 600 032

Eric Paul Rajendran
Senior Officer (HRD)
Hindustan Motors Ltd (E.E.D.)
Thiruvellore 602 004.

TENTATIVE PROGRAMME

DAY ONE, THURSDAY, SEPTEMBER 10, 1987

Forenoon

INAUGURATION : Hon'ble Minister
Shri P. Chidambaram* to Inaugurate,
Shri V. Krishnamurthy to Preside

Keynote addresses by :
Chief Executives : "HRD Philosophy, Values and Experiences"

Chairperson : Shri Suresh Krishna
Speakers : R. K. Daga V. R. Deenadayalu, V. Krishnamurthy, C. S. Kalyanasundaram, S. L. Khosla.

Afternoon (Session 1)

Chairperson : Shri N. M. Desai,* Chairman & President, Larsen & Toubro Limited.
Speakers : K. K. Nohria, S. V. S. Raghvan, R. N. Sharma*, Venu Srinivasan.

(Session 2)

Chairperson : Shri N. M. Desai*
Speakers : N. Vaghul, Col. S. P. Wahi, Dr. Ram S. Tarneja, C. R. Ramakrishnan, Rajendra Pawar
Mr. S. n. Bagai, RBI.

DAY TWO, FRIDAY, SEPTEMBER 11, 1987

Forenoon (Session 1)

Panel Discussion : "HRD Philosophy, Systems and Processes"
Chairperson : Dr. Rolf P. Lynton
Panelists : Dr. M. B. Athreya
Dr. S. Chandra, and Dr. T. V. Rao

(Session 2)

Papers :
(1) HRD in IOC by Mr. Bimal Kapoor,
(2) Role Analysis Exercises in IOC by Mr. P. K. Sarangi.
(3) HRD in Crompton Greaves by Ms. Susan Varughese.

*Confirmation awaited
Please refer to Committee of Patrons for information on Companies represented by Chief Executives.

Afternoon — Papers :

(1) HRD in Larsen and Toubro Ltd. by C. M. Srivastava

(2) Managing change through OD by S. Chandarasekar.
BILT experience by Anil K. Dixit.

(3) Organisational Renewal through HRD efforts :

(4) HRD in State Bank of India by T. P. Raman.

(5) HRD in Bank of Baroda by K. K. Verma.

(6) Training and HRD : an experience in symbiosis by Y. K. Bhushan.

DAY THREE, SATURDAY, SEPTEMBER 12, 1987

Forenoon — Papers :

(1) Major HRD initiatives in SAIL by, M. R. R. Nair

(2) HRD in Sundram Fasteners by M. S. Sambamurty.

(3) HRD in Eicher Goodearth Ltd. By Anil Sachdev

(4) Comparative Study of Japanese Management and HRD Practices in Sundaram Clayton by PVR Murthy.

Afternoon — Papers :

(1) HRD in Richardson Hindustan Ltd. by Ginil Shirodkar.

(2) HRD in BHEL by Parth Sarathi & S. S. Rao.

(3) HRD in R & D organisations by M. B. Puranik.

(4) Career Development Strategies in Lipton India by R. R. Nair.

(5) HRD in ONGC by Mr. Moolchand & Mr. S. Ramanathan.

SATURDAY SEPTEMBER 12, 1987

A PARALLEL FULL DAY WORKSHOP ON HRD IN GOVT. SYSTEMS FOR GOVT. OFFICIALS

- **National HRD Network Executive Board Meeting held in Jaipur on 7th June, 1987.**
    - **Members present were:**

Dr. T.V.Rao	Mr. I.G. Kannan
Mr. S. Chandrashekar	Mr. Philip Irudayaraj
Dr. Keith D'souza	Mr. Anil Trivedi
Mr. Anil Khandelwal	Ms. Susan Verughese
Mr.E. Abhraham	Mr. Pratik Roy
Mr. Rakesh Kumar	Ms. Kalpana Parikh
Ms. Uma Jain	Ms. Kokila Parthasarthy

1988

- **National HRD Network Annual Report**
    - Accomplishments
        - 1987 conference in Bombay brought many HRD managers to gather
        - Networking among many organizations and HRD managers through meetings, national conventions, newsletters and chapter programmes.
        - Orientation programmes conducted in several chapters to orient HR managers.
        - HRD & OD Facilators Lab offered in collaboration with ISABS for last 3 years.
        - Schemes of research grants, research support and awards to recognize and generate interest in the area of HRD.
        - Creation of sound financial base for network activities
    - Office Bearers
        - **Ex-officio member:** Dr T V Rao (Chairman PGP, IIM A)
        - **Elected Members:**

NAME	COMPANY
Mr. S. Chandrashekar	Dy. General Manager, L&T Ltd. ECC Construction Group
Mr. K Verma	Principal, Bank of Baroda Staff College
Prof S. R. Bijoor	Faculty, IIMA

- **Chapter presidents:**

CHAPTER	CHAPTER PRESIDENT	COMPANY
Ahmedabad	Mr. Anil Khandelwal	Chief Manager, Bank of Baroda Staff College
Bangalore	Mr. R. R. Nair	VP Personnel, Lipton India Ltd.
Baroda	Mr. Leo A. Singh	Personnel Manager
Bombay	Mr. Ginil Shirodhkar	VP Personnel, Procter & Gamble India Ltd.
Calcutta	Mr. Robin Basu	Personnel Executive, Infar India Ltd.
Delhi	Mr. Anil Sachdev	General Manager (Personnel), Eicher Goodearth Ltd.
Hyderabad	Mr. V N Kanatha Tao	Manager (HRD), Vijai Electricals Pvt. Ltd.
Madras	Dr. P. V. R. Murthy	Dy. Manager (HRD) Sundaram Clayton
Indore	Mr. Ajit Madhur	Indore Management Association

- **National HRD Network Scholarship was proposed**
  - Objectives, Target group and criteria for the Selection were decided, Selection Committee was formed and the amount to be given for the Scholarship was also raised.
- National HRD Network started giving Awards to individuals as well as organizations that have done some extra ordinary work in the area of HRD. These awards were given every year to encourage and promote individuals and organizations that have demonstrated some exemplary work in area of HRD.

National HRD Network

Announces

HRD Awards for Outstanding contributions to the promotion of Human Resources Development in Organizations, Groups and Society

The awards are for the following categories:

- **Individuals**
    - CEOs including Unit Heads, SBU Heads, Heads of Institutions, NGOs and Professional Bodies that have contributed outstandingly to the growth of Human resources
    - HRD Managers, Line Managers, and HR Professionals who mad eoutstanding contributions to Developing people
    - Academicians, Researchers, Scholars and Trainers
- **Organizations**
    - Any organisation from Public Sector, MNCs, Private sector, Small and Medium Enterprises ec. that have made outstanding contributions to the development of Human resources
    - Not for Profit Organizations, Academic Institutions, Professional Bodies and Associations

These awards are being given in recognition of outstanding work done by the originations or Individuals.

The single most important criterion for these awards is that the *work or service or contribution should be in the area of developing other people in terms of their competencies, commitment, values and leadership etc. and make them available for the larger cause or as larger resources.*

Other criteria that contribute to the outstanding nature of the contributions are:

1. *The nature of contribution should be considered as outstanding by any standards and by a variety of outsiders including the jury of the awards*
2. *It should have benefited a large number of people or should have the potential of benefiting with some evidence to that effect*
3. *It should have made a lasting impact on those that are aimed at already*
4. *It should have left some marks and lessons for others to learn*
5. *It should have the potential of being emulated or ahs already been emulated by other people*
6. *It should also have a local, global or national value*

Organizational Awards

- The organization should have a long-term vision and mission, which promotes continuous development of competencies and creation of culture (Development of 3Cs Competencies, Commitment and Culture) in the organization, society or neighborhood. The larger the sphere of influence individual developing HRD the more the potential to be awarded. For example Developing systems that have benefited a few of its managers will be considered as not great contributions as compared to another organization that have focused on workmen, and all other categories of managers. If HRD efforts are extended to the larger society or the neighborhood such an organization scores higher. In other words width of coverage of HRD and the depth of coverage (technical knowledge, values, leadership, soft issues, commitment etc.)
- HRD systems (High maturity of systems including implementation of the systems). Organizations that have used systems demonstrate the replicability and extensibility. Those organizations that have institutionalized the systems and have indicted that they have very mature and institutionalized systems are considered as outstanding.
- Should have shown a high degree of commitment to HRD. These may be indicted through statements, annual reports, vision mission statements and other published and internally circulated literature. The commitment is also indicated by the investments made on HRD practices for the benefit of the people. Excessive profit orientation without concern for long-term institution building, competence development is considered as negative to HRD. Pursuance of narrow goals without concern for people. The way the VRS is handled for example with concern for people will be an indictor of HRD orientation. Those who have taken VRS will be surveyed on a sample basis for determining the HRD philosophy and orientation. The circulars and d efforts made for VRS will be examined.
- Demonstrated that investment on people and people processes and systems yields organizational benefits. This may be justified by the organization
- Should have created a great work atmosphere. This may be indicted by surveys of Gallop, Business Magazines etc. Wherever available such evidence will be sued.
- Should have built leaders and supplied leaders to the society for promotion of peace and prosperity. Supply of leaders and change agents for internal or external consumption will be used a s criteria,
- Employee turn over rate or retention rates will be sued a some of the indicators for creation of work atmosphere and commitment
- Quick survey may be conducted for short listed organizations.

Individual Awards (CEOs, Heads of Organisations, Promotors of NGOs, Institutions etc.)

- A clear cut personal HRD philosophy- as stated in speeches, annual reports, actions and availability to serve the larger cause, and as reflected in personal style (360 degree data may be used)

- Role model in terms of setting standards and following the same (internal assessment and external customer and supplier assessment)
- Values people, people processes (evidence to be gathered by interviews and expert comments)
- High Integrity, Trust and Trustworthiness (will be considered most important quality for eligibility)
- Respect for local talent and free of biases in favor of the source of knowledge and promotion on indigenous knowledge
- Readily willing to share information and pass on benefits to others
- Donates times and available for servicing the society and larger causes
- Influences people with his own people philosophy and people practices
- Does not play politics in terms of using opportunities for self aggrandizement and personal promotion and even if he does puts larger causes in front than narrow interests

Individual Awards (HRD managers and Line Managers)

- Has a clear cut HRD philosophy
- Empowers his staff and encourages them to make larger contributions. Does not compete with the rather encourages them to build themselves and others.
- Systems driven
- Does right things
- Is a role model for HRD youth
- Influences the thinking of the juniors
- Available for promoting others
- Has a large circle of influence
- Sacrifices personal goals for larger causes
- Reads and writes
- Takes active interest in furthering the HRD Profession
- Has right values needed for HRD Manager
- Influences the thinking of the Top management
- Walks the talk
- Proud possession for the HRD profession
- Has capability to be a good line managers
- Has credibility
- Keeps in touch with latest developments in the field and disseminates his learning's
- Has made an impact on line managers and others
- Has made an impact in professional circles
- Innovative and Networking type

Individual Awards for Researchers, Scholars, Trainers, and Facilitators

- Generates new knowledge through research (basic and applied)

- Writes and Disseminates knowledge
- Works relentlessly for the spread of knowledge
- Provides assistance
- Develops the youth and works as a mentor for the youth
- Easily accessible
- Scholarly writings
- Originality of ideas

Methodology: Organizations

- Invite write ups
- Conduct assessment in a scientific way using a sample of HRD managers drawn from that city and the rest of the country
- Ask for nominations from HRD Managers not belonging to that organization
- Make preliminary enquiries and if necessary visit
- Examine evidence and circulate to a jury (the jury may extend beyond the team)
- Examine any confidential consultancy reports or published papers
- Examine hard data and case studies published in magazines etc.

Methodology for Individuals

- Invite nominations
- Conduct a 360 degree appraisal
- Examine publications and evidence
- Interview people (role set members, professional bodies, and colleagues)
- Talk to line managers from the organizations
- Get statistics right

❖ Mr. M R Nair (Director Personnel, SAIL) was appointed as the new president of NHRDN in 1987.

BIODATA OF SHRI M.R.R. NAIR

1. Shri M.R.R. Nair is the Chairman, Steel Authority of India Limited - the largest Public Sector Enterprise in India, with an investment of about Rs.14,000 crores, turnover of over Rs.10,000 crores, manpower of over 2,30,000 employees - a Company figuring in the 'Fortune 500 top Companies of the World'. Shri Nair has been associated with the Public Sector Steel Industry, right from its inception and has grown with the organisation. He joined the erstwhile Hindustan Steel Limited in 1960 and has worked in various capacities. He took over as General Manager (Personnel & Administration) in 1977 and became Director (Personnel) on the SAIL Board in 1981. He became the Managing Director of Bokaro Steel Plant in 1990. He took over as Chairman, SAIL, on November 01, 1992.

2. Shri Nair believed that the greatest strength of the organisation was the 'human resource' and the synergy of this resource could be used effectively to improve the performance of the Company. He took a number of steps including building up a new work culture, enhancing manpower utilisation through rationalisation, re-deployment and multi-skilling. All these resulted in the improvement of production, productivity, quality of products and services, cost reduction, attainment of capacity utilisation and generation of profits. Shri Nair provided the leadership in achieving the turn-around of SAIL.

3. Besides being one of the most successful managers in Indian Industry today, Shri Nair is also one of the top HRD professionals in the world. Widely travelled, Shri Nair is a visiting faculty of International Centre for Public Enterprises in Ljubljana, Slovania and member of the Committee on Industrial Relations of International Iron & Steel Institute, Brussels. At home, he is the founder member of Academy of Human Resource Development and was President of HRD Network in 1989-90. Recently, he has been made a Member of the Empowered Committee of the National Renewal Fund of the Government of India. He is also the Member of the Governing Body of XLRI.

4. Shri Nair is the recipient of a number of awards; to name a few, the National HRD Award 1989; Mother India International Gold Award 1991; International Excellence Award 1991; Vikas Ratna Award 1992; Rajiv Gandhi Excellence Award 1992; Rashtriya Udyog Award 1992; the Most Distinguished Service Award 1992, Shiromani Award, 1992.

❖ **Activities in National HRD Network**

- Indore Chapter of National HRD Network began in 1988. Mr. Ajit Mathur becomes the first president of Indore Chapter.

- Hyderabad Chapter conducts HRD climate survey of various industries in and around Hyderabad.

❖ **Books Launched**

- Book **"Human Resource Development: The Indian Experience"** by Mr. D. M. Silvera was launched. The book is about HR philosophies, HRD concepts, practices and traditions that are evolved in Indian context.
- Book **"Human Resource Development in Banks"** by Mr. Anil K. Khandelwal was launched. This book was first major book in this field.

1989

❖ **Dr. Rao had served as the president of ISABS from 1986–1989.**

INDIAN SOCIETY FOR
APPLIED BEHAVIOURAL SCIENCE

Dr. TV Rao
President

January 16, 1989

Dear

It is more than two year since I was elected as President of ISABS. This is the first time that the term of the President is extending over two years due to the new constitution. I feel that ISABS needs fresh air and new leadership. I also have some difficulty in finding time to work for the Society due to increasing demands on my time from my own Institute and others.

I strongly feel that there is a need for ISABS to have one full time paid Dean or Executive Director who can take full charge of the Society. I am scheduling a 3-day workshop for ISABS professionals to think of its future as a part of the summer event.

As I have difficulties in continuing as ISABS president beyond this summer, I request the Executive Board to appoint a Returing Officer and get the new President elected by May, 1989.

Thanking you and with regards,

Sincerely yours,

T V Rao

To: All Board Members of ISABS Board

- National HRD Network conducted Conference on "Towards Organizational Excellence through HRD" was held on 9th-11th Feb, 1989 at Hotel Taj Palace, New Delhi.
- ISABS conducted Summer Event from May 1–13, 1989 at Hotel Clarks Amer, Jaipur on
  1) Basic Human Process Laboratory
  2) Advance Human Process Laboratory
  3) Internship
  4) HRD-OD Facilitators Laboratory (jointly organized with the National HRD Network)

To :	Deepankar Roy A.S. Vasudevan Aroon Joshi Udai Pareek	Kirpal Singh Sushma Sharma MMP Akhouri Uma Jain Bhanu	All other ISABS members

From : T.V. Rao

Date : 12.12.1988

1. We have already decided that summer event will be held from May 1 to 13 at Clarks Hotel, Jaipur and the necessary bookings have already been made.

2. I propose that we hold that following programmes: BHP, AHP, Phases A and B and Internship. In addition we should make serious efforts to hold and get participants for a programme for women (or women trainers) and another for union leaders. The HRD programme will be held by HRD Network during the same time and independently at the same place. Hence the brochures will be separate and listing could be made of ISABS programmes in the Network Brochure and the Network Programme in ISABS Brochure.

3. The Brochure of the Summer event should be ready positively by the end of January for distribution in the HRD Conference at Delhi on February 9, 10 and 11 and Alumni Conference at IIMA on 10, 11 and 12 February.

4. The ISABS programmes will be advertised in the following professional journals (Indian Management, HRD Newsletter, IIMA Alumnus, ISTD Journal) and if possible in Economic Times. (Cost = Rs,4,500/- excluding Economic Times).

5. All programmes (except Phase A and B) are to be offered in the first week. The second week will be kept free (starting on Sunday) for a ISABS workshop (May 7 to 9). I request Udai to coordinate this workshop. This workshop is for discussing ISABS as an institution, sharing of thoughts, commitments and deciding a future course of action. ISABS Institute, Membership, Professional Development for university teachers etc. are additional items for this.

6. AGM and Board meeting will take place on 9th May afternoon to pass all resolutions required on the basis of the workshop. The design of Phase A and Phase B will be modified to suit this.

7. Akhouri and N.P. Singh may please explore the need and feasibility of a 5-day workshop for Trainers of Entrepreneurs to develop Human Process Competencies and to make them better trainers. If any of them agree they may please draft an announcement objectives, content, participants etc. and send to Deepankar.

8. Sushma, Bhanu and Uma may explore the possibility of Workshop for Trainers in Women's Development Programmes. Some international participation is possible as Commonwealth Secretariat indicated the possibility. Alternately a women's development programme (which we dropped last year) could be offered. As we need to finalise brochure material I request Bhanu to coordinate this and send the matter to Deepankar for inclusion in the Brochure.

9. I also request ISABS members/trainers who will be available for the summer event to send their acceptance to Deepankar Roy immediately for inclusion in the brochure and please keep May 1-13 free for ISABS event.

10. The term of the present team will get over by the end of 1989. We will be proposing in the next Board Meting (scheduled tentatively for February 8) to coincide with HRD Conference) the election process to start so that the new team is elected by '89 May and will have at least six months of overlap with the present team.

11. Responsibilities for 1989 Summer event. I suggest the following:

    11.1 Deepankar to coordinate finalisation of brochure, printing, mailing, advertisements and all other support for the event.

    11.2 Vasu to be in touch with Deepankar, identify faculty, new programmes and Dean the event.

    11.3 Aroon to write invitation letters for Phase A to all those who attended BHPs/AHPs in the last two years (specially this Winter event) and are found eligible for Phase A. AHP should be only for those whom it is absolutely essential and BHP to be taken as selection lab as per PDP guidelines. Aroon to write to all those who are eligible to come to Phase B and internship and also available from May 1 to 13 at Jaipur. In case it is difficult for Aroon to be present Isuggest Oriol Pujol to substitute and details may be worked out between them.

    11.4 Udai to explore cheaper accommodation at SIPA, Jaipur or University to offer low-cost programmes for those who cannot afford to pay for Clarks and inform Deepankar for costing etc.

2

11.5 Kirpal to get audited statements upto 31st March 1989 ready for the AGM and send necessary remainders etc.

11.6 Akhouri/N.P. Singh/Bhanu/Uma/Sushma to finalise new programmes and send brochure material to Deepankar.

11.7 Regional representatives to send their annual reports by April 15, 1989.

11.8 Syed to bring out the Newsletter. Summer event issue.

- National HRD Network Awards (1988–1989)
  - Organizational Awards

AWARD WINNING ORGANISATION
Crompton Greaves Limited
Larsen & Toubro Limited
Steel Authority of India
Sundram Fasteners Limited
TELCO

  - Individual Awards

AWARD WINING INDIVIDUAL
Mr. M. R. R. Nair
Dr. Udai Pareek
Mr. B. Ratnakar
Dr. Dennyson F. Pereira
Mr. P. K. Sarangi

- **Activities in National HRD Network Chapters**
  - **Ahmedabad Chapter**
    - Ahmedabad Chapter in collaboration with ISTD and NIPM organized a talk on "Training for New Technologies" by Prof. Sheila Rothwell, Director, Center for Employment Policy Studies, UK on 10th Oct, 1988.

- Mr. M. R. R. Nair, the then newly appointed Director of National HRD Network and Director (Personnel), SAIL gave a presentation on "HRD in SAIL" on 26th Dec, 1989. The session was chaired by Dr. N. R. Seth, Director IIMA. About 60 persons attended it.
- Dr. T.V. Rao, professor, IIM A addressed a joint gathering of members of ISTD and National HRD Network on "Organizational Renewal-Beyond Training" on Jan 18, 1989.

➢ **Baroda Chapter**

- "A Day of HRD Awareness" was organized for professionals in and around Baroda on 7th Jan, 1989.

➢ **Hyderabad Chapter**

- The Hyderabad Chapter, in collaboration with Rural Development Advisory Services of Hyderabad, had organized a one day workshop on "Searching for HRD Models for voluntary Actions in Rural Settings" on 2nd April, 1989 in Secunderabad.

❖ **Amendments in Rules and Regulations of Network**

➢ At the General Body Meeting of the Network held in New Delhi on 10th Feb,1989, an amendment in the rules and regulations was made to form an Executive Board consisting of the President, Secretary, Past President, Treasurer, three members elected by the General Body and Chapter Presidents and three members coopted by the National President. In addition to this freedom was given to the Executive Board can coopt maximum of three more members from among those who undertake significant responsibilities in furtherance of Network's objectives.

Phase VII: Strengthening the Academic Base: The Academy of HRD (1990–2008)

1990

❖ HRD Facilitators Programme

➢ HRD Facilitators' Lab was conducted from 4–16 June, 1990 and the programme was coordinated by Dr. Udai Pareek.

Phase I lasted for one week, consisted of human processes lab work. Dr. Rajan Gupta of IIM Lucknow and Dr. Keith D'Souza of XLRI were the facilitators in the first week. Phase II was conducted in the second week consisted of concepts, applications and experiences in HRD. It was taken by Dr. Udai Pareek, Dr. T.V. Rao, Ms Susan Varughese, Mr. Manohar Nadkarni, Mr. Arvind Agrawal and Mr. A. A. Niazi.

- National Institute of Personnel Management organized the 10th Annual Conference on the theme "Integrative Approaches to Human Resource Management" from 24th-27th Oct, 1990 in Krishna Oberoi Hotel, Hyderabad.
- **Activities in National HRD Network Chapters**
  - **Ahmedabad Chapter**
    - Mr. Parikh, Director General, Gandhi Labour Institute had delivered a talk to Ahmedabad Chapter on "Training of Civil Servants".
    - Ms. Harismita Trivedi delivered a talk on "Self Awareness, Development as HRD professionals" on 10th March, 1990.
    - Dr. Anjali Mehta, B.K. School of Management delivered a talk on "Self Awareness, for HRD professionals".
    - Dr. G. K. Suri, Director General, National Productivity Council gave a lecture on "HRD for Better Productivity".
    - Mr. I. M. Blachandani, Manager (Personnel), Blue Star had shared his experiences in initiating HR Department in Gandhinagar unit of Blue Star.
    - Ms. Harismita Trivedi of Ahmedabad Electricity Company had taken over as secretary of Ahmedabad Chapter from Mr. G.K. Ghosh.
  - **Bangalore Chapter**
    - Many lectures were organized by the Bangalore chapter on varied topics such as "Motivation in a Large Corporation", "HRD Systems & Practices in Digital Equipment", "New Priorities in HRD", and "Coming to Grips with Corporate Value System". The speakers include Mr. Shridhar Subhramanyam (President of Mudra Coats), Mr. V. G. Ratnam

(Group VP of UB Group), Ms. Maya Reddy (VP, HR of Digital Equipment), Mr. Ashit Sarkar (VP, HR of Britannia Industries), Dr. S. Subramanyam (Director of Manpower Development Centre, Amalgamations Group) and Prof. Vijay Padki (Consultant).

- Workshops arranged in that year:

<table>
<tr><th>DATE</th><th>WORKSHOP TITLE</th><th>RESOURCE PERSONS IN THE WORKSHOP</th></tr>
<tr><td>29 Jun, 1990</td><td>Role of HR manager: Key Issues</td><td rowspan="2">Mr. R. R. Nair (VP, Personnel, Lipton India)
Mr. K. S. Rao (President of Mudra Coats)
Mr. D.T. Devare (HRD Manager of Grindwell Nortell)
Mrs. Shobha Sethuram (Manager, A F Ferguson)
Mr. K.V. Dadiseth (Executive Director, Personnel, HUL)
Mr. B. Jagdish (HRD Manager of Karnataka Antibiotics)</td></tr>
<tr><td>30 Jun, 1990</td><td>Challenges for Coping with Employee Turnover</td></tr>
<tr><td>20 Aug, 1990</td><td>Stress, Health and Managerial Effectiveness</td><td>Dr. Ramnik Parekh (Chief Medical Officer, HUL)</td></tr>
</table>

- **Bombay Chapter**
    - A seminar on "Integrating New Entrants in the Organization" was organized by Bombay Chapter on 14th July, 1990.
- **Hosur Chapter**
    - The new office bearers were elected in the chapter meeting on 7th Jan, 1990. Mr. S Ponnambalanathan (Sr. Manager, P&A in Facit Asia Ltd.) was appointed as the new president for Hosur Chapter.
- **Indore Chapter**
    - Mr. A. Murlidharan (Dy. Divisional Manager, Personnel in Hindustan Motors Ltd.) was appointed as the new president for Hosur Chapter.
- **Ranchi Chapter**
    - Ranchi chapter had invited Mr. Sharu Rangeshkar, a Management Expert to deliver a talk on "How to Learn Management from your Wife" on 16th Nov, 1990 at Management Training Institute, SAIL.

ACADEMY OF HUMAN RECOURCES DEVELOPMENT (AHRD)

A note on my involvement with the Academy of Human Resource Development from January to December 1991

1. In October 1990, I was requested by the National HRD Network (a professional body committed to the development of HRD movement in the country) to help them set up an Academy of Human Resource Development as Honorary Director of the Academy. After discussions in the Steering Committee of RMCEI it was decided to undertake this as an Institution Building project of RMCEI. Director also approved my giving time for this project with an understanding that I will document the Institution Building experience as a part of RMCEI's work.

2. The Academy was since then established as an autonomous academic centre of the National HRD Network with a separate Board of Governors, Academic Council and a Diploma Committee. Within the last one year period the following activities have been initiated:

   2.1 A one year diploma programme in HRD has been started to provide academic preparation for those performing HRD roles without adequate professional background. This is being done on a distance education mode. Experiments are being conducted on making distance education more involving and useful.

   2.2 Workshops and round tables on priority areas have been initiated to bring together different categories of HRD professionals, reflect and document their experiences and suggestions. One workshop was conducted on "Role of Unions and Officers' Associations in HRD" in collaboration with XLRI. For the first time in the country Trade Union leaders and Officers' Association representatives got together to examine the role of unions and associations in HRD. The proceedings are being published in the HRD Newsletter.

   Another Round Table on 'Promotion Policies and Career Development' was organised in which HRD and Personnel managers from leading public sector, private sector and multinational corporations participated to examine the adequacies/inadequacies of promotion policies and career development strategies. The papers and proceedings are being published for wider use. The recommendations have been sent to CEOs of several organisations.

   2.3 A two-phase HRD facilitators development programme was initiated to develop HRD facilitation competencies in HRD staff.

2.4 A research-cum-documentation project on the "OD Experience of L&T ECC" has been initiated. This is likely to result in a book giving detailed description of the organisation development experience of L&T, ECC.

2.5 A research project on HRD Needs of Cooperation Sector was initiated with the help of NDDB.

2.6 Short term research projects have also been undertaken by the Fellows at the Academy. Atleast four such projects have been undertaken resulting in research papers.

2.7 Attempts are being made to develop trainers in Value Clarification and Personal Growth in Education and Voluntary Sectors.

2.8 An Annual Handbook for HRD Facilitators has been planned and the first volume is expected by mid-1992.

2.9 A data bank containing HRD profiles of different organisations has been started.

2.10 Attempts are also being made to build a small library of reference material in HRD.

2.11 A project to produce video films on "Excellence through HRD" has been initiated.

2.12 A cooperative research project on HRD Audit was initiated.

Of all these activities I have been personally involved in the following:

1. Conceptualisation and starting of various activities of the Academy.

2. Diploma Programme in HRD.

3. HRD Facilitators Programme - June 1-15, 1991.

4. Contact workshops for the Diploma and feedback to Diploma students.

5. Round Table on Career Development and Promotion Policies (other faculty : Profs. Jerome Joseph and Udai Pareek).

6. Workshop on Role of Unions in HRD (other faculty : Prof. N.R. Sheth (IIMA), Prof. Keith D'Souza (XLRI), Prof. Udai Pareek (IIHMR), Mr. Anil Khandelwal (BoB) and Mr. Nihar Ranjan Ghosh (NDDB).

I am preparing a separate note on the Role of IIMA with regard to the Academy of HRD.

Academy of Human Resources Development

Appeal for Membership of the Academy of Human Resources Development Society

Dear Sir,

The Academy of Human Resources Development is now a separately registered institution to conduct research and education in the field of HRD.

We understand that the Academy is first of its kind in this part of the world. We would like to make this a great institution with your support. We appeal to you to join the Society as a patron member and support its work.

We are enclosing details of the Academy. We look forward to your joining us.

Thank you,

M.R.R. Nair	***T.V. Rao***	***Udai Pareek***	***Ishwar Dayal***	***Rajesh Vidyasagar***
Chairman	*Hon. Director*	*Member*	*Member*	*President*
Board of Governors		*Board of Governors*	*Board of Governors*	*National HRD Network*

Encls : as above

12, Cosmo Ville, Satyagrah Marg, Ahmedabad - 380 054 Phone 648218 Fax 272-640681

Academy of Human Resources Development

Membership Brochure

Mission

The Academy was established in 1990 to conduct research in HRD, undertake education and training programmes to develop HRD professionals, and professionalise the HRD staff and provide technical services to industry, government, cooperatives,. NGOs and other agencies involved in developing people. The Academy's mission is to become an international centre for HRD where practitioners, andscholars from all over the world would like to visit and learn about HRD.

The Academy believes that continuous learning is the core of development. Most of us are not sensitive to the learning opportunities we have in our day to day living. There are several ways in which people can learn. Academy promotes, particularly, learning from each other (individuals, groups, organisations and institutions).

Origin

The Academy was established by the National HRD Network with initial institution building support from Ravi Mathai Centre for Educational Innovations, Indian Institute of Management, Ahmedabad, and Ahmedabad Management Association. Fellowships were provided by Steel Authority of India Limited, National Dairy Development Board, Excel Industries, Larsen & Toubro Construction Group, IBP Limited, and Ballarpur Industries Limited.

Early years

In a short period of time of its establishment, the Academy started a Diploma Programme in HRD, stabilized the HRD Facilitators Programme and conducted a few short duration programmes. The Academy also started researching into areas like the HRD needs of cooperatives, HRD needs of NGOs, communications as instruments of HRD, re-orienting personnel function to HRD, assessment of OD and its impact etc.

Future Plans

The Academy has the following plans for future :

* Doctoral Programme - Starting a doctoral programme for practicing HRD managers to equip them with research capabilities and orientation required to perform their roles well, and to contribute to the knowledge base in HRD.

Shri S. N. Sawaikar
DMD & CDO
SBI Central Office, Mumbai

Dear Mr. Sawaikar:

The Academy of HRD has been conducting a Doctoral Programme jointly with XLRI Jamshedpur. This is meant for HRD Managers, researchers and trainers. This programme has six weeks of course work. The first one was conducted at the IIMA campus. The second one at XLRI Jamshedpur last year. This year we planned to have it at Hyderabad. Unfortunaltely our buildings are not ready. This contact programme is expected to start from April 28 and close on June 7th. I am writing this as a special request to you to kindly allow us to use the SBI Staff College facilities for this programme. We need from April 28 to June 7 the following facilities:

1. Two Classrooms (if it is difficult atleast one).
2. Access to Library
3. Accomodation to about 35 participants in your ordinary rooms.

I understand that summer in Hyderabad is a slack period for the Staff College.
We will be paying all the expences involved within the reach of an educational institution like us. In return for your kind gesture we can offer the following to the SBI Staff college faculty.

1. They could attend freely any of our classes. The faculty names are given below.
2. Access to AHRD library for SBI Staff College Faculty

The faculty teaching in this programme include Dr. Udai Pareek, My self, Prof. jerome Joseph(IIMA), Omer-bin Sayeed (NITIE), Dr. Parameswaran (Osmania), Dr. Y. R. K. Reddy, K. Srinivas (Canada), Dr. Irudayaraj, Dr. Sethumadhavan (AHRD) etc. We all donate our time and consider as our contribution to build this profession. SBI is one of the founder members of National HRD Network which is the parent body of the HRD Academy. Considering the support provided in the past by institutions like the IIMA and your own institution I am sure you will be considerate enough to provide us this support.

We will be most grateful to you sir for this help. I look forward to a favourable reply from your side. With warm regards.

Sincerely,

T. V. Rao
March 10, 1997

* Assessment Centre - Providing Facilities and programmes for assessment of individuals, groups and organizations on dimensions that are critical for their effectiveness and providing feedback and intervention assistance.

* Library - Establishing a library that has all books, reports, films, and other documents relating to HRD from all over the world.

* Data Bank - Establishing a data bank providing information about the HRD practices of various organizations / Agencies.

* Social Development Centre and NGO Cell - starting a Social Development Centre that does research on Social development issues, and establishing a cell that works exclusively on NGOs.

Funds

To outline the above objectives the Academy requires to have its own Corpus Fund, support for building, and other infrastructure. At present, the Academy is housed in a row house purchased with the help of National HRD Network. The objective is to have its own small campus with minimal residential accommodation. The Corpus is expected to be raised through membership of the Academy. The Academy is registered under Bombay Societies Registration Act 1860 and Bombay Public Trust Act of 1950. The Academy has its own Board and Academic Council.

Membership

Since the Academy is now registered separately, it is enrolling members who are willing to support its activities. The membership fee fixed by the Board, at present, is:

Patron Members (Institutional)	-	Rs. 5 lakhs
Ordinary Members	-	Rs. 1 lakh
Foreign Patron Members (Institutional)	-	US $ 30,000
Foreign Ordinary Members	-	US $ 10,000

Privileges and Benefits of Members

The members of the Society are essentially contributing to the establishment of a research and education institution in HRD that will strive to be a global institution. As members they will have an opportunity to influence the activities of the Academy through representation in the Board. In addition, they will keep receiving all publications of the Academy and free participation in an annual event that acquaints the members with all developments in HRD in the year. The Academy also proposes to offer various programmes and activities to serve its members.

- **Books Launched**
  - Book "**Excellence through Human Resources Development**" written by Mr. M R. R. Nair and Dr. T.V. Rao was launched. This book is a compilation of the papers presented in the symposium, held at Madras in Feb, 1990.
  - A Book "HRD Missionary" written by Dr. T. V. Rao was launched. The book presents an outline on HRD, HRD Functions, carves out the roles and responsibilities of HR Professional, and presents some HR instruments that can be used to measure the effectiveness of HR Department.
  - Another Book "Performance Planning Analysis and Review: Skills Workbook" was launched in the same year. This book gave a new approach to Performance Appraisal, suited to the needs of the changing organizations.
  - Book "Organizational Behaviour" written by Mr. K. K. Mehta. This volume consists of case studies of situations and individuals about Organizational Climate and Culture.
- **National HRD Network Awards (1989–1990)**
  - Organizational Awards

AWARD WINNING ORGANISATION
Canara Bank
Eicher Goodearth Ltd.
Petrofils Cooperative
TISCO

  - Individual Awards

AWARD WINING INDIVIDUAL
Mr. S. Chandrasheker
Mr. V. Krishnamurthy
Dr. T. V. Rao
Mr. M.V. Subbiah
Ms. Susan Varughese

- **Dr. T.V. Rao had attended International Congress on Education in Mexico from 26th to 30th March, 1990 where he visited the president of NTL.**

IIMA
January 2, 1990

To : Prof. T.V. Rao

From : Director

Thank you for your note of December 27. I am happy to convey approval for your participation in the International Congress on Education to be held in Mexico from March 26 to 30, 1990.

Thank you.

1991

- **Dr. Udai Pareek of Indian Institute of Health Management Research became the new president of National HRD Network for the period 1991–1993.**
- **The General Body Meeting of National HRD Network was held on 16th June, 1991 at Hotel Clarks Ajmer, Jaipur.**
- **International Conference on "Human Resource Development for Management of Change" was organized by National HRD Network in Hyderabad from 7th-9th Feb, 1991.**
- **A joint programme was formulated by four public enterprises-BHEL, MRL, NLC, HMT on "PSU Consortium: A Unique HRD Effort" to develop young executives**
- **Activities in National HRD Network Chapters**
  - **Bangalore Chapter**
    - Bangalore Chapter was fully involved in organizing the National Symposium in Feb, 1992.
    - Bangalore Chapter had also kept several Open House Sessions where the members made presentations on varied topics like
      1) There is no such thing like objective Performance Appraisal System
      2) Career Planning and Development
  - **Pune Chapter**
    - Pune Chapter organized series of lectures for Symbiosis Institute of Business Management, Pune.

- An interactive session was organized by this chapter for management students "What do young HR professionals and management expect from each other"

➢ **Ananthpur Chapter**

- Ananthpur Chapter of National HRD Network began in the year 1991.

➢ **Koraput Chapter**

- The first meeting of the Koraput Chapter of National HRD Network was held on 7th May, 1991. The office bearers of the chapter were elected. Shri K.S. Venkateshwaran, DGM (Personnel) HAL was elected as the first president of Koraput chapter.

➢ **Calcutta Chapter**

- Calcultta chapter in collaboration with ISABS organized a 4 day residential training programme on "Basic Human Process Laboratory" from 20–23 Nov,1991

➢ **All Students Chapter in Lucknow**

- 32 students of IIM Lucknow started this in1992.

❖ **NHRDN and AHRD conducted HRD Facilitators Programme on June 10–22, 1991 at Hotel Clarks Ajmer in Jaipur.**

➢ In phase I was conducted in first week where conceptual and experiential inputs on organizational diagnosis, OD interventions were shared by the experts. OD skill development Lab and action plan workshop were also conducted. Phase II was conducted in the second week. It was named "Action Facilitation Phase" because the participants spend applying what they had learned in Phase I by preparing action plans for their organizations.

➢ Certification- On successful completion of the project report and its presentation, participants were certified.

❖ **AHRD announced several programmes**

➢ AHRD announces to offer Diploma in Human Resources Development (one year distance education course with contact sessions)

➢ AHRD announces Research Fellowship

- SAIL Research Fellowship
- IBP Research Fellowship

(Each Fellowship under the above two categories offer ₹3000-₹5000 depending on the qualification and experience of the candidate plus ₹1000 as housing allowance)

- BILT Research cum Fellow Management Trainee (Monthly stipend of ₹3500 was offered under this fellowship)

❖ **AHRD had conducted project on "Stress Audit".**

In this conference experts scientifically and systematically study, explore and manage various occupational stresses which the executives of the participating organizations experience. (Organizations willing to participate had to contribute ₹22,500). This was conducted in four phases:

- ➢ Phase I Data collection
- ➢ Phase II Statistical Analysis of Data
- ➢ Phase III Sharing of the findings with the organization
- ➢ Phase IV suggestions and action plan for the organizations

❖ **AHRD had conducted Cooperative Research Project on "HRD Audit".**

In this conference research is undertaken by a group of individuals along with organizations that are willing to participate (Organizations willing to participate had to contribute ₹40,000). This was conducted in four phases:

- ➢ Phase I Research Planning Workshop
- ➢ Phase II Data collection and Statistical Analysis of Data
- ➢ Phase III Workshop to decide Action plans
- ➢ Phase IV Review workshop

❖ **AHRD jointly with XLRI, Jamshedpur had organized a programme on "Role of Unions and Officers' Associations in HRD" IN Hotel Clarks Ajmer, Jaipur from 12th -15th Sept, 1991.**

❖ **AHRD sets up a search committee to recruit new Executive Director.**

❖ **AHRD had also conducted two workshops in that year**

- ➢ Personal Growth through value clarification exclusively for Trade Unions and Officer Associations

- Personal Growth through value clarification exclusively for HRD and Personnel Professionals.
- AHRD was shifted to its new permanent location. A property in Cosmoville Row Houses was purchased. Research center-cum-guesthouse was inaugurated.

1992

- **National HRD Network conducted a symposium on "Transitions in Indian Society: HRD Trends and Innovations" from 20–22, 1992 at Taj Residency, Bangalore.**
- **National HRD Network Awards (1990–1991)**
  - Organizational Awards

AWARD WINNING ORGANISATION
CMC Limited
Modi Xerox
ITC Limited
Thermax Limited
C-DoT
XLRI, Jamshedpur
Baroda Productivity Council

  - Individual Awards

AWARD WINING INDIVIDUAL
Dr. P. P. Gupta
Mr. Arvind Agrawal
Dr. K.N. Sharma
Dr. Ram Nath Sharma
Prof. Ishwar Dayal

- **Dr. Udai Pareek, President of National HRD Network had instituted the "President's Best Chapter Award" to be awarded to the chapter which contributes maximum towards furthering the objectives of National HRD Network.**
- **Members Honoris Causa**
  - The Executive Board of the Network had decided to invite eminent persons to join as MEMBER HONORIS

CAUSA. These were eminent persons who had contributed significantly in the HRD and their contribution to enhance the learning process through the National HRD Network.

MEMBER HONORIS CAUSA	ORGANIZATION
Prof. Abad Ahmed	FMS, University of Delhi
Ms Ela Bhatt	SEWA, Ahmedabad
Mr. R.C. Bhargav	Chairman & MD, Maruti Udhyog
Prof. S.K. Chakroborty	Professor, IIM Calcutta
Prof. S. Chattopadhyay	University of Delhi
Mr. K.L. Chugh	Chairman ITC, Calcutta
Mr. V.N. Jikhar	CMD, Petrofills Cooperative Ltd., Baroda
Prof. V.N. Khandwalla	Professor, IIM Ahmedabad
Mr. Vikram Lal	Eicher Goodearth Ltd., New Delhi
Dr. B.L. Maheshwari	Director, Center for Organization Development, Hyderabad
Mr. Vijay Mahajan	University of Delhi
Dr. Prayag Mehta	Participation and Development Center, New Delhi
Mr. Aftab Niazi	Chairman, IBP Company Ltd., Calcutta
Mr. Arvind Pandey	Director (Pers & Corp. Plg.), SAIL, New Delhi
Dr. S.N. Pandey	Executive Director (IR) TISCO, Jamsedpur
Dr. Amrita Patel	MD, NDDB
Mr. Atul Shroff	Tranpek Industries Ltd., Baroda
Dr. A.C. Shah	CMD, Bank of Baroda, Bombay
Mr. N. Vittal	IAS, Secretary to the Govt. of India, Dept. of Electronics, New Delhi

- **The Annual General Body Meeting of National HRD Network was held on 22nd Feb, 1992 at Hotel Clarks Ajmer, Jaipur.**
- **The Executive Board of the Network had formed a Search Committee for selecting the next president (1992–93) who**

would take over from Dr. Udai Pareek who was the president at that time.

- ➢ The Search Committee consisted of Mr. K.K. Nohria, Mr. M.R.R. Nair, Dr. Udai Pareek, Dr. T.V. Rao and Prof. Rajen Gupta.

❖ **Dr. T.V. Rao gave lecture on "Role of Young Professionals in HRD" in the Annual Convention of Xavier's Institute of Social Service (AXICON'92) held in Ranchi.**

❖ **The Board of Governors of AHRD met at Jaipur on 13th Jun, 1992.**

- ➢ Dr. Keith D'Souza became the Executive Director of AHRD in June, 1992.
- ➢ Dr. Geeta Saxena (Faculty of Organizational Behaviour, XLRI) had been appointed as the Coordinator of XLRI's Center for HRD from 20th June, 1992.

❖ **NHRDN and AHRD conducted HRD Facilitators Programme on June 1–13, 1992 at Hotel Clarks Ajmer in Jaipur.**

- ➢ In phase I was conducted in first two week where Group learnings based on Group –L Approach sessions were conducted on conceptual and experiential inputs on organizational diagnosis, OD interventions were shared by the experts. OD skill development Lab and action plan workshop were also conducted. Phase II was conducted in the second week. It was named "Action Facilitation Phase" because the participants spend applying what they had learned in Phase I by preparing action plans for their organizations.
- ➢ Certification- On successful completion of the project report and its presentation, participants were certified.

❖ **AHRD conducted a four day contact programmes on "Introduction to HRD" at New Delhi, Madras, Calcutta, Bombay in 1992.**

❖ **AHRD had conducted Diploma Contact Programmes at Ranchi and Bokaro.**

- ➢ The programme at Ranchi had 40 Diploma participants
- ➢ The programme at Ranchi had 40 Diploma participants

Prof Keith D'Souza, Dr. T.V. Rao, Mr. Ashok Kumar and Mr. Nihar Ghosh were the resource persons for this programme.

- **AHRD had begun promoting the establishment of Consortium of HRD Consultants.**
  - The purpose behind doing this was to develop HRD Managers as consultants.
- **AHRD had also conducted Value Clarification workshops in that year**
  - Personal Growth through value clarification exclusively for Leaders of Trade Unions and Officer Associations
  - Personal Growth through value clarification exclusively for HRD and Personnel Professionals.
  - AHRD was shifted to its new permanent location. A property in Cosmoville Row Houses was purchased. Research center-cum-guesthouse was inaugurated.
- **Dr. T.V. Rao, Member of Academy Board and former Honorary Director of the Academy had visited Institute of Developmental Studies, University of Sussex, UK as Visiting Fellow to carry out research and prepare a book on the subject HRD in Developmental Sector.**

Prof. T.V. Rao
Organizational Behaviour Area

July 7, 1992

Dear

Subsequent to the Working Group meeting held at London from 27th to 30th January this year on "HRD Strategies: Developing National Policy and Planning Guidelines", I have been requested by the Commonwealth Secretariat, London to prepare the proposed book. I visited the Secretariat and a few other institutions in UK, particularly the Institute of Development Studies at Sussex. On the basis of my discussions with various experts in other institutions and the HRD Group at the Commonwealth Secretariat, I have prepared the enclosed note on the book.

I plan to start working on this book from mid-August or early September. I am likely to be stationed at the Institute of Development Studies, Sussex. I need your help and cooperation to make this book a very useful one to different countries. I request you specifically for the following:

i) Your comments on the proposed outline of the book;

ii) Details of any reference material, case studies, experience and other literature you expect me to summarise or include in the book; and

iii) Any other comments/suggestions you have, to make the book useful.

I would appreciate your response as soon as possible. If you reply after August 15, you may write to the following address: Prof. T.V. Rao, Visiting Fellow, C/o. Mr. Christopher Colclough, Institute of Development Studies, University of Sussex, Brighton BN1 9RE, England [Fax (0273) 621202].

I am enclosing a short resume of mine for information.

I look forward to your support.

With professional regards,

Yours sincerely,

T.V. Rao

Encl: a.a.

24 JUL '92 9:49 PAGE.002

IDS SUSSEX

The Institute of Development Studie
at the University of Sussex
Brighton BN1 9RE England

Telephone: Brighton (0273) 606261
Direct Line

Telex: 877997 IDSBTN G
Fax: (0273) 621202
(0273) 691647

Dr. T.V. Rao
Indian Institute of Management
Vastrapur
AHMEDABAD 380015
India

Our ref: SD/fah

23 July 1992

Dear Dr. Rao,

I am pleased to let you know that your application has been approved and we would therefore like to invite you to the Institute as a Visiting Fellow for a 6-month period from mid August 1992. You will be preparing a draft for a book on human resource development strategies, as outlined in your application.
Dr. Christopher Colclough will act as your academic Sponsor.

It is understood that your visit will be funded by the Commonwealth Secretariat including the usual IDS fee of £200 per month for the provision of office services, which includes the use of an office and basic facilities such as a copy card for 96 photocopies each month, postage for letters, UK telephone calls, stationery and limited secretarial assistance (i.e. for the typing of research material). The Institute cannot provide you with the use of your own computer, but you will have access to the facilities in our computer room.

If you accept this invitation, please confirm the dates of your visit in due course and let me know whether you would like temporary accommodation to be reserved for you by Ms Felicity Harrison (Secretary, Visitors Programme). A room can be reserved for the first week of your visit, either in the IDS building if available (brochure enclosed) or in a guest house in Brighton. The University's Accommodation Office will be able to supply you on arrival with the current list of local properties for rent during the remainder of your stay.

We look forward to hearing from you.

With best wishes,

Yours sincerely,

Susanna Davies

Dr. Susanna Davies
Deputy Director

c.c. Mr. S. Packer, Commonwealth Secretariat, London

Resume of T.V. Rao

Prof. T.V. Rao is Professor of Organisational Behaviour and Chairman of the Ravi Matthai Centre for Educational Innovation. He also held the position of Honorary Director of Academy of Human Resource Development at Ahmedabad till recently and is likely to direct its Centre for Social Development in future. He holds a Ph.D. in Psychology. He was on the faculty of the National Institute of Health Administration and Education, New Delhi; University of Udaipur and Xavier Labour Relations Institute, Jamshedpur where he worked as L&T Professor of HRD and Head of the Centre for HRD. He has been on the faculty of the Indian Institute of Management, Ahmedabad since 1973 and held different positions at the Institute. He worked as a Consultant in the first India Population Project in U.P., UNFPA Project in Rajasthan, UNICEF Project on Social Development in Gujarat and several projects of UNESCO. His areas of interest include self-employment and entrepreneurship, education systems, health and population management, adult literacy and HRD in corporate sector. He is founder President of the National HRD Network and also was President of the Indian Society for Applied Behavioural Science. He authored or co-authored over 20 books on Human Resource Development, Health and Population Management, Entrepreneurship Development, Adult Education and Education Systems. He served as USAID Consultant to the HTRD Project of Ministry of Health, Indonesia; as UNIDO Consultant to the National Entrepreneurial Research and Development Association, Malaysia and also worked as a short-term Consultant to the International Committee on Management of Population Programmes, Kuala Lumpur.

HUMAN RESOURCE DEVELOPMENT PLANNING AND IMPLEMENTATION

A) Book Outline

This book is expected to cover the following:

- Review the concept of HRD and how it has been viewed by different agencies/writers all over the world. Highlight commonalities and differences and present rationale behind the views;

- Present a coherent and integrated concept of HRD building on the available thinking. This concept should be simple, comprehensive and usable by policy makers;

- Present a description of various HRD strategies (both sectoral and multi-sectoral) that have been used in the past and that could be used for future HRD planning. The strategies should focus on integrated and cross-sectoral policies and their implementation. However, as such literature may be scant, they could be derived from sectoral experiences. The sectoral strategies that may form the base could be limited to Education (including primary, secondary and tertiary), Science and Technology, Industry (private and public sector), Agriculture, Health (including infant mortality, health care, mother's health and nutrition), Population, Employment, particularly self-employment (and other forms of human resources utilisation), Women and the Disadvantaged Groups (including the poor and the under-privileged), and any others that may emerge during the work;

- Present guidelines for formulating policies and implementation strategies in each of the sectors;

- Present guidelines for policies and mechanisms of integrating the sectoral strategies and action plans into a comprehensive overall national and local level HRD plans;

- Outline the various processes involved in an effective implementation of the HRD strategy and provide guidelines for an effective management of these processes.

  The processes may include:

  > Structuring/restructuring of sectoral administration (including merger of departments/ministries), coordination mechanisms, roles to be played by the policy-makers, planners, administrators/programme managers, monitoring mechanisms needed, developing indicators and managing the implementation review mechanisms, etc.

The book could be presented in the following two parts:

Part I: Section 1 - Concepts, Policies and Strategies

- Activities in National HRD Network Chapters
  - **Pune Chapter**
    - A meeting was organized by the Pune chapter on "HRD in Classroom" on 3rd Feb, 1992. It was aimed to create link between school teachers and HRD professionals to improve the quality of education.
  - **Koraput Chapter**
    - Koraput chapter had conducted several programmes in that year on varied subjects:
      1) Creativity
      2) Transactional Analysis for Teachers
      3) Effective presentation skills for school/college teachers
    - Koratpur Chapter had also organized two programmes on "Success through Effective Speaking" for school/ college students.
  - **Anand Chapter**
    - Mr. Ravi Shankar, MD, National Dairy Cooperative Federation of India Limited had taken over as the president of Anad Chapter succeeding Mr. Shailendrakumar, Manager (HRD) of NDDB.

      Other office bearers:

      Mr. Sarad Amin, Managing Partner, Warm Stream, Vallabh Vidhyanagar (VP)

      Mr. Thomas Benjamin, Sr. Executive, NDDB (Secretary)
  - **Madras Chapter**
    - A presentation on "HRD for Workmen" was made by Mr. Francis Fernandez, a consultant on 14th Feb, 1992.
  - **Bokaro Chapter**
    - Bokaro Chapter organized a one day workshop for middle level managers on time management on 14th Feb, 1992. The workshop was conducted by Dr. Geeta Saxena of XLRI, Jamshedpur.
  - **Ahmedabad Chapter**
    - One day workshop was conducted on "Promotion Policies and Career Development" on 7th March, 1992.
  - **Bangalore Chapter**
    - A discussion on "HRD Implications of Exit Policy" was conducted on 14th Aug, 1992.

- Prof K.K. Swaminathan, president at S. A. Management Institute, Hyderabad delivered a lecture on Computerized Skill Gap Analysis Technique on 11th Sept, 1992.
- In a meeting jointly arranged by Bangalore Management Associations and Bangalore Chapter, Mr. M.R.R. Nair (V.P. Lipton, India Ltd.) had given a talk on "HRD-Global Prospects" on 22nd Sept, 1992 in which he had summarized the presentation made by him at the World Personnel Congress at Madrid, Spain.

➢ **Madras Chapter**

- Madras Chapter organized a workshop was conducted on "Empowerment" on 22nd May, 1992. Mr. C. M. Srivastava (President, Bombay Chapter) and Prof. Nadkarni were the resource persons in that workshop.

➢ **Jaipur Chapter**

- Jaipur Chapter organized a two day workshop was conducted on "Total Quality Management" on 1st & 2nd May, 1992. Dr. Ashok Agrawal had inaugurated the workshop. Dr. Udai Pareek, Mr. M. L. Gulati, Mr. R.P. Singh and Mr. R. Chandra Shekhar were the resource persons in that workshop.

➢ **Ranchi Chapter**

- Ranchi Chapter organized one day programme on Appreciation of ISO 9000 on 12th Dec, 1992 at Management Training Institute, Ranchi.
- A joint meeting of the members of the Ranchi Chapter and Ranchi Management Association was organized on 27th Nov, 1992. The session was addressed by Dr. T.V. Rao.

1993

❖ **A National Conference on HRD for Workers was conducted in Bhillai on 5th& 6th June, 1993.**

➢ The conference was conducted by Bhillai Steel Plant in collaboration with National HRD Network.

❖ **Books Launched**

➢ Dr. T. V. Rao was working on a book **"Leadership Styles"** and it was launched.

Prof. T.V. Rao
Organizational Behaviour Area

September 3, 1993

Dear

A team of us at IIMA (Profs. P.N. Khandwalla, S. Ramnarayan, J.P. Singh and myself) are in the process of preparing a book on "**Leadership Styles**" of CEOs and top level managers in the country.

As a part of this book, we would like to give short caselets of some of the outstanding managers who exhibited leadership qualities and made things happen. We would like to give an account of some of the things they have done, their personal philosophy and beliefs about people (employees and people in general), the situations they took charge and influenced, their leadership styles and decision-making styles.

Such caselets are likely to provide insights about leadership and also serve as role-models for other managers. We would like to include you in this series of case studies. I would appreciate your consent. On receiving your approval, I will make arrangements to meet you to interview you and collect some data. I will need about 2 hours time for such interview.

Look forward to your response.

With regards,

Yours sincerely,

T.V. Rao

- **Mr. Manoj Kumar had joined AHRD as Executive Secretary from 20th Mar, 1993, succeeding Mr. K. Raghu.**
- **Management Development Programmes were conducted by the AHRD**
  - A MDP on "Introduction to Human Resource Development-I" was organized at the Sterling City Club, Ahmedabad. It was meant for executives and managers that were new to HRD function. Faculty for this programme included:

Dr. Keith D'Souza	Executive Director, AHRD
Mr. P Kumar	Chief HRD, Arvind Mills
Mr. Anil Khandelwal	Chief Manager Training, BOB Staff College
Prof C. Balaji	Professor, IRMA

- A Personal Growth Laboratory was conducted during 10th-13th March, 1993 at Hotel Harsha, Bangalore. Facilitators for this programme were:

Dr. Keith D'Souza	Executive Director, AHRD
Dr. C. N. Daftuar	IBP Fellow, AHRD

- A MDP on "Team Building for Organizational Excellence" was conducted during 15th-18th March, 1993 at Hotel Harsha, Bangalore. This programme was mostly for the line managers responsible for team functioning. Facilitators for this programme were:

Mr. R. Mukundan	Corporate Manager HR & Administration, Gaitonde Group of Companies
Dr. C. N. Daftuar	IBP Fellow, AHRD

- **Activities in National HRD Network Chapters**
  - **Jaipur Chapter**
    - Jaipur Chapter conducted a two day workshop on "Quality Circle" on 23th & 24th Jan, 1993. This work-shop focused on improving the quality of work life and product quality.
  - **Jaipur Chapter**
    - Jaipur Chapter conducted a two day workshop on "Quality Circle" on 23th & 24th Jan, 1993. This work-shop focused on improving the quality of work life and product quality.
- **NHRDN and AHRD conducted HRD Facilitators Programme on June 7–19, 1993 at Hotel Clarks Ajmer in Jaipur.**
  - In phase I was conducted in first two week where Group learnings based on Group –L Approach sessions were conducted on conceptual and experiential inputs on

organizational diagnosis, OD interventions were shared by the experts. OD skill development Lab and action plan workshop were also conducted. Phase II was conducted in the second week. It was named "Action Facilitation Phase" because the participants spend applying what they had learned in Phase I by preparing action plans for their organizations.

- Certification- On successful completion of the project report and its presentation, participants were certified.

❖ **AHRD had organized two round table conferences in 1993.**

- First round table conference was on "HRD Implications of ISO 9000" and it was held in New Delhi from 27th -29th May, 1993.
- Second round table conference was on "HRD in Emerging Industrial Context" and it was held in Madras from 22nd -24th May, 1993.

❖ **In 1993, Dr. T.V. Rao had written a paper on the status of HRD in South Asia and the position of India in the South Asia region in the area of HRD.**

1994

❖ **Pune Chapter received the Best National HRD Network Award.**

❖ **National HRD Network Awards (1993–1994)**

- Organizational Awards

AWARD WINNING ORGANISATION
Widia (India) Ltd.
Marico Industries Ltd.
Vijay Wires and Filaments Pvt. Ltd.

- Individual Awards

AWARD WINING INDIVIDUAL
Mr. M. R. R. Nair
Mr. K. L. Chugh
Suresh Krishna

❖ The Executive Board Meeting of the National HRD Network was held on 21st Jan, 1994 at Hotel Taj, Bombay.

NATIONAL HRD NETWORK

12, Cosmo Ville, Satyagrah Marg, Ahmedabad - 380 054 Phone : 648218 Fax : 640681

MINUTES OF EXECUTIVE BOARD MEETING
at 6.00 P.M. on January 21, 1994 at Hotel Taj, Bombay

Members Present:

Rajesh Vidyasagar	-	National President
V S Mahesh	-	Past National President.
T V Rao	-	Hon. Director, Academy of HRD.
G P Rao	-	President, Delhi HRD Network.
D T Devare	-	President, Bangalore HRD Network.
C M Srivastava	-	President, Bombay HRD Network.
Arun Wakhlu	-	President, Pune HRD Network.
Udai Pareek	-	President, Jaipur HRD Network
T S Rajamani	-	President, Hosur HRD Network
R Ramachandran	-	President, Bokaro HRD Network.
Col. Ramesh Pathak	-	Hon. Secretary, Pune HRD Network.
Ashok Agarwal	-	Member, Jaipur HRD Network.
P V R Murthy	-	Member, Madras HRD Network.
S Chandrasekhar	-	Member, Vizag HRD Network
J M Sampath	-	Member, Bangalore HRD Network.
V B Jhala	-	Member, Baroda HRD Network.
Bharat D Mehta	-	Member, Baroda HRD Network.
C V R Murthy	-	Hon. Treasurer, Calcutta HRD Network.
Manohar Nadkarni	-	Member, Bombay HRD Network.
Baburaj V Nair	-	Executive Secretary,National HRD Network.

(Prof. Keith C D' Souza, Former Executive Director of Academy of HRD, regretted his inability to attend the meeting).

The Executive Board Meeting, chaired by Mr. Rajesh Vidyasagar, the National President, started after a formal introduction of all members present.

The following items, as per agenda, were taken for deliberation and subsequent ratifications/ resolutions were made.

1 Ratification of statement of accounts of National HRD Network for the years 1991, 1992, and 1993.

The audited statements for the years mentioned above was read out by the National President and the ratification of these audited statements were proposed by Mr. D T Devare, and seconded by Mr. Arun Wakhlu.

While clarifying that these audited statements are of National Secretariat of the National HRD Network, Dr. T V Rao raised the concern of non-receipt of audited statements from local Networks, and requested the members present to send the audited statements to the National Secretariat at Ahmedabad, for accounts purpose.

2 Nomination of three members by the Natinonal President.

The National President nominated Mr. Satish Pradhan, General Manager- HR of ICIM, Pune, Mr. Marcel Parker, General Manager -HRD of Modi Xerox Limited, New Delhi, and Mr. Anand Nayak, General Manager (Corporate Personnel) of ITC Limited, Calcutta as Executive Members of the National HRD Network; and invited them to join the Board.

- **Books Launched**
  - Book **"Designing HRD Systems"** written by Dr. Ishwar Dayal Professor, Management Development Institute, Gurgaon was launched in 1994.
- **AHRD had stated Center for Social Development (CSD). The center was established to exclusively function in areas related to social issues.**
- **AHRD had conducted a workshop on "Understanding HRD needs of NGOs" on 19th Mar, 1994.**
- **A round table conference on "Executive Performance Appraisal Systems" on 6th-8th May, 1994 was organized at Hotel Clarks Ajmer, Jaipur.**
- **The Network had also organized a lecture meeting by Ms Carol Nelson, Interact Consultant, Canada on the topic "Understanding your Personal Styles" on 22nd Sept, 1994.**
- **NHRDN and AHRD conducted HRD Facilitators Programme on 2nd- 14th May, 1994 at Hotel Clarks Ajmer in Jaipur.**
  - In phase I was conducted in first two week where Group learnings based on Group –L Approach sessions were conducted on conceptual and experiential inputs on organizational diagnosis, OD interventions were shared by the experts. OD skill development Lab and action plan workshop were also conducted. Phase II was conducted in the second week. It was named "Action Facilitation Phase" because the participants spend applying what they had learned in Phase I by preparing action plans for their organizations.
  - Certification- On successful completion of the project report and its presentation, participants were certified.
  - Dr. T.V. Rao and Mr. P V R Murthy were coordinators of this programme.
  - The core faculties of the programme were Dr. T.V. Rao, Dr. Udai Pareek, Prof. S. Ramnarayan and Mr. P V R Murthy.
- **AHRD had four round table conferences.**
  - The first one was on "HRD Implications of Business Restructuring" jointly organized by AHRD and Delhi Management Association.

- The second conference was on "Executive Performance Appraisal Systems: Meeting the Challenges of New Economic Environment" and it was held in Jaipur.
- "Retention & utilization of Human Resources" was held on 19th Aug, 1995 at Hotel Green Park Hyderabad.
- Round Table Conference on HRD for workers and support staff.

- **AHRD had also conducted a workshop on "Performance Appraisal" on 12th-13th Aug, 1994 at Hotel Nest, Ahmedabad.**
- **AHRD had launched its first bulletin "Renewal" to promote and share theory and practices in OD, HRD, organizational building and other human and organizational practices.**
- **AHRD had also conducted another workshop on "Use of Instruments in Improving Organizational and Managerial Effectiveness" on 16th-17th Sept, 1994 at Hotel Rivera, Ahmedabad.**
- **AHRD had taken a project on "Organizational Renewal for NGOs in Developmental Action (ORENGODA)" supported by Evangeliche ZentralstelleFur Entwicklungshilf (EZE), Germany.**
- **Fr. E. Abraham S.J, former director of XLRI, Jamshedpur had joined AHRD as vising professor and joint Director to revitalize AHRD.**
- **Activities in National HRD Network Chapters**
  - **Ahmedabad Chapter**
    - Ahmedabad chapter had organized annual chapter get together in which 50 members of the chapter participated.
    - Ahmedabad chapter had also organized three lectures in 1993.
      1) One was on " HRD –Transcending the organizational boundaries by Mr. VRS Cowlagi (Director of Gandhi Labour Institute)
      2) Second lecture was on "Value Engineering and Value Management- what is it all about" by Mr. Jayanth Murthy, Value Engineering Consultant.
      3) Third lecture was on "HRD for Customer Orientation-The Amtrex Experience" by Mr. Arvind Nair, Chief Executive of Amtrex Appliances Limited.

- Ahmedabad chapter had organized several lectures and meetings in collaboration with NIPM.
- Annual General Body Meeting of Ahmedabad Chapter was held on 6th July, 1994.

➢ **Anand Chapter**

- Anand Chapter had organized a group discussion on "You as an Organizational Change Agent" facilitated by Sonu Soni of Amul on 30th Aug, 1994.

➢ **Delhi Chapter**

- Delhi chapter had organized several meetings and conferences in 1994.
  1) "Contribution of HRD in increasing Market Share" by Mr. A R Deshpande and Dr. K. B. Mehra of BHEL.
  2) "Culture Building" by Mr. Vivek Paranjape of HP.
  3) "Flexibility as a way of work" by Dr. C. S. Venkatratnam of IMI
  4) "People Orientation in MUL" by Mr. R. Vasudevan
  5) "Employee Development" by Mr. Sanjay Jain and Mr. Rakesh Sharma of Indian Shaving Products.
- Delhi chapter had organized and managed the programme "Young Professionals' Meet" which was held in Dec 1994.

➢ **Baroda Chapter**

- Baroda Chapter had conducted elections were new office bearers were selected. Dr. N. S. Pathak (Management Consultant) as the president.

➢ **Koraput Chapter**

- Koraput Chapter had conducted elections were new office bearers were selected. Mr. T.N. Surendranathan (DGM P&A, Hindustan Aeronautics Ltd., Koraput) as the president.

➢ **Pune Chapter**

- They had organized two seminars in1994.
  1) First seminar was on "Group Think on New Vistas and Perspectives in HRD" on 8th Sept, 1994.

2) The second seminar was on "HRD-What We Preach &What We Practice" on 18th Aug, 1994.

- **Ranchi Chapter**
  - Ranchi chapter in collaboration with Ranchi Management Association had organized a lecture on "Information, Organization- Challanges" by Prof. Wolfgang Schuelo from University of Bielefeld, Germany and Prof. M.P. Vitthal, IIM C on 6th April, 1994 at Ranchi.

1995

- **The Board of Governors of AHRD had met on 19th Aug, 1995 in Dr. Reddy's Lab R&D center at Miyapur, Hyderabad.**
  - Dr. Anjali Reddy, the than Chairman of Dr. Reddy's Lab had formally given the letter to Mr. M.R. R. Nair, Chairman of Board of Governors of Academy offering 10 acres of land on a 99 year lease for establishing Academy.
- **AHRD had organized a six day contact workshop for the Candidates of Diploma in HRD (1994–96 batch) at Gandhi Labour Institute, Ahmedabad from 3rd – 8th Apr, 1995.**
  - This was coordinated by Mr. S. Shreepathy, SAIL Fellow, who is diploma coordinator.
- **Dr. P. Sethumadhavan had joined AHRD as Associate Professor on full time basis and team leader for the Hyderabad Center. Prior to that he was associated with Center of Development (COD), Hyderabad and IIMA.**
- **Dr. P.V.S. Kumar had joined AHRD as part of its Secretariat Staff.**
- **Dr. P. Subramanyam had joined AHRD as Administrative Manager leader for the Hyderabad Center. Prior to that he was associated with ICRISAT, Hyderabad.**
- **Dr. M.G. Jarmon (a full time participant of Fellow Programme in HRD at AHRD) had also joined AHRD.**
- **Ms. Arpan Kulkarni (BSc. Zoology, MS University) had joined Social Development Center of the Academy.**
- **Dr. S. Shreepathy and Ms. Archana Sharma (SAIL Fellows) who were at AHRD, Ahmedabad from April 1994 had shifted to Hyderabad Center.**

- **Dr. Kuldeep Singh, Faculty, Dept. of Management Studies, Uni of Jammu had joined AHRD and had worked on series of video cassettes produced jointly by Academy and Suvik Communications on themes like:**
  - HRD for Institution Building
  - OD: An Indian Experience
  - HRD for R&D Institutions
  - HRD for grooming Professionals

  He had also edited two books:
  - "Organizational Effectiveness by HRD" along with Prof. Jerome of IIM A
  - "Principles and Practices of Organizational Development" along with Prof. S. Ramnarayan of IIMA.
- **NHRDN and AHRD conducted HRD Facilitators Programme on 17th-22nd Apr, at Green Park Hotel in Hyderabad.**
  - In phase I was conducted in first two week where Group learnings based on Group –L Approach sessions were conducted on conceptual and experiential inputs on organizational diagnosis, OD interventions were shared by the experts. OD skill development Lab and action plan workshop were also conducted. Phase II was conducted in the second week. It was named "Action Facilitation Phase" because the participants spend applying what they had learned in Phase I by preparing action plans for their organizations.
  - Certification- On successful completion of the project report and its presentation, participants were certified.
  - Dr. T.V. Rao and Mr. P V R Murthy were coordinators of this programme.
  - The core faculties of the programme were Dr. T.V. Rao, Dr. Udai Pareek, Prof. S. Ramnarayan and Mr. P V R Murthy.
- **Activities in National HRD Network Chapters**
  - **Ahmedabad Chapter**
    - Ahmedabad Chapter had organized Value Clarification Workshop for "Culture Building in Organizations" on 11th March, 1995 by Dr. Uma Jain.

- **Anand Chapter**
  - Dr. Prasad Kalpa of Mithya Institute of Learning, Campbell, California, USA had given a talk on "Organizational Growth through People Development" on 20th June, 1995.
  - Anand chapter had organized a meeting by Peter Block to talk about and for sharing experience on "HRD for TQM and Culture Change" by Mr. Hemant Kaushik and IVNS Raju.
- **Bangalore Chapter**
  - Bangalore Chapter had conducted elections in their Annual General Meeting of the Executive Board were new office bearers (1995–97) were selected. Dr. Rupande Padki as the president.
  - John S. Mr. Hamilton (MD of Cargil Seeds Pvt. Ltd.) had organized a talk on "Problem Solving and Decision Making: A team Approach" on 4th Feb, 1995.
- **Baroda Chapter**
  - Baroda Chapter had organized a talk on "HRD Approach to Management of Discipline" by Mr. J.B. Kabra, Deputy Gen. Manager of Polychem Limited on 24th Mar, 1995.
  - Mr. N.R. Nadkarni the pioneer of 'Industrial Kirtankaar' had made a presentation on "Managerial Training through Edukirtan" on 25th Mar, 1995. It was jointly organized by NIPM, ISTD and Baroda chapter of Network.
- **Bombay Chapter**
  - Bombay Chapter had conducted elections in their Annual General Meeting were new office bearers (1995–97) were selected. Dr. P. V. Bhide (VP, HR of Bombay Dyeing Ltd.) as the president.
- **Hyderabad Chapter**
  - Hyderabad Chapter had organized a talk on "Productivity and HRD" by Mr. R.C. Shastry (VP VST Industries Ltd.) on 16th Mar, 1995.

- Another lecture was also organized by Hyderabad chapter. The talk was given by Dr. G.N. Rao, Dir of L.V. Institute on HRD concepts he introduced in the institute on 20th Apr, 1995.

➢ **Ranchi Chapter**

- Ranchi Chapter had conducted elections in their Annual General Meeting were new office bearers (1995–97) were selected. Dr. S.D. Tyagraj, Jt. Dir HRD of MTI, SAIL as the president.

➢ **Hosur Chapter**

- Hosur Chapter had conducted elections in their Annual General Meeting of the Executive Board were new office bearers (1995–97) were selected. Mr. M. N. Ramanathan (Works Manager of SUVA) as the president.

➢ **Jaipur Chapter**

- Jaipur Chapter had conducted elections in their Annual General Meeting of the Executive Board were new office bearers (1995–97) were selected. Mr. A.K. Gupta (GM of Hotel Clarks Ajmer, Jaipur) as the president.
- Jaipur Chapter had conducted a three day Trainer's Training Programme for Community Participation Unit (CPU) consisting of programme officers of community participation unit (CPU) consisting of programme officers from different backgrounds like Health Education, Sanitation, Water Distribution etc. from 10th-12th July,1995 at Hotel Clarks, Ajmer, Jaipur. Dr. Hem K. Bhargava coordinated the programme. Dr. Virendra Sisodia, Dr. Rameshwar Sharma, Dr. T.P. Jain and Dr. D.K. Jagdev were the facilitators of the programme.
- Social Sciences Research Center and, Indian Institute of Public Research (Regional Branch of Rajasthan) and ISTD, Jaipur had jointly organized a lecture on "Management of Conflict" by Shri H.S. Oberoi (Dy. Dir. ISTD) in Sept 1995.

- Jaipur Chapter and IIHMR organized one day training on "Work Ethics" on 18th Nov, 1995.

➢ **Madras Chapter**

- Madras Chapter again started getting active. Chapter had decided to start its seperate Madras chapter news-letter. It had also organized lectures on varied topics.
  1) "Outdoor Action Development" on 12th April, 1995.
  2) "Reiki- a Management Tool of 21st century" by Mr. R. Chandran on 3rd May, 1995.
  3) "Multimedia Applications in HRD" by K Ramchandran, Sr. Dy. Gen Manager- Multi Media and Mr. M. Gunaseelan, Manager HRDPentafour Software and Exports Ltd.
  4) "Re-engineering the HR processes" by Mr. N Swaminathan, Center for Creative Thinking, Dubai.

➢ **Pune Chapter**

- Pune Chapter had conducted elections in their Annual General Meeting of the Executive Board were new office bearers (1995–97) were selected. Mr. Kiran Gandhi as the president.
- Pune chapter had also organized a meeting by Dr. Naushad Forbes, director Forbes Marshall on "Do Organizations Need to have HRD Departments?" on 16th Sept, 1995.

1996

❖ **National HRD Network organized its 5th National Conference from 4th-6th Jan, 1996 at Hotel Krishna Oberoi at Hyderabad on "Challenges of Development- Aligning Human Resources Processes" on following sub-themes:**

➢ Reskilling HR Professionals
➢ Recruitment & Selection
➢ Remuneration & Rewards
➢ Competency Building
➢ Productivity & Quality
➢ Communications in Organization

- Culture Building
- IT for HR
- Women at Work
- HR Issues in Public Systems Management
- HR for Voluntary Sector
- National Policies for HRD
- Restructuring, Delaying, Downsizing,
- M&A and Joint Venture-HR Issues

Mr. Ramesh Galli, Chairman of the Global Trust Bank was the Conference Chairman.

- **Network had organized a two day seminar on "Employee Retention: The Key to Business Success" in collaboration with Asia Pacific Center for Management & Education at Hotel Taj Palace in Aug 1996.**
- **Individual And Organizational Assessment Center of AHRD started the first Professional Development Programme on "Individual and Organization Assessment" leading to certification at La Paz Gardens, Vasco, Goa from 4th-9th Mar, 1996. Faculties in this programme were:**
  - Dr. T.V. Rao
  - Mr. Aroon Joshi
  - Dr. Udai Pareek
  - Dr. P. Sethumadhavan
- Dr. Rao reviewing some of the activities of AHRD.

Dr. Sethumadhavan
Director, AHRD
Hyderabad

November 3, 96

Dear Sethu:

I could not get a seat on the Hyderabad flight yesterday and I returned home. I am planning to take the mid-night flight from Ahmedabad reaching there tomorrow morning 4.00 am. In case Keith is staying on it will be nice. I do not yet have the agenda of the meeting. My suggestions for discussion are as follows:

1. I suggest that we do not admit any students this year as we need to concentrate on the existing candidates. However, I am open in case the committee strongly feels that we should maintain the continuity. Please note that it is not an unusual practice on the part of Universities to take candidates for Doctoral programmes once in two to three years.

2. I suggest that the second year of the programme be held at a place where the students have good library facilities. I also suggest that the second year students be given adequate time to do library work and writing during the contact programme. There should be enough faculty available for guiding them. Hyderabad has more resources than Jamshedpur. I recommend that we appoint two or three faculty (Eg. Dr. Parameswaran, Dr. B. G. Reddy, Dr. Ravichandra, Dr. Sayeed etc. if necessary to work for the entire six week period to act as mentors and guide the students). I recommend that there should not be excessive concern about management and monitoring of the programme. What we should monitor is the quality of the work.

3. I would like to propose Fr. Abraham and Dr. Udai Pareek to be made members of the Doctoral Programme Committee and I also suggest that Dr. Pareek be requested to take over as Chairman of the Committee if it is acceptable to XLRI.

4. Keith mentioned that there continue to be some doubts in the minds of XLRI faculty about this programme. I do not anymore like half-hearted participation from XLRI. I also feel uncomfortable if they want to play a big brother role all the time criticising the AHRD rather than supporting it. As you have seen at Singapore these are days of joint ventures and collaboration. If XLRI has still doubts I feel we could review the arrangements, but such a review has to be commissioned by the Board of Governors of AHRD or XLRI or both as the programmes have been approved by the Boards. The DPC could make their recommendation for such a review. I personally feel that it is too early.

In the event of the DPC making such recommendation I would now actively look for one of the American or Australian Universities. I discussed with a Professor from George Washington University and he said that most U.S. Universities are coming to India and are actively looking for collaborators. It is not difficult to get one of them associated. Actually tomorrow is the inauguration of an M.B. A. Programme of Deakin University of Australia and the Vice-Chancellor is here. Ministry of HRD is supporting their Executive M.B. A. in India. My personal preference is to continue with the existing arrangements and XLRI should get recognition of this programme as per our M.O.U.

4. Mr. Jomon is submitting his proposal. Mr. Ghosh also is likely to submit it soon. I have seen their drafts. Please decide the procedure of approving the thesis proposal. If I recollect XLRI's role here is critical as it is at this stage and the thesis defence stage we have asked them to have a considerable say to ensure quality. I suggest that every proposal should be referred to some expert outside India as we may get some good suggestions about the literature and studies conducted earlier.

Please convey my regrets to the committee for not being able to make it on time for this meeting.

With warm regards

Sincerely,
T. V. Rao

November 14, 96
Dear Sethu:

Sub: Review of Academic Activities

As suggested by you during my last visit to AHRD I have planned to review the Academic Activities of AHRD. I would like to address the following issues for the review.
1. Is AHRD moving in the direction of its mission and objectives with which it was originally set up? Are the various activities of AHRD in the direction of developing HRD professionals and the HRD Profession?

2. Has AHRD been able to influence the thinking of HRD professionals and CEOs in various sectors or atleast well on way to do so? Is the current pace excellent or good enough or could be better?

3. Are the various activities well balanced or are some important things getting neglected? For example is there a good degree of balancing between education (Diploma, FPHRD), research, training and extension or consulting activities?

4. Is there a good balancing between meeting the institution and individual needs? Are people contributing to the institution and putting institutional needs first or are they overconcerned about their individual needs and trying to eat fruit even before they nurture the young tree?

5. Are we paying adequate attention to the Doctoral and Degree programmes? Are we able to synergise these with the other activities?

6. Have we been able to network well with the other educational institutions and use them as strategic avenues to disseminate our HRD knowledge?

7. Are the academic staff sharing information and learning from each other or are they building walls around them and becoming possessive of their territories, sectors and knowledge?

8. Are the administrative systems supporting academic work or are they hindering? Are people able to understand the resource constraints and be having cost consciously?

9. Is there adequate quality consciousness? Cost-consciousness? and Collegiate culture?

10. What more can be done to get the best contributions from all of us?

These are just a few issues that come to my mind. I request others to add to this list. I would appreciate if you can circulate this to all the staff of the AHRD with a request to use this and get ready for individual interaction with me during my stay there between 15th and 19 the November. As mentioned to you on phone I have a session with the Police Academy on 18th 11.00 to 1330. The rest of the time I will be available. I hope I will be able to meet each and every member at AHRD and take their concerns. Thanks.

T.V.Rao

- **AHRD with the support of Samtel India Ltd. had organized a three day Round Table Conference at YMCA, New Delhi for HRD Workers and Support Staff.**
- **AHRD with the support of Eicher Consultancy Services Ltd. and Danne Miller Tyson, USA had organized a three day Round Table Conference at YMCA, New Delhi for "HRD Workers and Support Staff".**
- **AHRD had started its consultancy division in 1996.**
- **Activities in National HRD Network Chapters**
    - **Baroda Chapter**
        - Baroda Chapter had conducted elections in their Annual General Meeting of the Executive Board were new office bearers were selected. Mr.N.S.Pathak was elected as the president on 31st Aug 1996.
    - **Bombay Chapter**
        - Bombay Chapter had networked with Grid Consultants Pvt. Ltd. in connection with Steven Covey's Programme and had also networked with AHRD in connection with Programme on Human Capital Accounting by Prof. Keith Bradley.
        - Bombay Chapter had formed three LANs to effectively network with various professionals spread across the city. These LANs had organized several programmes.
            1) South Bombay LAN
            2) Western Suburban LAN
            3) Navi Mumbai LAN
    - **Delhi Chapter**
        - Delhi Chapter had organized a lecture on "Psychological Testing: Recruitment & Career Development" by Mr. M. D. G. Koreth, Sr. VP-HRD, Ranbaxy and Ms. Kiron Wadhera, Executive Director of Asian Center for Organizational Research and Development.
        - The network had also organized a family get together on 22nd June. A talk on "Effect of Stress on our Health" by Mr. Samir Makkar (Health Consultant).
        - A lecture was delivered on "Corporate Restructuring-HR Implications" by Mr. M.R.R. Nair, Director- Personnel, Lipton India Ltd in Aug 1996.

- Chapter had organized a lecture on "Relevance of Indian Ethos in Modern Management" by Swami Someshwaranad.
- Chapter had also organized a lecture on "A vision 2000 plus for Indian HRD Professionals" by Dr. M. B. Atherya on 25th Sept, 1996.

➢ **Jaipur Chapter**
- Dr. Udai Pareek had been invited as a speaker in OD Network Annual Conference held in Orlando, Florida, USA held from 5th -9th Oct, 1996.

➢ **Hyderabad Chapter**
- **Four lectures were organized by the Hyderabad chapter.**
  1) "Chief Executives' Perspectives on HRD" by Mr. S. Bhattacharya, Chairman & MD ITW Signode in May, 1996.
  2) "Current Trends in culture, life & HR Practices" by Dr. S. Chandrashekhar, GM- HRD, Pennar Group, USA in June, 1996.
  3) "Attitudes and Altitudes" by Mr. Venkati P. Rao in July, 1996.
- Hyderabad network and TMI Network (consultancy specializing in Recruitment Advertising) jointly organized a half day workshop was organized on "Recruitment Advertising" on 14th Sept, 1996 at Hotel Krishna Oberoi, Hyderabad.
- The chapter had also started honoring persons for their commitment towards profession, integrity and honesty.

➢ **Pune Chapter**
- Pune chapter had organized a talk on "Value based Transformational Processes- Experiments & Experiences" by Prof. M.S. Pillai in Aug, 1996.

❖ **Books Launched**

➢ Book **"Selected Readings in HRD"** by Mr. Kuldeep Singh, Dr. T.V. Rao, and Mr. Baburaj Nair and published by Tata McGraw Hill Publications was launched.

- Book **"Assessment of Organizational Climate"** by Mr. Sethumadhavan, Dr. T.V. Rao and published by AHRD was launched.
- Jaipur chapter foundation had supported Dr. Udai Pareek for his book **"Training Instruments for HRD"** published by TATA McGraw Hill.
- Book **"Assessment of Organizational Climate"** by Dr. Sethumadhavan, Dr. T.V. Rao and Mrs. Sarupriya which was published by AHRD was launched.
- Another book **"Evaluation of HRD"** was also launched.

1997

- **Network had organized a workshop on "Executive Stress Management" by Prof. D.M. Pestonjee of IIM A**
- **Network had organized five lecture meetings**
  - "Tackling HR issues during M&A" by Mr. M.R.R. Nair on 17th Oct, 1997.
  - "Economic reforms by- Challenges for HRD Professionals" by Dr. Nrupendra Rao, Chairman Pennar Group.
  - "Recent Developments in OD" by Ms. Kristine Sullivan and Mr. Rolland Sullivan, experts in OD.
  - "Public Interest Litigations-HRD Concerns" by Mr. L. Ravichander.
  - "Role of HR-A CEO's Perspective" by Mr. R.S. Nanda, President & MD, Coromandel Fertilizers Ltd.
- **Activities in National HRD Network Chapters**
  - **Jaipur Chapter**
    - Mr. Manohar Nadkarni had been invited as a key speaker in World Conference on Individual and Organization Development Association (IOAD) held from 21st-25th Sept, 1997.
    - Jaipur Chapter had organized a two day workshop on "New Dimensions in Supervision" on 14th-15th Feb, 1997 at IIHMR Jaipur.
  - **Koraput Chapter**
    - Koraput Chapter had conducted elections in their Annual General Meeting were new office bearers were

selected. Mr. M.L. Malaviya was elected as the new president.

- **Madras Chapter**
  - Madras Chapter rejuvenated under the guidance of Mr. P.V.R. Murthy, the founder member of the Madras Chapter.
  - The Chapter had organized two day workshop on "Concepts & Practices in HRD" on 29th and 30th Nov, 1997.
- **Pune Chapter**
  - Pune Chapter had organized a lecture on "Learning Organizations" by Mr. Arun Wakhlu.
  - The chapter had also organized annual workshop on "The Fall and Rise of Human Resource Management" on 15th March at Thermax Ltd.
  - Pune Chapter had conducted elections in their Annual General Meeting were new office bearers were selected (1997–1999). Mr. Suhas Palekar was elected as the new president.
- **Calcutta Chapter**
  - Calcutta Chapter had organized three lectures in 1997
    1) "Turnaround Strategy" by Mr. S.P. Mukherjee, Director Personnel Hindustan Cables Ltd. in Oct.
    2) "Reiki for HR Pacilitators by Ms. Parul Dutta" in Nov, 1997.
    3) "HRD in Service Industry" by Mr. Surojit Banerjee of Oberoi Grand
  - Calcutta Chapter had organized a meeting and Mr. G.P. Rao had apprised the committee regarding the National Conference at Delhi in 1998.
  - The chapter had organized a talk on "Empowerment: J K Corp" by Mr. G.P. Rao, GM (HRD), J K Corp in Nov 1997.
- **Delhi Chapter**
  - Delhi Networks sub chapter was inaugurated on 14th March, 1997. Mr. S.N. Shukla of Amity University was appointed as the coordinator.

- Delhi Chapter had organized a talk on "Empowerment Audit" by Dr. Udai Pareek on 14th Feb, 1997.

➢ **Hyderabad Chapter**

- The Jan meeting of the Hyderabad chapter was addressed by Padmashri Rajesh Gelli, Chairman of Global Trust Bank at FAPCCI Auditorium on "Explosive growth of Service Sector- HR Implication".
- A workshop on "Benchmarking for Competitive Advantage" was conducted by the chapter president Dr. Y.R.K. Reddy
- Chapter had organized a lecture on "Common Law and Mordern Management" by Justice Prabha Shakar Misra, the than Chief Justice of Andhra Pradesh
- Hyderabad chapter had launched its second issue of directory of Members for the year 1996–97.

➢ **Ahmedabad Chapter**

- Ahmedabad Chapter started getting rejuvenated under the leadership of Mr. Madan Saluja. The executive board had started meeting regurlarly.
- A seminar on "360 degree Performance Appraisals" was organized.

➢ **Bangalore Chapter**

- Bangalore Chapter had organized a lecture on "Corporate Social Performance" by Mr. John Bickell, Director Community Affairs, Allied Dunbar Assurance plc. UK.

❖ **AHRD had launched a directory of HRD Professionals (in India) which contained information about 232 HR Professionals.**

❖ **AHRD had conducted the fifth PDP on Individual and Organizational Assessment Center (IOAC) at Hotel Centaur Airport, Mumbai from 27th Jan -1st Feb, 1997.**

❖ **AHRD had organized its 6th Individual and Organizational Assessment Programme from 8th- 13th Sept, 1997at Maurya Sheraton, New Delhi.**

❖ **The I and II contact program for 1996–97 batch of Doctoral Fellow Program in HRD had been held from 28th Apr- 8th June, 1997 at Inst. Of Public Enterprises, Hyderabad.**

- **AHRD had conducted a five day in-house training programme at Vishakhapatnam Steel Plant on "Leadership through Team Development" from 17th – 21st March, 1997.**
- **AHRD's Doctoral Committee under the leadership of Mr. E.G. Paremeshwaran had met at Hotel Viceroy on 8th Mar, 1997 to discuss the about the Research Proposals for the first batch of Doctoral level Fellow Programme.**
- **AHRD had conducted Round Table Conference on "Transperency in NGOs" on 5th-6th Dec, 1997.**
- **AHRD had also conducted Supervisory Development Programmes for the Staff of ONIDA Branch Office Hyderabad on 28th -29th Dec, 1997.**
- **AHRD had organized the Ravi Matthai Memorial lecture on "How and What of Institutions Transformations, Ravi Matthai Revisited". It was delivered by Dr. Udai Pareek on 6th June, 1997 at Hyderabad.**
- **AHRD had organized a three day unique learning event on "Designing the Strategic Training Systems: Re-engineering Training for Results" from 24th-26th Feb, 1997 at Hotel Oberoi Towers, Mumbai.**
- **A meeting of Board of governors of AHRD was held on 27th Feb, 1997. Prof. C. Balaji was appointed as the first full time director of AHRD.**

ACADEMY OF HUMAN RESOURCES DEVELOPMENT
(An Institute of the National HRD Network)

12, COSMOVILLE, SATYAGRAH MARG, AHMEDABAD - 380 054. PHONE 079-648218, 640341 FAX: 079-640681

May 27, 97

Dear Prof. Balaji:

Congratulations and belated Best Wishes for wonderful Institution Building years at AHRD. You are the first Full Time Full term Director at AHRD. Keith D'Souza came on a one year leave and stayed for one and half years. Sethu was an acting Director. You have taken over at a very crucial time. The entire AHRD's future depends on you and I am very confident you will do a wonderful job.

The AHRD is very unlike most other institutions. On the positive side it is an innovative institution and the only one in the world. The American AHRD is not entirely comparable to us as they are only a network and do not have Doctoral and other programmes. They are willing to collaborate with us I understand. The uniqueness of this institution is in its goals, resources (or lack of them), support of professionals, applications to all sectors besides business sector etc. The absence of Tatas, Birlas , Governament, Ford Foundation , International agencies or any other Business house house to back it financially at this stage puts more difficulties, challenges as well as opportunities in the lap of the Director. Wish you all the best.

The Doctoral Programme is a unique one and it may set a new model for several others. Consultancy is needed but has the dangers of distracting the faculty from other productive work. Balancing this and other priorities and ones own professional work requires a lot of tight rope walking, personal example and sacrifices. My good wishes to you on this also.

We started AHRD culture as one that attempts to practice what it preaches. It is not always easy to do this. Discipline is important. Hard work on the part of every one will be a constant need for growth of AHRD as well as personal growth of every one. I realised that Trustworthiness of everyone is the most critical factor among the OCTAPACE culture.

Best wishes for a happy and eventful tenure and Successful Institution Building and generation of new knowledge through your experiments and experiences.

TV Rao

T. V. Rao

June 15. 97

To: Prof. C. Balaji

From : T. V. Rao

Sub: Academic Council of AHRD

As you are aware the last meeting of the Academic Council was held one and a half years ago. We have not yet scheduled the next AC meeting as NHRDN has not yet planned its meeting. In the last Board meeting of AHRD we decided to continue the existing AC as it is. My informal discussions with a few of the members of AC indicate that this could be made a useful body to advise AHRD and its Board on various Academic matters. We need to hold the next AC meeting on a date convenient to AHRD. As AHRD now has a full time Director, I recommend the following:

1. The Director of AHRD takes over as the Vice-chairman of the AC and also appoints one of the AHRD faculty as the Member-Secretary. I have checked with a few memebrs of AC about the Director taking over as Chairman. A consistent view was that anoutsider should be the Chairman like in the case of the Board to bring external inputs as Director is already Chairman of the Faculty Council.

2. The Academic Council is re-constituted with its original constitution intact. The membership includes: Council of Guides, HRD Network President and Chapter Presidents, Representatives of XLRI (two), ISTD, ISABS, ISISD, NIPM, IGNOU, TISS, AIMA, AMA, All Faculty and Professors Emiritus of AHRD, Outstanding HRD Managers etc.

I would appreciate your views and recommendations of the names on this so that a letter of invitation could be sent to them. The letter of invitation could also go from the Director's office as AHRD should eventually be the Secretariat of the AC. You may like to discuss this further among the faculty. In case the faculty wish to change the constitution of the AC it may need to be taken to the Board. If not, further action in terms of rejuvinating it, reconstituting the membersship and convening a meeting could be initiated by the Director.

Please let me know in case you would like me to take initiative in this regard in terms of writing letters etc. I would prefer this to be done at your end so that you could slowly take charge of AC.

We should be sending a communication to AC memebers soon about:
FPHRD update, Joining of the New Director, Academic Programmes planned for this year, Idea of the two year PGP in HRD, Possible dates of next meeting etc. The HRD News letter used to be sent all our AC members on a complimenatary basis as it gives news about AHRD. Catch up and the Diploma news letters also used to be sent. i hope these conventions are continuing.

Thanks

1998

- **Books Launched**
  - Book "Pioneering Human Resources Development: The L&T System" by Dr. Udai Pareek and Dr. T.V. Rao was launched.
- **The Executive Board meeting of Network was held on 17th Feb, 1998 at Taj Palace, New Delhi.**

- **AHRD had also conducted a programme on Developing & Managerial Excellence for Top and Senior Executives of JT Mobiles Ltd, Hyderabad on 9th Jan, 1998.**
- **AHRD had also conducted a programme on Developing & Managerial Excellence for Senior Executives of Awarpur Cement Works of L&T Group, Awarpur on 1st- 2nd Feb, 1998.**
- **AHRD had conducted the Individual and Organizational Assessment Center (IOAC) at Harmony Cyber Convention Center, Mumbai from 20th -21st Apr, 1998.**
  - Facilitators of the programme were Dr. T.V. Rao and Prof. C. Balagi
  - The speakers were:

SPEAKER	COMPANY
Mr. Aroon D Joshi	R.P.G Enterprises
Mr. George Kunnath	Mahindra & Mahindra Ltd.
Mr. Nihar R Ghosh	Johnson & Johnson Ltd.
Mr. R.S. Singh	L&T
Mr. R.K. Premranjan	XLRI
Mr. Rajan Acharya	Wipro Ltd.

- **Activities in National HRD Network Chapters**
  - **Ahmedabad Chapter**
    - Many activities were conducted in Ahmedabad Chapter in 1998.Many talks meetings and presentations were made in that year.
    - Ahmedabad Chapter in collaboration with NIS Ahmedabad organized a long term training programme "Personality and Communication Effectiveness"
    - The chapter had also organized a lecture on "Managing TIME: Return on Time Invested" by Mr. Shymal Taneja, Regional Director, Leadership Management International India.
  - **Ranchi Chapter**
    - The chapter had organized a talk on "Lockheed Martin's Survival Story" by Mr. Satyajit Jena, Faculty Member, MTI, and SAIL.

- The chapter had also organized a talk on "Total Excuse Control" by Mr. E.I. Ravindranath, GM-HRD, Martin Industries Ltd.

1999

- **The first National HRD Network Foundation Day Lecture series was inaugurated by Dr. Anjali Reddy, Chairman Dr. Reddy Labs. The Lecture was delivered by Mr. YRK Reddy, Chairman Yaga Consulting.**
- **A National Conference of Young HR Professionals "HR in next Millennium" was organized on 3rd -4th Dec, 1999.**
- **In 1999 there was a need to revitalize National HRD Network so the Interim Management Committee was set up.**
  - The Interim Management Committee of National HRD Network was set up to look after the matters till the new President was elected.

From: T.V.Rao <tvrao@adl.vsnl.net.in>
To: tvrao@adl.vsnl.net.in <tvrao@adl.vsnl.net.in>; iimhraj@jpl.vsnl.net.in <iimhraj@jpl.vsnl.net.in>; ksnhrd@usa.net <ksnhrd@usa.net>; arvind@rpgnet.com <arvind@rpgnet.com>
Cc: ezobob@cal2.vsnl.net.in <ezobob@cal2.vsnl.net.in>; > <<Aquil.Busrai@motorola.com>; > <<gprao@jkmail.com>; > <<yaga@hdl.vsnl.net.in>; > <<nghosh@jnjin.jnj.com>; Pareek <anagat@infozech.com>
Date: 20 December 1999 16:00
Subject: Re: National HRD Network

Dear Udai, Anil, GP, Aquil, Nihar, YRK and Arvind;

I am sending the enclosed letter to all Chapter Presidents and other office bearers. This for your information. KSN has requested me to do the same. regards
T V Rao

Dear Professional Colleague:

I am writing this on behalf of the Interim Management Committee set up be the Executive Board of the National HRD Network. As you are aware Mr. Arvind Agarwal has been appointed as the next President of the National HRD Network. He will take over from April 1, 2000. He has just shifted from escorts to RPG Group as Director Corporate Development. Mr. Agarwal was Treasurer and a very active member of the National HRD Network in the early years. He was associated with HRD, Corporate Planning, as well as Marketing functions in Modi Xerox and subsequently moved as the CEO of one of the businesses in Escorts.* His coming into HRD and Corporate development and National HRD Network are excellent coincidences and we are all hopeful that he will provide us the right kind of leadership and put the national HRD Network as a world class quality professional body to be benchmarked by others. Please join the current Board and the Interim committee in wishing him all success in both his new assignments.

I am taking this opportunity to also inform you that Mr. K. Satyanarayana of Hyderabad HRD Network has taken over as Executive Director of the National HRD Network. His appointment is in pursuance of the recommendations of the Executive Board and has been finalized by the Interim Management Committee. I am enclosing a short note on role of the Executive Director. He will be operating from the Hyderabad HRD Network's office and work in close association with the Academy. He has a critical role to play. All of us need to support him in rejuvenating National HRD Network and making it a world class benchmarking body. I am enclosing the contact addresses of both the new President and the Executive Director. I request you to be in touch with them and provide all the support.

26/03/01

In the last three months the Interim committee has done a few things. Many chapters are not functioning well and those functioning have not been sending information. We prepared a renewal agenda and sent to some of the chapters. We have not yet been able to contact some more chapters, which need attention. We began with those, which have recently become less active and have a lot of potential. I am enclosing a short note on the renewal agenda we have set up for ourselves. I hope you will give all support and cooperation in taking HRD forward. I hope we will start a new era of cooperation and voluntary action.

With warm professional regards, and good wishes for the year 2000.

T. V. Rao
Chairman, Interim Management Committee
National HRD Network

Enclosures: *(i)Role of Executive Director. (ii) Contact Addresses of President and ED. (iii)Renewal agenda of NHRDN. (iv) Note on Interim Management Committee's activities so far.*

From: T.V.Rao <tvrao@ad1.vsnl.net.in>
To: Academy <ahrdhd1@hd1.vsnl.net.in>
Date: 29 October 1999 15:21
Subject: Fw: National HRD Network

Please take a print out and give to K Satyanarayana on Novemebr 1, 99
T V Rao

From: T.V.Rao <tvrao@ad1.vsnl.net.in >
To: nghosh@jnjin.jnj ; nihar <nghosh@jnjin.jnj.com >
Cc: tvrao@ad1.vsnl.net.in
Subject: Fw: National HRD Network
Date: 23 September 1999 22:36

Dear Nihar:
Thank you for agreeing to be on the Interim management Committee of the National HRD Network. The Committee is authorised to take all decisions to rejuvinate the network. I hope you can help us do the same in Mumbai as well as in other chapters. Regards
T V Rao

From: T.V.Rao <tvrao@ad1.vsnl.net.in >
To: Rupa Padki < padaki@blr.vsnl.net.in >
Cc: gopal.mahapatra@bplnet.com
Subject: Fw: National HRD Network
Date: 18 September 1999 10:29

Agenda for Renewal and Transformation of National HRD Network

Who will do it?

The Empowered Interim Management Committee. The proposed Members include:

Anil Khandelwal
Aquil Busrai
Nihar Ghosh
Udai Pareek
T V Rao
G P Rao

Others are to be finalised

With the help of the current Executive Committee and S earch Committee for the President, National HRD Networ (Arvind Pande, Aquil Buhrai, Udai pareek, GP Rao)

Strategy:

- Enrolling new members. Target: Every one with HRD in their title should be a member of this body.
- Inactive chapters should be activated.
- Active chapters should be encouraged and used as role models. Prepared to be bench-marked by others.
- New chapters should be started.
- Create new hope for the members about the need for and advantages of being a professional member

- New agenda should be created for chapters and the body.
- Networking should be the primary agenda. - Future will be that of knowledge workers and HRD professional are knowledge workers and in addition human service professionals. This profession needs preparation. NHRDN helps members to prepare for the future. If you are a member it can help you prepare for future and prevent you from becoming obsolete. It is a means of preparation for the future challenges, rejuvination and reorientation of HR managers to new roles demanded by the changing environment, strict ethical standards, regulation of the profession like the Indian Medical Association, certification

- Performance of the office bearers should be appraised and non-performing office bearers should be encouraged to step asisde in the interests of the body.

- Using students and student bodies to enrol meemebrs and facilitate activities.

Activities of the HRD Network:

1. **Networking through Internet**: Features of the Internet HRD Network:

    - About HRD Network
    - Update on the world trends in HRD.
    - News and views,- including short articles, internet talks, events etc,
    - HRD Library : Books and Book Summaries,
    - HRD Newslettter,
    - Membership Directory,
    - Employment Opportunities - this feature actually helps organisations in placements etc.,
    - Professional Ethics and values for HRD professionals,
    - HRD Education - India and Abroad
    - Links with Universities and other professional bodies
    - HRD Helpline
    - Dialogue Box ; Dialogue with personalities - this feature has a monthly personalities from India and abroad who willl answer quiries on the areas of specialisation
    - Benchmarks- this section introduces bench marks of some of the HRD systems and also highlights new practicesnew practices
    - Other professional bodies - introduces other professional bodies like the OD Network, ASTD, ISTD, NIPM etc and membership details
    - NGO network
    - Other networks

2. HRD Newsletter

3. National and International Conferences, seminars and symposia

4. Academy of HRD

5. Setting and Maintaining professional Standards

6. Certification through Academy

7. Comopetency testing for HRD Professionals

7. Meetings and other professional activities

8. Promoting other networks (NGO Network, Teachers Network)

9. HRD Awards

10. Scholarships

From: T.V.Rao <tvrao@ad1.vsnl.net.in>
To: Academy <ahrdhd1@hd1.vsnl.net.in>
Cc: ksnhrd@usa.net <ksnhrd@usa.net>
Date: 29 October 1999 14:59
Subject: Fw: Re:National HRD Network : attention Balaji and Ravi

---

Dear Mr Murthy;

I never got a full reply to this.
Please take a print out of this and give to Mr Satyanarayana
He may not be able to access this from his hot mail.
Regards

T V Rao

From: T.V.Rao <tvrao@ad1.vsnl.net.in >
To: M/S ACADEMY OF HUMAN RESOURCE DEVT. <ahrdhd1@hd1.vsnl.net.in >
Cc: gprao@jkmail.com
Subject: Re:National HRD Network : attention Balaji and Ravi
Date: 07 September 1999 21:59

Dear Balaji and Ravi;

I have been nformed by GP Rao that the Executive Board of NHRDN have asked me to Chiar the Interim Management Committee and have authorised me take all steps needed for rejuvination of the Network. As you will notice from the e-mails sent I am getting into action. i need all the support from you as I would like do a few things to start the rejuvination and renewal process going. I need immediately the following:
1. The updated lists of addresses of of all the members of the Network and its executive Board
2. Any briefing on the current status of activities etc. of each of the chapters
3. Names and addresses of contact persons and executive Boards of each of the chapters
4. Financil position of the Network
5. A copy of all the Board meeting minutes of the last five years or as much as you can give.
6. Amended (uptil now) constitution of HRD Network
and any other details you may think as of use.

Warm regards
T V Rao

Other HRD Networks

We have not received any news from other Networks. Some activities took place in Calcutta and Bombay Networks but details are not available. Attempts are being made to form a Kerala Network of HRD. Some activities have started but the Network needs to be formalised.

Membership

The membership of the Network has grown quite a bit during this year. We have nearly one thousand members in the National HRD Network with Bangalore, Pune, Bombay, Hyderabad and Delhi Networks having more than a hundred members each.

I thank all the office bearers, members and others who played an active role and supported various activities at the HRD Network during this period.

I close with the good wishes to the new team.

T. V. Rao
Interim President

ADDING VALUE TO THE HR PROFESSION- AN ACTION PLAN

ADDING VALUE TO THE HR PROFESSION - AN ACTION PLAN

1. Improving HR education.
2. Moving HR from a 'function' to a 'profession'.
3. Giving HR Managers 'Line' experience.
4. Building HR as a 'strategic business partner'.
4. Celebrating successful HR professionals as role models.

1. IMPROVING HR EDUCATION

- Select leading MBA/Management Education institutions in Delhi,Mumbai,Kolkata,Chennai, Bangalore, Hyderabad and Pune respectively which offer a 2 year course with HR specialisation. TISS and XLRI should be included.
- Formally communicate with the Management of these institutions on behalf of NHRD Network and offer to 'adopt' them.
- Name 2 persons from within HR profession who will be the mentors of that institution, on behalf of the NHRDN. (Ideally one of them should be the President of the Network chapter nearest to the institution).

- Create a mentoring framework and put all these mentors - from across the country-together and agree on a common mentoring process for these educational institutions.
The mentoring task to include syllabus review and addition of content relevant to Industry.
(For eg. Interviewing skills as a subject for an MBA in HR)
-Faculty evaluation and faculty development plan
-Arranging visiting/adjunct faculty for full courses after -rigorous selection process
-Arranging for faculty internship in companies by using personal contacts with the companies.

-Set up an official process of empanelling working professionals to write/contribute to HR text book and case study development. Offer this panel to Universities, MBA colleges etc.
-Make special efforts to "place" students of "adopted institutions" into firms and take responsibility for the performance of those candidates.

2. FROM A 'FUNCTION' TO A 'PROFESSION'

-Collaborate and strengthen the CII Work on HR competency model. Take a position around desired HR competencies and announce/offer it to members.
-Build a certification program for in-company HR professionals integrated with our recommended 'Competencies"
- Outsource this task to an eminent HR training institution though a standard evaluation process.

Establish a Code of Ethics

- Study the code of ethics for HR professionals in US, Canada, UK (China?) Japan, Australia and any other exemplary work anywhere in the world.
- Create a draft code of ethics applicable in India.
- Circulate it to chapters and all members. Circulate it to at least 200 CEO's, owners, promoters and opinion leaders from all walks of life - Government, NGO set-up, politics, academia, corporate sector (including public sector), armed forces etc.
- Conduct chapter level workshops with members and others from industries in validating and improving the proposed draft.
- Based on inputs finalise a code of ethics for NHRD Network and publish.
- Create a formal mechanism for acceptance and allegiance to the code of ethics by full time members of the HRD Network including of the institutional members.
- Link the certification program with the code of ethics.

Recommend standard Template documents

- Create an index of templates around core HR functions like HR Planning, Recruitment and Seléction, compensation policy, incentive plans/variable plans, performance management system etc.
- Set up subject matter experts to design and recommend templates.
- Create another panel to evaluate the templates and finalise them by putting the stamp of NHRD on that.
- Make them available to HR community and other users on HR portal, initially as a few downloads and eventually as pay-per-use model.

3. GIVING HR MANAGERS 'LINE' EXPERIENCE

Select 5 to 10 companies which will offer to pilot a model of HR functionaries at the middle level to take up line roles and vice-versa.

Create and offer a framework of rotation and learning and evaluation.

Create sponsors for each of the firm where pilot takes place, who will work with CEO/HR lead who is running the pilot.

Study the learnings, evaluate the impact and finalise a ready to use format as a recommendation from HRD Network to Industry.

4. PARTNERING WITH BUSINESS

- Choose 2 firms each in the start-up, growth, mature and declining environments from both the sectors of manufacturing and services. Thus create about 15 to 20 firms where HR partnership with business - from a strategic sense - will be formally piloted and a case study eventually published.
- Agree on a methodology of deriving and aligning HR strategies from/with the business plan.
- Agree on a framework of validating the methodology and an execution plan.
- Formally invite companies to participate in this experiment.
- Publish results after the end of a Financial Year and celebrate success stories with data on business improvement.
- Ask academy of HRD to document and offer this experience and approach as a standard product.

5. CELEBRATING SUCCESSFUL HR PROFESSIONALS

- Create a large no. of "Excellence in HR practices awards". Broaden identification process.
- Segment the various types of firms/organisations and areas of contribution across the country and create at least 30-50 types of excellence 'awards' for proven work in defined areas of HR.
- Make these excellence awards a coveted, objective and competitive process.
- Create a 'hall of fame' for HR professionals which can be published (e.g.Eco Times)
- Find academic institutions across the country who will invite the members of Hall of Fame as adjunct faculty. Make it mandatory for those selected to offer x no. of free talks/courses.

❖ Some important changes were made in the governance of AHRD.

From: T.V.Rao <tvrao@ad1.vsnl.net.in>
To: yaga@hd1.vsnl.net.in <yaga@hd1.vsnl.net.in>
Cc: ahrdhd1@hd1.vsnl.net.in <ahrdhd1@hd1.vsnl.net.in>
Date: 19 May 1999 13:18
Subject: Academy of HRD and Its Governance

Dear RK:

The Personnel and Finance Committee has been merged into the newly formed Executive Committee of the Board of the Academy. Unfortunately we did not have an opportunity to meet since the time the new Committee was formed. AHRD was to organise the new Board meeting some time in January or February 1999. This has also not taken place so far and thus I did not have much of an opportunity to brief you. As you are new to the AHRD Board and as I was Chairman of the Personnel & Finance Committee I wish to brief you a few matters. As the P&F Committee is merged to form the EC all the functions performed by the P&F Committee should be performed by the EC for which you are the chairman.

The Personnel and Finance Committee is the main policy making body for all personnel and finance matters and acts on behalf of the Board. I think it is now the Executive Committee which has to take up this role and its role is enhanced to include building and other fund management.

The Financial management at AHRD in the last few years after it has moved to Hyderabad could have been more efficient. A lot of money was kept in savings account and interest loss had taken place. Investments may not have always been paid attention to maximize the benefits. The P&F Committee did not exercise controls and the Directors were perhaps less knowledgeable or did not give priority to this. I have not paid attention to these as I perhaps felt that it would be interfering with the Director. The Director may have lacked guidance and may not have paid attention.

AHRD was supposed to send monthly statement of income and expenditure which they did some times but some times had to be asked. I hope they are sub mitting to you monthly statements of receipts and expenditure. These need to be seen and any suggestions made.

Director was empowered to spend only upto Rs 20,000 (to the best of my recollection) at a time on capital expenditure and needed the permission of P&F. There is a note giving the delegation of financial powers to the Director prepared during Sethumadhavan's time. This was done to make sure financial systems are followed and the P&F Committee guides the Director and his team.

The P&F Committee approved all the permanent appointments and also made recruitment policies. In the recent past the Director prepared such policies and sent for approval to P&F. The Executive Committee should naturally be the approving body of all permanent

26/03/01

appointments of Faculty. The Director is authorized to appoint any faculty only for temporary period of one year.

The P&F Committee reviewed all promotion decisions and raised performance related issues. They also insisted on annual activity plans to be prepared by AHRD and sent for P&F Committees information. Each individual faculty was supposed to make such plans and also reviewed annually. Attempts were made but quality of initiative and compliance could always be more.

The Director is required to send all his travel plans as well as Consultancy involvement for approval to P&F Chairman. This is in the interest of the Director himself as there is no one else to supervise. Infact this point has been specially made in the last Board meeting and in place of the Chairman who is busy the EC was suggested to take up this role. I hope this is being done. This specially important to ensure proper accountabilities.
Consultancy rules are also the prerogative of the P&F Committee as such matters cannot be left for the Faculty and the Director in terms of the long term implications of any such policies. We have generally honored the suggestions of Director and faculty as the P&F Committee had not found the necessity to make any drastic changes as long as the faculty generate its resource.

Mr. Murthy could give you the files containing all the decisions and minutes etc. of P&F Committee from the beginning. The files must be there from day one as this (P&F) Committee existed from the beginning and I was actively involved in it. You may also like to go through the Board minutes of the previous years if you have time.

I am marking a copy of this note to Balaji so that he knows the brief I have given you and it also helps him to recapitulate the safeguards and norms. I strongly believe that while these committees are not supervisory or control bodies they cannot also ignore their role in creating appropriate systems, norms and culture, enforce accountabilities . Some of the issues the EC would deal with cannot be taken lightly and the EC should play an active role in guiding the Director and his faculty. The role of EC becomes important specially in view of the fact that our Board does not meet frequently and relies heavily on the Academics to provide leadership.

You may also be aware that there is an Academic Council for which I am supposed to be the Chairman. It consists of all the Council of Guides, HRD Network executive, Nominees of other Professional bodies, HRD Award winners etc. It is a large body and is supposed to meet once a year to coincide with the annual conference of HRD Network or NIPM or ISTD (to save travel costs as AHRD cannot afford the same). The AC has taken all important decisions in the past. For example the decision to start the diploma, the decision to start the Doctoral Program and collaborate with XLRI, etc. were all taken there. It was active and is the only forum where all those who contribute to AHRD as visiting faculty etc. have a say. I have stayed away from activating it as I wanted AHRD Director and full-time faculty to take the drivers seat. I am not sure if that was the wise thing to do. I have been proposing a discussion on this

26/03/01

for the last few times but it did not get the priority it deserved. I am not giving it up. I talked to a number of well wishers of AHRD and got the feeling that it should be activated. I am preparing a paper on the same and propose to discuss preferably in the next Board meeting.

This note is meant to give you some background. With this I have done my duty and the rest is upto the Executive Committee, the Director and the Board to take it forward.

Warm Regards
T V Rao

From: T.V.Rao <tvrao@adl.vsnl.net.in>
To: Yaga Consulting Pvt. Ltd. <yaga@hdl.vsnl.net.in>
Date: 07 September 1999 05:35
Subject: Re: Academic Council

Dear YRK: I am enclosing a communication I have prepared and sent for comments and suggestions to Balaji. I would appreciate any suggestions on this. Also I am sending this to coordiante with you as Chairman of the executive Committess and keep you informed of the initiatives.
Regards
T V Rao

Academic Council of the Academy of Human Resources Development

Dear ------

The Academy of HRD is reconstituting its Academic Council. I am approaching you with a request to you to be a member of this Council. The Academic Council is the main academic decision making and advisory body. Currently it consists of eminent HRD professionals including Practitioners, Professors, Researchers, Scholars, All members of the National HRD Network Executive Committee, Representatives of professional bodies, all Doctoral program guides and Consultants. All the Academic staff of the Academy is its members and the Director is Member Secretary.

One of the missions of AHRD is to improve the standards of the HRD profession and professional education in the country. The Academy is governed by a Board of Governors who are industrialists and representatives of members of the Academy's Society. While the Board looks after the overall governance of the Academy, the AC looks after the Academic affairs.

The AC is being reconstituted to make it a much smaller and viable body. The AC members should be able to provide guidance periodically. It is proposed to have meetings and conferences over the net using e-mail and meet physically once a year. There will be steering committee, which will meet more frequently. I request you to give your consent to be a member of this council. You will be contributing by your presence and advice to the upliftment of the standards of HRD profession in this country and also to promote HRD for national development. I take your consent as indicative of your willingness to devote a few days in a year for the promotion of HRD profession. Your name will appear on the brochure of the Academy and the term will be for three years. We need to undertake some Academic Renewal exercise for the Academy and I am enclosing the agenda for the next meeting or Internet dialogue. Please send me your consent by e-mail.

With professional Regards

26/03/01

- AHRD in association with Symbiosis Center for Management had HRD, Pune for 1 year Diploma Programme in HRD.
- **AHRD had organized seventh HRD Facilitators Programme. Mr. Baburaj Nair had coordinated the programme.**
- **AHRD had conducted the ninth PDP on Individual and Organizational Assessment Center (IOAC) in Bangalore from 29th Nov -4th Dec, 1999.**
- **AHRD had organized a five day workshop on "Monitoring and Evaluation and Organizational Development" was coordinated by Prof. Balaji for the executives of CRY and its partner NGOs.**
- **AHRD had conducted the PDP on Individual and Organizational Assessment Center (IOAC) at Hyderabad from 21st – 26th June, 1999.**
  - Coordinator for the programme was Mr. Himank Priyadarshi.
  - Faculties were Dr. Udai Pareek, Dr. T.V.Rao, Dr. Ohja, Dr. E.G. Parmeshwaran, Prof. E. Abrahm S.J., Dr. Keith D'Souza, Mr. Ujawala Peendes, Mr. Aroon Joshi, Dr. Balaji, Dr. R.N. Saxena, Col. T.N. Reddy, Ms. Dipti Sethi, Mr. P.C. George, Mr. V.K. Verma, and Mr. R.K. Koner.
- **Activities in National HRD Network Chapters**
  - **Ahmedabad Chapter**
    - Two lecture were conducted in Ahmedabad chapter
      1) Audio Visual presentation and role play on "Enriching Boss- Subordinate Relationships" was done by the HR team of the Adani Exports.
      2) Prof. Nina Mancherji of NIRMA University had given a lecture on "Leadership".
      3) Mr. Ashok Chanda made a presentation on "Evolving HR Strategies for Growth" in Dec, 1999.
    - A Programme for the development of the Line Managers was facilitated by Mr. Rohit Thakker.
  - **Cochin Chapter**
    - Cochin Chapter along with NIPM had organized a lecture on "HRD Score Card" which was delivered by Dr. T.V. Rao.

- **Ranchi Chapter**
  - Ranchi Chapter had conducted elections were new office bearers were selected. Mr. S.C.L. Das (Executive Director HRD, SAIL) as the president.

2000

- **The Second Foundation Day Lecture was organized on 20th July, 2000 at Harihara Kala Bhavan. The lecture was delivered by Shri Ramalingan Raju, Chairman Satyam Computer Services.**
- **National HRD Network organized 7th National Conference "Going Global-Leveraging Human Potential" at Hotel Taj Krishna, Hyderabad from 17th-19th Aug, 2000.**
- **New Life Members had joined National HRD Network in 2000.**

SPEAKER	COMPANY
Mr. Ajay Sharma	Globerena IT Knowledge
Mr. Ajit Kumar	Centrax Services
Mr. Aurn Gour	Grasim Industries
Mr. Deendayalan S.	Center for Excellence
Mr. Harsha Chandra	Dayanad Institute of Vedic Studies
Mr. Raja Mahendra T.	GVK Petro Services
Mr. Renu Vijayanad	Tech Pacific India
Mr. Sharma S. S.	Indian Overseas Bank
Mr. Somashekhar Rao	Nizam Sugars
Mr. Surath S. Malhotra	Namdhari X'bit Systems
Mr. Veera Raghava Reddy K.	Electrolux India
Mr. Venkat Subha Rao	Govt. of Andhra Pradesh

❖ National HRD Network had organized a Vision Mission meeting to plan the future of National HRD Network.

From: T.V.Rao <tvrao@adl.vsnl.net.in>
To: tvrao@adl.vsnl.net.in <tvrao@adl.vsnl.net.in>
Date: 09 February 2000 18:49
Subject: Vision-Mission Future planning meeting of National HRD Network April 15, 2000

To: Executive Board of National HRD Network
Memebrs of Interim Management Committee
Shri Manab Bose, Dr. Santrupth Mishra, Shashi Khanna, P. K. Sarangi,
Fr. E Abraham, Anil Khandelwal, Udai Pareek, Y R K Reddy, Aquil Busrai, D. M. Silveira, G. P. Rao, V. K. Mahajan, Anil Sachdev

From: T. V. Rao (Chairman Interim Management Committee, National HRD Network) and Arvind Agarwal (President Elect, National HRD Network)

As you are aware the National HRD Network founded in 1985 have contributed a great deal to facilitate netwroking and knowledge dissemination in HRD filed. It has brought out 14 books in the form of Conference papers, set up an academy of HRD and has held over twenty Conferences and seminars, developed a large number of professionals through HRD Facilitator programmes and has made a mark in the HRD field.

The increased use of Internet, availability of alternate forms of learning, speed in learning and increased sensitivity to human capital throws up more challenges and opportunities for HR filed. It is recognised that HRD filed has to change its gear and also the national HRD Network has to revisit its own vision and reformulate its Mission if necessary.

Towards this purpose a one day event is planned on 15th April at Hyderabad. The event will focus on reviewing the activities of the National HRD Network and developing a Vision, Mission and list of activities for the next few years. We would like this body to amke a mark once agin by contributing its best to the knowledge base of HR in this country and actoss the world.

The meeting will begin with a presentation and review of the activities of various functionaries (Executive Director, Secretary, Director AHRD, Editor Newsletter, Chapter Preesidents, Hyderabad Conference etc.). The Board meeting of the outgoing Board is also expected to take place in the morning fololwed by the new Board with shri Arvind Agarwal taking over.

I am writing this to request you to keep 15th April free and plan to attend the meeting on that day. The exact venue of the meeting will be communicated to you soon.

Arvind wishes to have an Advisory Board to guide the National HRD

26/03/01

- **Shri S.V. Ramachandran Rao, Shri B. Ashok Reddy, Shri V.K. Mahajan had been elected to join the National Executive Board.**
- **AHRD collaborated with Search Net and AHRD-USA to remain in touch with the global trends and Global Best Practices in HRD.**
- **AHRD became the coordinator of the Indian Chapter of Academy- USA to disseminate systematic learning in HR.**
- **AHRD was facing some financial and other problems in the year 2000. So there was need to revitalize it. Some of the key issues were identified and probable solutions for these problems were suggested. Many efforts were made to revitalize AHRD, one of them being that Dr. T.V. Rao was appointed as the interim president.**

From: T.V.Rao <tvrao@ad1.vsnl.net.in>
To: poodles@satyam.net.in <poodles@satyam.net.in>
Date: 16 June 2000 08:13

Dear Sreenivasulu garu:

I need your help at this point of time on a voluntary basis to reconstruct the AHRD. I am requesting this on a voluntary basis as I am not sure of the financial situation and the direction in whcih the AHRD will go. One thing I am sure is that AHRD will do only some service to Industry on a commercial basis. In other words it may set up a separate consulting division headed by some one with a high salary and profit sharing basis as an independent entity. But that is the lowest priority area for us.
The most important is to give it a new life and direction. It should contribute to social development issues. My need at present is to have a team of friends and well wishers of the academy to work with me, donate some of their time and steer it to pput it in shape. I donot know the task. It may be an advisory group or a AHRD Renewal Group or a strategic thinking and implementation group. The group has to think of both intellectual directions as well as physical facilities, administrative amnagement etc. I need your help only as think tank and also for some running around until we put it is shape. Something a like an advisor or OSD or a revival team member. Please think about it .. we will discuss more when I come there on 21st.
Regards
T V Rao

T. V. Rao Learning Systems Pvt. Ltd.
12 Cosmoville, Satyagrah Marg
Ahmedabad 380 054, India
Phone 91-79-6748218 Fax 6740681
website: http://www.indiatrade.com/tvrls
Fax 91-79-6740681

From: T.V.Rao <tvrao@adl.vsnl.net.in>
To: Yaga Consulting Pvt. Ltd. <yaga@hdl.vsnl.net.in>
Date: 30 January 2000 09:08
Subject: Re: sent mails of the last few days for your info

Dear Prof. Balaji:

We have requested Dr. Himank to take the muinutes of the Academic Council meeting after you have left. Unfortuntely by the time we closed at 6.30 pm none of the administrative staff or research scholars were there. I expected Ruchi atleast to be there as she helped in summarising the suggestions from memebrs. I was very disappointed to see this lack of involement. I think we need to do something urgently to change this work culture.

I would also appreciate if Ruchi can be put in-charge of Academic Council activity to coordinate from the Academy's side. Her tasks for this could be maintaining all the correspondence in relation to Academic Council in coordination with me.
Warm regards
T V Rao

Dear YRK:

I have been thinking about the AHRD and various things. As I think the follwoing seems to be come clear:
1. The demoralisation in AHRD seems to have increased. Uncertainity is there. Himank and such others seem to think of leaving. He mentioned that as there is no leader in AHRD now the future is uncertain and therefore they get tempted to search for jobs.
2. We are not likely to have the Director in the next six months and this period is critical. Balaji would in all likelyhood throw up his hands and may unconsciously take it out to prove that things weere better under his leadership. I hope he is mature enough not to do that. It looks that he has withdrawn considerably.
3. The implication of the above two is that our decisions of starting the Executive MBA etc. may not get pushed unless you take some interest. I also think that the work culuure of the AHRD that has deteriorated needs to be arrested.
4. I am wondering what we should do under these circumstances. Would you like to have a chat with all the faculty and Balaji and prepare an action plan for the next few months with responsibilities. I will provide whatever assistance I can. I am tied up till the end of March particularly due to the long visit to Vietnam. I will try my best to visit once again if the same is neded and spend a couple of days or more.
Please let me know your views.
regards
T V Rao

T. V. Rao Learning Systems Pvt. Ltd.
12 Cosmoville, Satyagrah Marg
Ahmedabad 380 054, India

26/03/01

From: T.V.Rao <tvrao@adl.vsnl.net.in>
To: soumya dixit <soumyadixit@usa.net>
Date: 16 June 2000 04:25
Subject: Re: date of joining

Dear Soumya:
I am also taking charge of the Academy at Hyderabad as balaji is leaving and we need to do some rejuvination there. I am loking for some Research fellows there. Please encourage your class fellows to consider working there for two years. We are offering two year Fellowships of rs 5,000 per month. They will have good trainig ground there. I would need to interview them for final selection. We await here your joining.

I will be in Hyderabad from 21st to 23rd and if any of your classmates are interested in exploring the Fellowship they could fix an appointment and meet me at Hyderabad. they could also vist the place. Selected candidates will be asked to join immediately. They could also plan to meet me at Ahmedabad for interviews. I also need some of them to work here. Best wishes for your exams.
T V Rao
T. V. Rao Learning Systems Pvt. Ltd.
12 Cosmoville, Satyagrah Marg
Ahmedabad 380 054, India
Phone 91-79-6748218 Fax 6740681
website: http://www.indiatrade.com/tvrls
Fax 91-79-6740681

From: T.V.Rao <tvrao@adl.vsnl.net.in>
To: pvss kumar <kumarpvss@yahoo.com>
Cc: tvrao@adl.vsnl.net.in <tvrao@adl.vsnl.net.in>
Date: 13 July 2000 08:13
Subject: Re: about ahrd

Dear Mr. kumar:
This refers to another e-mail you sent whcih I saw this morning. I have received no other resignation apart from yours.

I do not wish to increase the salaries of any one under threat of resignations. Any of you are most welcome to do what you feel fit. AHRD will be wound up from there sooner than I thought thanks to the contributions of all of you. No one will be relieved without the required one month notice which is the minimum time needed for alternate arrangements.

I do not wixh to come in the way of any of you in building your careers. You may leave after the due date and after handing over all the matters to the person designated for this purpose.

My request to any of you is please give us adequate to wind up the AHRD center there.

Best wishes
T V Rao

T. V. Rao Learning Systems Pvt. Ltd.
12 Cosmoville, Satyagrah Marg
Ahmedabad 380 054, India
Phone 91-79-6748218 Fax 6740681
website: http://www.tvrls.com
Fax 91-79-6740681

From: T.V.Rao <tvrao@adl.vsnl.net.in>
To: Yaga Consulting Pvt. Ltd. <yaga@hdl.vsnl.net.in>
Date: 30 January 2000 09:04
Subject: Re:

There seems to be some problem wiht our e-mails. I sent about four messages to you since I returned. Hope you got all of them. This message was returned from your mail bos.
Rgeards
T V Rao
Dear YRK;
Having experienced several times the leadership change at IIMA, I think that the interim period could be very frustrating to many and we run the risk of losing people. I suggest the following to manage the change process.
1. Clarify the role of Balaji till the time a new Director or Interim Director is appointed.
2. Calrify your own role as the Chairman of the search committee as well as Chairman of the executive Committee. A circular may be of use.
3. Brief all the staff of the decisions taken at the Board and the Academic Council including the attendance etc. They need to know and also to ensure that there is a new spirit generated than frustration and uncertainity.
4. Advertise imediately in Human capital and other appropriate places for the Psoition of Director and Faculty. The advertisement should also be used to talk about the Courses we are planning to offer and highlight other activities of the AHRD.
5. Get some of us involved in developing and implementing the planned activities. I will be happy to do whatever I can.
6. I am even tempted to come there for the next six months and take charge as suggested by you once. I have commitments until April 1. Do you think it is worth thinking about it for atleast some time. If you are bale to devote enough time then there is no worry.
Regards
T V Rao

Regards
T V Rao

T. V. Rao Learning Systems Pvt. Ltd.
12 Cosmoville, Satyagrah Marg
Ahmedabad 380 054, India
Phone 91-79-6748218 Fax 6740681
website: http://www.indiatrade.com/tvrls
Fax 91-79-6740681

From: T. V. Rao <tvrao@ad1.vsnl.net.in>
To: Academy <ahrdhd1@hd1.vsnl.net.in>
Cc: ahrdad1@satyam.net.in <ahrdad1@satyam.net.in>; arvind@rpgnet.com <arvind@rpgnet.com>; iihmr@iihmr.org <iihmr@iihmr.org>; TAPASH SENGUPTA <tapash@attglobal.net>
Date: 07 August 2000 03:43
Subject: AHRD Newsletter, August 2000

Academy of HRD
Monthly Bulletin of News and Information
August 7, 2000

To: Members of the Board of Governors
Academic Council Members, Professors Emiritus
Ex-Faculty and Well wishers of AHRD

From: T. V. Rao, Chairman Academic Council

I am writing this to keep you informed of the various developments at the Academy of HRD.

- I was at AHRD Hyderabad from 28th to 30th July for shifting and again on 4th and 5th August for sorting out a few things including disbursement of salaries etc.
- The Academy's Knowledge Management Center and most of the furniture, books, and computers have been shifted to Ahmedabad. Dr. D. S. Sarupriya, Reader from the Management School, M. S. University, Baroda and Shishir Mishra newly joined Research Fellow at AHRD Ahmedabad assisted and supervised the shifting. Dr. Sarupriya has taken special leave for this purpose, travelled to Hyderabad on train at his own cost and have assisted in shifting the materials. Gati Cargo have shifted the materials at a highly concessional rates (at cost). All staff at AHRD have assisted in this process. I thank all of them for the assistance and making it so smooth. It was a painful process for me and for every one involved. Some of the members were in tears. I thank all of these individuals for their support. Special thanks to Dalpat and Mr. Mahindra Agarwal, MD of Gati and his team at Hyderabad regional office.
- Dr. Udai Pareek and Shri Arvind Agarwal (President National HRD Network) have kindly agreed to be members of the new Executive Committee in place of the Dissolved Executive Committee. This committee will act as the Personnel & Finance committee and will formulate all policies relating to Personnel, Finance, Buildings etc. The Bank Accounts will be signed hereafter by two of the following: Prof. T. V. Rao, Chairman AC & EC (Compulsory), Mr. Mahendra Agarwal (Member of Board); Mr. Arvind Agarwal, (Board member); Prof. D. M. Pestonjee (IIMA, Founder Trustee)
- Prof. Satya Prakash Agarwal, Senior Consultant from Fergusons has kindly agreed to conduct the Financial and Management Audit of AHRD and review the financial situation as well as the systems in operation. He visited AHRD on 29th and 30th July and examined all the books of Accounts and other documents. He interviewed the AHRD Auditors, Ex-Director, staff available at AHRD. He examined various records and had detailed discussions with me. His report is expected at any time.
- The response to our advertisement for Faculty and Research Staff is very good. We are likely to call the candidates for interview in September. I am requesting Dr. E.G. Parameswaran, Dr. Udai Pareek and Prof. D. M. Pestonjee to form the selection committee for the Faculty and Research Staff.
- I am happy to inform you that the Search Committee has decided to invite Mr. Tapash Sengupta to head the Academy of HRD. Mr. Tapash Sengupta has accepted the offer and has indicated that he will be joining as Director of AHRD from December 1, 2000. He is currently in Indonesia. A brief biographic sketch of Mr. Tapash Sengupta is presented below:

❖ As 'Change is the only constant thing' so some changes were also proposed to adapt AHRD to the changing times.

From: T.V.Rao <tvrao@ad1.vsnl.net.in>
To: abraham enthemkuzy <abrahame@yahoo.com
Date: 01 January 2000 10:06
Subject: Re: Happy 2000

Dear Abe:
Happy New Millennium. I would appreciate if you can give your views on the following issues of AHRD. V need these to decide the future directions of AHRD.
Regards
T V Rao
January 1, 2000
Ahmedabad

To: Academic Council Members
Academy of HRD

From: T. V. Rao, Chairman, Academic Council

Dear Memebr:

We thank you for your acceptance to be a memebr of the Council. We are proposing to hold the first meeting of the newly constituted Academic Council on 24th of January at the AHRD premises in Hyderabad. As indicated to you earlier the meeting will be limited to those who can be in Hyderabad on that day and will be mainly to finalise the decisions/recommendations of the Academic Council on the basis of the inputs received from the memebrs by e-mail or mail. You may recollect my indication that we request the memebrs to give their inputs on e-mail to conduct a virtual meeting. To facilitate this meeting I am circulating the agenda for this meeting. The agenda has some definite questions for which we need your views. The views will be used to finalise our recommendations and take decisions on 24th. The Board meeting of theAcademy is scheduled on the 25th and the inputs of the Academci Council will be used as inputs for the Board. Even if you are unable to physically attend the meeting, your views will be taken as equivalent to your presence. I would appreicate a quick response.

Any suggestions on the technology of electronic meetings will be welcome.

Warm Regards
T V Rao
Chairman, AC

Item 1:

1. **Doctoral Level Fellow program jointly with XLRI**. This program has admitted so far 70 candidates. Only two candidates have completed and about 20 more are active as per our records. Considering the large number who are already in the program and the smaller number who are in the process of completion, it has been decided by XLRI to stop admitting any new candidates for this program. For all practical purposes the collaboration may be closed after the last candidate graduates or the stipulated time is over, whichever is earlier.

In the light of this, Should AHRD announce its own Fellow program? Nirma Institute and such other Institutes have gone ahead and announced such Fellow programmes without formal approval from AICTE. Apparently AICTE has informally indicated to them that they themselves have some doubts about their own role in recognising Fellow programmes and a Committee is looking into this matter. They seem to have suggested that till such time the matter is cleared any one may go ahead and announce such programmes. There is a lot of confusion on this aspect.

In early ninties Doctoral program was conceived as most practicing managers were interested in a Research degree. Post-liberalisation the scenario seem to have changed. Managers seem to undr pressure to perform

21/03/01

and their organisations ar less willing to give them time for research. Our experience with the Felllow programme indicates that a Doctoral programme for practicing managers is not anymore attractive for them. It is difficult for practicing managers to do a good job of thesis work as the work pressures are high and there is no definite advantage of having a doctorate from a career point of view. Infact those who have completed so far and are in the process of completion are the full time students or those who have academic associations (lecturers, consulltants etc.) There are only a few exceptions of practicing managers being able to sustain their interest and do the hard work required by the programme.

2. **Joint Diploma program with AIMA.** AHRD has not played any significant role in the recent years after it has given away its old Diploma program to AIMA and suggested the course design. A strategy needs to be worked out for more active participation in this.

What are your suggestions about this program. Would you be interested in contributing to the contact sessions of this program?

3. Joint Diploma programs with Symbiosis Center for Management and HRD, TA PAI Institute of Management Studies, IPS Institute, Indore.

In this AHRD gives the curriculum for some courses and conducts an exam at the end of the second year to ascertain if the candidate has completed all the requirements and has acquired the knowledge. Candidates passing will be awarded a joint diploma by AHRD and the institute concerned. Should we continue to offer joint diplomas with these institutions? Should we enter into collaboration with other institutions? So far the turnout from these coursses has been marginal. About 20 in all.

4. **IOAC Forum** (set up by Dr. Sethumadhavan when he was Acting Director of AHRD)

What are the methods and suggestions for enhancing the effective use of this forum.
This consists of all those who have gone through the IOAC (assessment Center programs of AHRD). Should it focus on new areas? What are the other activities it should carry out besides conducting IOAC programs and consultancy projects. It si currently involved in developing In-baskets etc.

5. **Publication of a journal called Renewal under its Social Development Center to promote HRD in NGOs.**

This has become defunct for the last one and half years. Would you like to volunteer and take it up as an Editor. Any suggestions on taking this forward?

6. **Deciding the nature of the Academy and reviewing its course of progress and reformulating the same in the context of the changing global scenario and India's needs.**

Your suggestions on the future directions of the Academy. I am enclosing a note received from Dr. EG Parameswaran in this connection. Please comment on the proposals as well as give your own thoughts.

7. Deciding the strategies to influence and upgrade the quality of professional preparation and the quality standards of HRD professionals in the country. Should it be through Doctoral research only or are there any other ways? Should there be a certification of HRD professionals that can guide the corporate sector? What is the role AHRD can play?

8. Broad guidelines for the macro structure and processes of the Academy to respond to and meet the challenges. Should AHRD continue to be a consulting body or should it only be research institution? Should the Academy be separate from that of the Institute? Should it be appointing committees to review the academic standards? What will be its role vis-à-vis the Association of Indian Management Schools and AICTE? Should it influence the thinking of these bodies and be represented in them?

9. Should we start any other model education programs in HRD? Should we do it alone or network with some one else like TISS or Symbiosis? Etc.

10. What lessons can we learn from the Doctoral Fellow program so far? Could there be a different model? Should we collaborate with any other place like the University of Michigan or George Washington University? Can we have professional renewal programs conducted by the AHRD? Should we have renewal seminars on contemporary issues?

11. Should we network with HRD consultants like McBer, Hay, and Software agencies like People Soft, PCMMM, etc. Can we anticipate human factor related failures in SAP, ERP etc. and prepare for the same through research and guidance? Can we get some of the IT giants to fund research in these areas to help them and help several of those

❖ AHRD had conducted Academic Council Meeting to discuss some of the critical issues.

From: T.V.Rao <tvrao@ad1.vsnl.net.in>
To: Academy <ahrdhd1@hd1.vsnl.net.in>
Cc: tvrao@ad1.vsnl.net.in <tvrao@ad1.vsnl.net.in>
Date: 27 January 2000 18:33
Subject: Attn. Himank Priyadarshi

Dear Himank:

I would appreciate if the following minutes of the Academic Council are sent to all the members of the AC. Kindly add the names of those who responded to e-mail. I have only given the names I rememebred and there are more who responded to the e-mail. Please also alphabetise all the names while mentioning the same.
Please also add any points you have and I have forgotten.
Thanks
T V Rao

Minutes of the Academic Council Meeting held on 25-1-2000 at the Academy of HRD Premises, Hyderabad

The following members participated electronically and sendt their responses to items: FR. E. Abraham, Gopal Mahapatra, Santrupth Mishra, Ipsita Kathuria, Keith Bradely (U.K), Sethu Madhavan (Bahrain), GP Rao, Himank Priyadarshi, C. Balaji, Anil Sachdeva, Ravindran (Singapore), Kuldeep Singh, Prayag Mehta, Satish Kalra,

The following memebrts were present during the meeting:

Dr. E. G. Parameswaran
Prof. C. Balaji
Dr. Himank Priyadarshi
Dr. Sudarshan
Dr. Mathew manimala
Dr. T. V. Rao (Chairman, AC)
Dr. Y R K Reddy

During the meeting the e-mail was kept open and some of the memebrs have sent their messages also during the meeting.

1. The Chairman welcomed the members.
2. Dr Y R K Reddy briefed the memebrs about the decisons taken by the Executive Council and the Board indicating that there is no need for separating the Academy and its Academic center. Academy should be one and should strive to contribute to its mission of generating a body of knowledge and influencing the HR practices of Industry and all the other sectors of the economy including NGOs and the Government.
3. Dr. Rao summarised the responses received from all the members of the Academic Council in response to the agenda circulated for the meeting. The summary indicated the follwoing:
3.1 There is a feeling that the Fellow programe should be offered by AHRD by itself or in association with another institution (India or abroad).
3.2 There is need and scope for starting a PG program in HRD and the AHRD should do it for practicing managers.
3.3. IOAC has done good work and its activities should be stepped up.
3.4 Work in NGO and non-profit sectors should be attended to.
3.5 Quality of whatever is offered should be excellent and AHRD should work in new areas in tune with the changing trends of HR.
4. After a good deal of debate and discussion on the various issues the memebrs have suggested the follwoing to be implemented by the Academy:
4.1. Associateship Program in HRD (Equivalent to M. Phil). This shuld be of 18 months duration and is

intended to prepare rigorous researchers in the field of HRD. This should consist of six months of course work through contact sessions at the Academy follwed by one year of Dissertation work. There will be examinations and thesis evaluation. It shoudl admit only Masters Degree (or equivalent) holders and not graduates. Admission should be on the basis of passing the Junior Research Fellowship examination of UGC or an equivalent test to be conducted by AHRD.

4.2 Fellow Program in HRD to be awarded by AHRD. This should admit only those who have completed the Associateship as above. It should be of 18 months duration and should be on the basis of Thesis work. The objectives of both the programs is to prepare Researchers in the field of HRD. Not more than 8 full time students should be admitted to the above program. There should be no part time students.

4.3. Post Graduate Diploma in HRD (Executive MBA) which will be of one years duration and is meant for practicing executives intending to specialise in HRD. This should be of one year duration. Three alterantive designs were generated during the meeting. These three may be tested out in the market the AHRD may take the decsion on the fee as well as the design:

Design A: Two week Course work, Followed by 10 month project work in own company or elsewhere, followed by two weeks of course work.

Design B: Three weeks of Course work folllwoed by six months of project work, followed by three weeks of course work, followed by another six months of second project work and closing with three weeks of course work.

Design C: Four weeks of course work followed by six months of project work followed by one month of course work followed by six months of second project and ending with one week of course work.

In all these the courses should be advanced HRd courses including IOAC, Strategic HRD, 360 Degree Feedback, HRD Audit, OD Intervenetions, Competency mapping, IT Applications etc. The fee may be Rs 25,000 to Rs 1 lakh. It should be non-residential considering the practial issues involved in AHRD p[roviding accomodation etc.

5. The memebrs also recommended that the AHRD should have a minimum of about 4 core faculty to man these courses and conduct the programees as well as to do research. AHRD also should maintain a roster of its Resources persons drawn from Academic Council etc. and use them to conduct these courses.

6. IOAc activities should be stepped up as it has contributed a good deal to the HRD profession.

7 The Renewal Journal should be continued as an Annual.

8. Dr parameswaran volunteered to bring out an Annual Review of research in HRD. It could be publsihed as an issue of renewal.

9. The members stressed the need to select facutly after rigourously screening them to ensure quality of work at AHRD. It was also felt that the Research and dissemination should not be neglected. Faculty should be appraised on the basis of their publications and made accountable for conducting quality programmes.

10. The meeting ended with thanks to all the embers who resoponded to the meeting.

T. V. Rao Learning Systems Pvt. Ltd.
12 Cosmoville, Satyagrah Marg
Ahmedabad 380 054, India
Phone 91-79-6748218 Fax 6740681
website: http://www.indiatrade.com/tvrls
Fax 91-79-6740681

❖ Mr. Tapash Sen Gupta was appointed as the director of AHRD.

```
From:   T.V.Rao <tvrao@adl.vsnl.net.in>
To:     TAPASH SENGUPTA <tapash@attglobal.net>
Cc:     arvind@rpgnet.com <arvind@rpgnet.com>; iihmr@iihmr.org
        <iihmr@iihmr.org>; ahrdadl@satyam.net.in
        <ahrdadl@satyam.net.in>
Date:   06 August 2000 18:57
Subject: Thanks for Accepting the Directorship of AHRD
```

Dear Tapash:

Thnaks for accepting our offer to Direct AHRD. We have a lot of hope about its impact and the future. The Academy has a row house as well as a flat at present. They are likley to be vacated if we are able to find a good commercial place or an appropriate building for this purpose. Hence your accomodation will be no problem.

We look forward to your taking charge on December 1. We also look forward to your visit in Novemebr. I will make appropriate changes in the announcement and send the a copy of this to you. We are going ahead and announcing your acceptance.
Warm Regards
T V Rao

T. V. Rao Learning Systems Pvt. Ltd.
12 Cosmoville, Satyagrah Marg
Ahmedabad 380 054, India
Phone 91-79-6748218 Fax 6740681
website: http://www.tvrls.com
Fax 91-79-6740681

❖ Activities in National HRD Network Chapters

- Hyderabad Chapter
    - Sixth edition of the directory of the members of Hyderabad Chapter was released in 2000.
    - Mr. Ajay Chandra, Manager HR of Globarena IT knowledge spoke on leadership in e-organization.
    - 7th National Conference on the theme "Going Global-Leveraging Human Potential" inaugurated by Sri Ashok Gajapathi Raju, The than Minister of Revenue, Govt. of Andhra Pradesh
    - Hyderabad Chapter had conducted elections were new office bearers were selected (2000–2002). Mr. S.R. Tripathi (Chairman, NMDC) as the president.

- The chapter organized a lecture on "The New Maverik HR Manager" by Dr. Neeraj D.R. (Chairman, Nagaraj Management Services, Bangalore)
- Ms. Jayalakhmi of Qualcore Technologies spoke on Knowledge Management.
- The chapter also conducted an in-house development programme for the offices and staff of New India Assurance Company at Dream Valley Resorts, Gandipet.
- A special Meeting of the Hyderabad Chapter where speaker Dr. Francis Fernandez (Leading Consultant in OB Area in Malaysia) delivered the lecture on "Recent Trends in Training in Asia" at Surana Auditorium.

➢ **Rajkot Chapter**
- A new chapter was inaugurated at Rajkot. Mr. K. K. Anirudhan became the coordinator

➢ **Vishakhapatnam Chapter**
- Shri S. Hanumantha Rao, (GM-HRD, BHPV) had taken up the responsibility as the president to revitalize the Vishakhapatnam Chapter.

➢ **Ahmedabad Chapter**
- The chapter had conducted a program on "HRD score card" in 2000.

➢ **Jaipur Chapter**
- Jaipur Chapter had organized a workshop on "Learning Organization" from 21st-23rd July, 2000. Dr. Udai Pareek, Dr. Vinod Arora, Dr. Surabhi Purohit, Mr. D. K. Sen, Mr. Girdhari Gyani were the facilitators of the programme at Indian Institute of Quality Management, Jaipur.

➢ **Cochin Chapter**
- It had organized a programme on "Managerial Perspectives for 21st century" at Rivera Suits, Cochin.

➢ **Delhi Chapter**
- Delhi Chapter organized a lecture on "Changing Technology: Implications of HR" by Mr. Atul Kunwar, CEO Mantraonline.

Delhi Chapter had hosted a conference on "People Issues in Telecom and IT" on the theme "m-powering the e-wave minds"

2001

- **National HRD Network appointed new office Bearers**
  - Dr. Santrup Mishra was appointed as The Regional president of the western region in 2001.
  - Mr. Acquil Busrai was appointed as The Regional president of the Northern region in 2001.
  - Dr. YRK Reddy was appointed as National Treasurer by National Executive Board in 2001.
  - Mr. GP Rao was appointed as National Secretary by National Executive Board in 2001.
- **National HRD Network organized an e-HR tools Conference and Exhibition on "Power your way through e-HR" from 1st Nov to 3rd Nov 2001.**
  - Mr. Vivek Kulkarni, the IT Secretary of the govt. of Karnataka inaugurated the exhibition and conference.
  - Mr. Arving Agrawal, National NHRD President and Mr. Sadagopan, the Founder Director of IIIT Bangalore gave the key note address.
  - Mr. D R Nagaraj, President NHRD Bangalore chapter welcomed and presented the backdrop of conference.
  - Mr. R Vidyasagar, Vice President NHRD Bangalore chapter gave the preview of the conference.
  - The conference was attended by over 200 delegates in the field of HR and IS from the various organizations.
  - 21 exhibitors participated in the exhibition where they had showcased their e-HR products in the exhibition. Companies like HP, People Soft, Ernst and Young, Mafoi Consultants, Hinduja TMT and others participated.
- **XLRI developed and launched HR Portal**

T V Rao

From: Arvind Agrawal <arvind@rpgnet.com>
To: Anil Sachdev <anilsachdev@growtalent.com>; Balaji_C <Balaji_C@satyam.com>; S Hanumantharao <gmhr%5Fbhpv@satyam.net.in>; R Sarangi <mti@dte.vsnl.net.in>; John Pulickan <Pulicks@forindia.com>; Dilip Misra <dilipmisra@finolex.com>; Shashi Muzumdar <ssmuzumdar@vsnl.com>; P K Panda <hindalco.rkt@rms.sprintrpg.ems.vsnl.net.in>; M G Gupta <sailemd@cal2.vsnl.net.in>; Ashok Agarwal <ashok@iihmr.org>; K G Shenoy <kgshenoy@bom4.vsnl.net.in>; S Ramadoss <srd@titan.co.in>; P R Tripathi <prtripathi@nmdc-india.com>; Bimal Rath <rathb@india.btap.bt.com>; Gilbert D'Souza <avthomco@giasmd01.vsnl.net.in>; K Sridhar <sridhark@ssi-technologies.com>; D R Nagaraj <nms@vsnl.com>; Ravi Shankar <rshankar@irm.ernet.in>; S S Bhatia <shyam.bhatia@johnsonpump.co.in>; Arvind Pandey <arvind.pande@sailor.com>; K Satyanarayana <
Cc: Dr. Jessy Fenn <fennfamily@yahoo.com>; Madhukar Shukla <madhukar@xlri.ac.in>
Sent: Friday, December 07, 2001 5:07 AM
Subject: HR Portal

As you are aware, we have been working with XLRI to develop and launch HR Portal over the last few months. This initiative has progressed well and I am happy to mention that the HR Portal will be launched during the forthcoming III National HRD Conference which is to be held on December 22 – 23, 2001 at XLRI, Jamshedpur. This is the biggest HR event which gets annually organized by XLRI. Prof Madhukar Shukla of XLRI, who has been the key contact and the champion on behalf of XLRI to develop this Portal, will be writing to you separately about the Conference. It will be great if you could personally attend the Conference and also participate in the launch of the Portal.

For taking charge of the ongoing responsibility for this Portal, National HRD Network has appointed Dr. Jessy Fenn as a full time resource person operating from XLRI campus in Jamshedpur. She is provided with all the infrastructure facilities by XLRI and is functioning under the overall guidance of Prof Madhukar Shukla. Jessy in consultation with XLRI faculty would be responsible for making sure that the content in the Portal is of high quality and of contemporary interest.

This will require ongoing involvement and support from all of you. High quality content from the various Chapters has to be mobilized on a regular basis and sent to Jessy. To ensure that this is done on a regular basis, it is essential that a resource person is specifically named in each Chapter towards this activity. Accordingly, I would appreciate your discussing this in your Chapter and appointing on a voluntary basis a suitable resource person and confirming to Jessy at the following email id (fennfamily@yahoo.com) at the earliest.

Looking forward to your whole hearted support in making this a success.

With all best wishes.

Arvind N Agrawal

Cc: Prof Madhukar Shukla: With a request to please sent the details of the December Conference to all concerned.

Cc: Dr Jessy Fenn: Please send the highlights of the HR Portal to all concerned for their information.

- **Mr. Tapas Sen Gupta had joined AHRD as the new Director on 16th January, 2001.**
- **AHRD had organized a one day seminar on Best Benchmarking practices by Dr. Robert C. Camp.**
- **Activities in National HRD Network Chapters**
    - **Cochin Chapter**
        - Cochin Chapter had organized a one day programe on 2/12/2000. Managerial perspective of the 21st

century by N.S. Ramaswamy, Director CARTMAN, Bangalore.

- Cochin Chapter had organized a seminar on "Evaluating Training Effectiveness" by Shri Alex.P. Lukose on 15th March, 2001, at Pandhal Restaurant, MG Road, Kochi.
- A meeting was also organized on 5th June 2001 at Hotel Sea Lord addressed by Shri. K Satyanarayan, Executive Director of the chapter.

➢ **Delhi Chapter**

- Delhi Chapter had organized a seminar "Retention through Up gradation: the win at your premises" by Mr. Arun Dang, on March 20, 2001.
- Delhi Chapter had organized a two day conference on "e-learning on Anytime, Anywhere learning for everyone: concepts, trends, tolls and cases, on 27th-28th April, 2001 at Le Meridien New Delhi.
- Delhi Chapter had conducted a workshop on building leadership was conducted by Mr. Peter Block and Mr. Anil Sachdev on 17–19 oct,2001 at Hotel Renaissance Goa Resort, Goa.
- National conference on Young HR professionals "Profession in transition: from Here to Where" on November 23rd April, 2001 at Hotel Park Royal.

➢ **Hyderabad Chapter**

- Dr. YRK Reddy delivered a lecture on "leadership development" on 16th august 2001.
- Hyderabad Chapter had organized a meeting where Ms. Lekha Systa spoke on "Internal marketing in organizations" on 5th Apr, 2001.
- Hyderabad Chapter Mr. Krishna Koneru was invited to deliver a lecture on "Negotiating your ways to success with Japanese- the cross cultural factors" on 19th April, 2001.
- Dr. YRK Reddy delivered a lecture on "leadership development" on 16th august 2001.
- Hyderabad Chapter had organized a seminar on "Nurturing Creativity and Innovation" by Mr. Shailender Jaiswal on 1st march, 2001.

- Hyderabad Chapter had organized a panel on "BUDGET 2001, the HR implications on 5th march, 2001 at FAPCCI auditorium, chaired by Shri. P.R. Tripathi.
- Hyderabad Chapter had organized a seminar on "The Future of IT Industry-The HR implications" by Mr. T. Hari on 15th march, 2001, at Surana Auditorium, FAPCCI.
- Training Need Analysis workshop conducted by Subra from SMR, Malaysia, on 24th April, 2001 at Hotel GRT Grand days.
- Third foundation day lecture of the Hyderabad chapter, National HRD network by Shri VS Rao on 17th May, 2001 at FAPCCI. The lecture was on "Ingredients for the success in emerging global economy."

➢ **Ahmedabad Chapter**

- Ahmedabad Chapter had organized a meeting where the newly appointed Director of AHRD, Mr. Tapash spoke on "Experience Sharing" on 17th April, 2001.
- Mr. Rakish Bhagwati, Director ATE group of Companies had delivered a lecture on Innovative HR practices on 24th Jan, 2001.
- Ahmedabad Chapter had invited Dr. Ramesh Kapadia, eminent cardiologist who had given a lecture on "Prevention of heart attack" on 21st Mar, 2001.
- There were many lectures organized by Ahmedabad Chapter in 2001:
    1) Mr. Mukesh Shah spoke on "Creative thinking" on 18th April, 2001.
    2) Mr. Sunil Handa spoke on "CEO's expectation from HR professional" on 24th April, 2001.
    3) Mr. Bala Bhaskaran spoke on "Preparation for the knowledge era" on 16th May, 2001.
    4) Another Meeting was organized by Ahmedabad Chapter on 20th June, 2001 where Mr. Saurabh Dixit on "Group HR and challenges for HR in business corporate communications call centre Adani".

- **Pune Chapter**
  - Pune Chapter had organized a session on 6th April, 2001 at Hotel Poonam where Mr. Shahi Alam on "Change Management".
- **Bangalore Chapter**
  - Bangalore Chapter had organized a symposium on "Where do you go from here" on 9th June, 2001at hostel Taj Residency.
  - The Chapter had conducted elections to elect new office bearers. Mr. D.R. Nagaraj was elected as the President of the new executive committee.
  - An executive committee meeting was held on 8th June, 2001 at Sasken communications Technology.
  - A Meeting was conducted by Mr. Ashok Dalwai on 20th Sept, 2001 on "Responses to challenges: HR initiatives in Public service institutions" at Hotel Taj Residency.
  - Bangalore Chapter started their own chapter newsletter "NHRD @ Bangalore" in 2001. The 1st issue of NHRD @ Bangalore was launched on 28th June, 2001 at Taj Residency. Also a lecture on "Globalisation and its impact on HR" was delivered.
  - Bangalore Chapter had organized a Debate on "Human side of downsizing" on 17th July, 2001. Persons present were Mr Guhan Sadashiva, Dr Nagaraj (retired Justice) and Mr C Ramachandran.
  - A one day workshop was conducted by High Impact Reward Strategies –Performance linked variable pay on 25th Aug, 2001 at Taj Residency, modulated by Mr. Pallab Bandopadhyay.
  - Bangalore Chapter had organized a Programme conducted on " HR initiatives in Public sector " held at Taj Residency during the September of 2001; attended Mr. Baliga, Mr. Nagaraj, Mr. K jai Raj
- **Bombay Chapter**
  - Mumbai Chapter had conducted elections in their Annual General Meeting were new office bearers were selected (1997–1999). Shri S.S. Majumdar was elected as the new president.

- Bombay Chapter had conducted a workshop on "Transforming the Organization: Strategic agenda and steps to make it happen."
- Bombay Chapter had conducted another lecture where Dr. Diwedi spoke on "e-HR" on 11th July, 2001 at AIPMA hall, Andheri, Mumbai.
- Mumbai Chapter had organized a lecture by Mr. Ramoli Mahajani and Mc Conkey on "Relevance of Competencies" at RPG, CEAT Mahal.

➢ **Chennai chapter**

- Chennai Chapter had organized on one day workshop on "HRD for IT industry" Mr. Lakshiminarayan on 10th April, 2001.

➢ **Hosur Chapter**

- Hosur Chapter had organized monthly meeting on 4th Jnauary, 2001 at Ashok Leyland MDC, Hosur.
- The Chapter had also organized a seminar on " Recent trends in HR" on 9th May, 2001
- Dr. TV Rao addressed the meeting on "Recent trends in HR" on 9th May, 2001 at Ashok Leyland MDC.
- A lecture on "CEO`s expectations from HR professionals" was addressed by Mr. Dipak Mane on 30th July, 2001.
- Hosur Chapter had also organized a seminar on "WEB enabled HR" by Mr. Shriram Krishna on 13th July, 2001.

➢ **Vishakapatnam Chapter**

- Vishakapatnam Chapter had organized a meeting on "Opportunities on New Millennium" on 12th July 2001.
- Vishakapatnam Chapter had organized a meeting in collaboration with NIPM and ISTD on 23rd august 2001. Prof. Ursula Schneider spoke on globalization and transnational corporations"

➢ **Lucknow Chapter**

- A new chapter was inaugurated in Lucknow by Dr. Pritam Singh, Dr. Udai Pareek, Mr. Arvind, Mr. GP Rao, Mr. Abha Chaturvedi and Mr. PK Panda.

- **AHRD had conducted the seventh professional development programme for HRD facilitators from October 30-Nov9, 2001.**

2002

- **National HRD network organized a two day conference on H.R. at Taj Residency, Lucknow from 22nd to 23rd Feb, 2002.** The theme of the conference was "Adding values to business through HR – Issues and Challenges". The Speakers list I s given below and indicates the popularity of NHRDN and the role of chapters. Dr. Pritam Singh played a very supportive role thereafter and he evens started a collaborative program at MDI Gurugram after he shifted to MDI. Originally the Academy of HRD proposed a joint program with IIM Lucknow. However NHRDN had the resources and strategic intent to collaborate with MDI. Understandably MDY preferred to collaborate with NHRDN in offering a joint master's level program and get NHRDN leaders to teach in the program. The role played by this conference in Lucknow went unnoticed by many in terms of subsequent collaborations.

Speaker	Designation and Organization
Dr. Pritam Singh	Director, IIM Lucknow
Mr. A.K. Agarwala	Director, Hindalco
Mr. G.N. Bajpai	Chairman, LIC India
Mr. Prashanto Banerjee	Chairman, GAIL
Mr. Rajat Gupta	Principal, McKinsey and co.
Mr. Ravi Sahi	CEO, BSEB
Mr. R.R. Nair	Advisor-Org. Dev., Hindustan Lever
Dr. Santrupt Misra	Director, Birla Mgmt. corp. ltd.
Mr. T.S. Palani Kumar	MD, New Holland Tractors
Dr. A Sahay	CMD, Scooters India Ltd.
Dr. T.V. Rao	Chairman, TVRLS, Ahmedabad
Mr. Anil Nadkarni	Executive Director, Siemens
Mr. Debasis Mitra	MD, Global Green Co., Bangalore
Mr. K Pandiarajan	MD, Ma Foi
Mr. Manoj Kohli	CEO, Escotel Mobile Comm.

Mr. Mahendra Swarup	CEO, Times Internet Ltd.
Dr. Zahid Gangjee	Mgmt. Consultant, Calcutta
Mr. Bimal Rath	Alliance Director, British Telecom
Mr. Aquil Busrai	Executive Director-HR, Motorola
Mr. K.K. Sinha	Director (Personnel), NTPC
Mr. Arvind N Agarwal	President Corp. Dev. And HR, RPG
Mr. Rajendra Sinha	President-HR, HFCL
Dr. Ranjan Das	IIM, Calcutta
Mr. G.P. Rao	Vice President-HR, Birla VXL Ltd.
Mr. Mahalingam.C.	V.P.-HR, Hewlett Packard
Mr. B.N. Sarangi	Chief-HR/IR, TISCO
Mr. Aadesh Goel	VP-HR, Hughes Software Systems

- **National HRD Network had organized 8th National Conference on on 28th Sept, 2002 at Powai, Mumbai.**

Page 1 of 1

TVRao.

From: Shashi Muzumdar <ssmuzumdar@vsnl.com>
To: Dr Santrupt Misra <santrupt@adityabirla.com>; Arvind Agrawal <arvind@rpgnet.com>; G.P.Rao <gpr@birla-vxl.com>; B.Ashok Reddy <bar@infotech.stph.net>; Fr.E.Abraham <abraham@ximb.ac.in>; Dr Udai Pareek <udai@iihmr.org>; Dr T.V.Rao <tvraoad1@sancharnet.in>; Dr Shashi Khanna <carasti@vsnl.net>; Manab Bose <manabbose@hotmail.com>; Ms Hema Ravichandar <hravichandar@infy.com>; Dr Anil Khandelwal <ed@bankofbaroda.com>; Dr Anil Sachdev <anilsachdev@growtalent.com>
Sent: Monday, September 23, 2002 1:31 PM
Subject: NHRDN Conference

To,
All NHRDN Executive Board/ Advisory Board/ Ex officio Members & Chapter Presidents

On behalf of the Conference Executive Committee, I have pleasure in inviting all of you to..the forthcoming 8th National Conference being held at Renaissance Convention Centre, Powai Mumbai, between 3 - 5 Oct'02.We are looking forward to your active participation and support during the conference.

We hope , you might have already registered your name thro` your respective organisation or are in the process of doing so in the next few days.

For any reason ,,should this.be not found feasible, we offer. to take over.your registration fee costs for the conference. We shall be thankful if those wishing to avail of this.offer would inform us by 28th Sept'02,so that the delegate passes/badges could be prepared in advance and handed over to them at the venue during the registration time.

We look forward to see you during the conference and help us in making this conference a grand success.

With Regards,

Shashi Muzumdar

❖ **National HRD Network had organized Executive board meeting on 5th Oct, 2002 at Mumbai. Some important changes and highlights of the same are given in the document below. By 2002 NHRDN evolved the culture of distributing the conference papers in a book form at the beginning of the Conference and also to sue the Conference as an opportunity to have the Executive Board meeting and also the Annual General Body Meeting. Conferences are usus ally attended by many NHRDN members and it is the best time to sense the pulse and needs of members and plan subsequent activities. It is in the 1987 conference when one member remarked about the neglect of HRD for workers that lead to 1889 conferences on HRD for workmen. It is the 1989 conference that sowed the seed for gaining International Perspectives and resulted in Peter Block and u such others attending and giving talks exposing global trends to NHRDN members.**

NATIONAL HRD NETWORK

1. At the Board meeting held on 5th October, 2002 at Mumbai, a Task force with Mr. HM Jha, Fr. Abraham and DR Nagaraj, as Convenor was appointed to recommend to the Board some solutions to this vexed issue of sharing of Membership Fee, Surplus from Conferences etc.

2. The Committee made its recommendations to the Board at the meting held on 2nd Feb at Pune. The Board, after listening to the recommendations and also the points on repositioning NHRD by Dr. Santrupt Misra, felt that this should also be considered along with the other major changes envisaged.

3. The Board also suggested some additions, in order to encourage Chapters, which are performing well and creating Benchmarks and accordingly some changes were thought of in the pattern of sharing of the fee between Chapters and the HQ.

4. This Committee has taken note of the suggestions made by different members at the board Meeting held at Pune and has made the following recommendations, which incorporates the earlier recommendations and the changes suggested.

National HRD Network

Minutes of the General Body Meeting held on 5th October'02

Venue : The Renaissance Convention Centre Powai, Mumbai

Quorum : There was a quorum present.

Chairman : The meeting was presided over by Dr.Santrupt Misra, National President.

Discussions held and decisions taken in the meeting:

1. Accounts and the Report on Activities: The General Body approved the audited Accounts and the Report on Activities for the period 2000-02.

2. Appointment of Auditors : The General Body approved the proposal for re-appointment of the present Auditors (.... name of the auditors) for the period 2002-2004.

3. Changes in the Memorandum of Association : The General Body took a note of and approved the changes (...list of changes attached) made in the Memorandum of Association and rules and regulations, based on the decisions taken at the Executive Board Meeting of March 2001.

4. Constitution of new Body : The General Body took note of constitution of new body with National President and 4 Regional Presidents etc.

5. Other Items :

   a) The General Body congratulated and complimented the Mumbai Chapter for successfully hosting the National Conference.

   b) The suggestion of a member for creating a Code of Conduct was noted. It was decided that the National Executive Board may discuss and do the needful.

6. Thanks : The meeting ended with thanks to the Chair.

National HRD Network

Minutes of the National Executive Board Meeting held on 4th October'02

Venue : The Renaissance Convention Centre Powai, Mumbai

Present:

1.	Dr.Santrupt Misra	President
2.	Mr.Arvind N Agrawal	Immediate past President
3.	Mr. P.Dwarakanath	Regional President .North
4.	Mr.Trideep Ranjeker	Regional President-South
5.	Mr.G.P.Rao	Secretary
6.	Mr.K.Satyanarayana	Executive Director
7.	Mr.V.K.Mahajan	Elected Member
8.	Dr.Anil Sachdev	Advisory Board Member
9.	Fr.Abraham	Co-opted Member
10.	Dr.Uma Jain	Ex-Officio Member
11.	Mr.Aquil Busrai	Advisory Board Member
12.	Mr.Dileep K Misra	President Pune Chapter
13.	Mr.Jha H M	President Delhi Chapter
14.	Mr.Madan Saluja	Representing Ahmedabad Chapter
15.	Mr.Muzumdar S	President Mumbai Chapter
16.	Mr.Nagaraj D R	President Bangalore Chapter
17.	Mr.Ravindra G K	Representing Kolkata Chapter
18.	Mr.Sukhjit S Pasricha	President Chandigarh Chapter
19.	Mr.Tripathi P R	President Hyderabad Chapter

Discussions held and decisions taken in the meeting:

1. **Minutes:** Minutes of the last Board meeting held at Chennai on 27th July'02 (already circulated) were confirmed.

2. **Regional Presidents :**

   a) National President informed the Board about the appointment of S/Shri P. Dwarkanath, Dileep Ranjekar, Anand Nayak and Marcel Parker as the Regional Presidents for North, South, East and West respectively. The Board welcomed them.

   b) The Board recorded thanks and appreciation for Shri Aquil Busrail for having served the Board as the Regional President - North during the last 2 years.

❖ **4th Ravi Matthai memorial lecture on "Reforms in higher education" was conducted by Academy of HRD.**

Mr. N.R. Narayana Murthi had delivered the lecture. Dr. Udai Pareek introduced the Chief Guest and also gave a brief about the background of the Ravi Matthai Memorial Lecture. The lecture was held at Indian Institute of Science, Bangalore and Dr. Uma Jain organized the same. The Ravi Matthai memorial talks were imitated to celebrate the association of RMCEI of IIMA that gave a helping hand to AHRD by lending the services of Dr. Rao in setting up AHRD. There was no fund and no attempt was made to generate the fund. It would not have been difficult to create an endowment. But no such effort was made, and the Ravi Matthai Memorial talks became rare events subsequently.

- **An International Conference was on "Human Resources Development in Asia: Trends and Challenges" was organized jointly by Academy of Human Resources Development, International, USA and Academy of Human Resources Development, India on 28th-29th Oct, 2002 at Bangalore.** The conference was held at the Indian Institute of Management, Bangalore. Subsequently both the Institutions collaborated in organizing other International Conferences but this was a land mark conference and laid foundations for cross-national collaboration. This isa very positive experience and the papers presented were published in a book form and is available at the Academy. AHRD India could have taken h this collaboration forward. An issue comes up is how does an institution leverage such institutional collaborations. Who has to paly a leadership role? Perhaps AHRD India could have played a lot more proactive role and leveraging a great body like AHRD USA which was started a couple of years later than AHRD India.

Academy of Human Resources Development

12, Cosmoville, Satyagrah Marg, Ahmedabad - 380 015 • Pl Phone : 6870213, 6871341 FAX. 079-6870681
E-mail: ahrdad1@satyam.net.in Website: www.academyofhrd.org

22nd August 2002

Joint Secretary
Foreigners IV Section
Ministry of Home Affairs
Govt. of India
North Block
NEW DELHI 110 003

Dear Sir:

Sub: First Asian Regional International Conference on Human Resource Development – Bangalore – October 2002 – Govt. of India's (MHA's) approval

We invite your attention to our communication of May 8 (copy attached) informing you that Academy of Human Resources Development, India, is jointly organizing an International Asian Conference on Human Resource Development at Bangalore – India during October 2002. Conference is scheduled on October 28-29, 2002 and pre-conference workshops on October 26-27 2002. We expect attendance(participation) from all Asian countries (including South Asia, USA and Europe and from Japan to New Zealand, and from Vietnam to Saudi Arabia). A copy of conference brochure is attached.

We sought vide our letter of May 8 Government of India's approval (MHA's). We had simultaneously written to Ministry of External Affairs, GOI. We are pleased to inform you that we have since received their permission/approval for holding the International Conference and for participation of foreign delegates. Copy of their approval letter is attached. They have suggested that we approach your section for visa clearance for foreign participants.

We are writing this to seek your Ministry's clearance for visa of foreign participants. If any procedure needs to be followed, please advise us.

Thanking you,

Yours faithfully,

T.V. Rao

TV Rao
Chairman - EC

AHRD

Academy of Human Resource Development, International, USA

Jointly with the

Academy of Human Resources Development, India

Announces the

First International Conference on
HUMAN RESOURCE DEVELOPMENT IN ASIA

Conference Theme:

Human Resource Development in Asia: Trends and Challenges

Conference Dates:
October 28-29, 2002 — Bangalore — India

(Pre-Conference Workshops: October 26-27, 2002)

Venue:
Indian Institute of Management, Bangalore, India

First International Conference on

Human Resource Development in Asia: Trends and Challenges

October 28-29, 2002 — Bangalore — India

The Asia Chapter of the Academy of Human Resource Development (the top global scholarly organization in the field of HRD), in cooperation with the Indian Academy of HRD, announces its first Asian Conference. The Conference will bring together researchers and practitioners in the field of HRD coming from various disciplines and fields of study (HRD and HRM, business management, education, IT, economics, psychology, sociology and others). It will also be an effective forum for networking and professional interactions among leading HRD researchers and practitioners from around the world who have interests in HRD in Asia. From throughout Asia, attendance is expected from Japan to New Zealand, from Vietnam to Saudia Arabia.

The Indian Academy of Human Resources Development (established in 1991), based in Ahmedabad, is a center for Research and Education in India. It holds round table and other conferences, conducts doctoral level fellowships and other education and training programs to prepare HRD professionals and has a number of publications.

The Academy of HRD, headquartered in the USA, is supported by four international publications: Human Resource Development Quarterly(HRDQ), Human Resource Development International(HRDI), Advances in Developing Human Resources, and the new Human Resource Development Review. All of these journals are published quarterly by reputed publishing houses in the USA and the UK. Selected papers from this conference may be considered for publication in these journals.

Conference Themes and Papers

More than 140 scholarly papers have been accepted from Indian and overseas authors for presentation at the Conference. The Conference theme will cover the following issues:

- HRD Concepts, Mechanisms and Processes
- HRD in Societies and Social Sectors
- HRD and Indigenous Culture
- Performance Management
- Learning Organization and Knowledge Management
- Training and Organization Development
- Leadership and Change Management
- Environmental and Cross-Cultural Issues
- Emerging Concerns and other Related Issues

Sixty of the papers are from Mainland China, Taiwan, Bangladesh, Korea, Sri Lanka, Malaysia, Singapore, Kyrgyzstan, USA, U.K., and such other countries. Eightyfive approved summaries are from India.

Prominent paper presenters and key note speakers include the following scholars and practitioners:

Dr. Gary McLean, Dr. Ronald Jacobs, Dr. Gene Roth, Dr. Larry Dooley, Dr. Monica Lee, Dr. Aahad M. Osman Gani, Dr. Young Lin Moon, Mr. Azim H. Premji, Dr. Udai Pareek, Dr. S. Ramnarayan, Dr. T.V. Rao and Dr. Madhukar Shukla.

Pre-conference Workshops and Skillshops

Pre-Conference Workshops and Skillshops will be held on October 26-27,2002, at the conference venue. Eight interactive workshops have been arranged on these two days as per the following schedule:

Pre-conference Workshops: October 26-27, 2002

Time	Workshop Topics	Leaders/Facilitators
	October 26, 2002	
09.00-13.00 hrs	1. Human Re-engineering & Development Using NLP	Mr.K.Prakash HAL Management Academy
	2. HRD Audit	Dr.T.V. Rao, Chairman,TVRLS
14.00-18.00 hrs	1. Mapping Competence for the Future	Ujjwala Pendse-Vernalis India
	2. Cultural Readiness for Knowledge Management: Understanding behaviour, attitudes, and values in knowledge sharing	Mrs. Waltraut Ritter Hong Kong
	October 27, 2002	
08.30-12.30 hrs	1. The Use of Full-Circle Feedback in Management Development and Performance Appraisal	Dr. Gary McLean, University Of Minnesota, USA
	2. Unleashing Human Potential Through Empowerment	Dr.K.S. Gupta, HAL Management Academy
13.00-16.30 hrs	1. Using Theory and Theory - Building to Improve HRD Research	Dr.Larry M Dooley, Texas A&M University
	2. Value Clarification as an HRD Intervention	Dr. Uma Jain,AHRD, India

* Pre-Conference workshop will be offered subject to a minimum registration of 10 participants.

Conference Chairs and Committees

CONFERENCE CEO AND ASIA CHAPTER CO-COORDINATOR:
Dr. Aahad M. Osman-Gani
Professor of HRD and International Business
Nanyang Business School
Nanyang Technological University, Singapore
Tel: (65) 6790-4982
E-mail: aahad@ntu.edu.sg

Advisor:
Dr. Gary McLean,
University of Minnesota, USA, and
Past-President, AHRD, International
420 Vo-Tech Building
1954 Buford Ave.
St. Paul, MN 55108 USA
Tel. 612-624-4901; Fax. 612-624-4720
mclea002@umn.edu

CONFERENCE SITE CO-CHAIRS:
Dr. T V Rao
Chairman,
T V Rao Learning Systems Pvt. Ltd.
603, 6th Floor, PARSHWA
Opp.Rajpath Club,
Sarkhej –Gandhinagar Highway
Ahmedabad 380 015 - India
Tel: 079: 6872718, 6870312, 6870687
E-mail: tvraoad1@sancharnet.in
talamvrao@rediffmail.com
&
Prof. N M Agrawal
Area Chairperson – OB HRM Area
Indian Institute of Management, Bangalore
Bannerghatta Road
Bangalore 560 076 - India
Tel: 080 – 6993037, 6993161 @ 6590125
E-mail: agrawal@IIMB.ERNET.IN

PROGRAMME COMMITTEE CO-CHAIRS:
Dr. Aahad Osman-Gani and **Dr. T.V. Rao**

PROGRAM ASSOCIATE CHAIRS:
- Dr. Rebecca Sta Maria, Malaysia: Rebecca@intanbk.intan.my
- Dr. Tan-Chiraprapha Akaraborworn, Thailand: chira123@hotmail.com
- Dr. Bella Ya-Hui Lien, Taiwan: bmayhl@ccunix.ccu.edu.tw
- Dr. Kiyoe Harada, Japan: HRDharada@aol.com
- Dr. Ahmad A. Ajarimah, Middle-East & Gulf: ajarimaa@aramco.com.sa
- Dr. David Ripley, NewZealand : d.ripley@mang.canterbury.ac.nz
- Dr. Eunsang Cho, South Korea: escho@krivet.re.kr

CONFERENCE PROCEEDINGS EDITORS:
Editor: Dr. Udai Pareek
Indian Institute of Health Management Research
1, Prabhu Dayal Marg
Sanganer Airport
Jaipur – 302 011 - India

Co-Editors:
Dr. Aahad Osman-Gani, Dr. T.V. Rao, and Dr. S. Ramnarayan

CONFERENCE SITE COMMITTEES:

Financial Assistance Committee:
- Mr. R. Vidyasagar – Chairperson
- Mr. Pallav Bandhopadhyay – Member
- Mr.S.V. Nathan – Member
- Mr. Ranjan Acharya – Member
- Mr.C. Mahalingam – Member

Limited financial support may be arranged for the presenters from developing countries. Participants whose papers have been accepted for the conference, requiring financial assistance (partial) or full programme registration fee waiver) may write to the Chairman of Financial Assistance Committee to the following Address:

Mr.R.Vidyasagar,
e-mail: r.vidyasagar@iflexsolutions.com

Programme Sub-Committee:
- Prof. K.B.Akhilesh – Chairperson
- Prof. Vasanthi Srinivasan – Member
- Dr. Rupandi Padaki – Member
- Dr.K.S. Gupta – Member
- Dr. Gopal Mahapatra – Member
- Mr. Subrabhi M.A. Member

Logistics Committee:
- Prof. Kalyani Gandhi – Chairperson
- Mr.J.R. Saligram – Member
- Mr.D.R. Nagaraj – Member
- Mr.H.N. Srinivas – Member
- Mr.S.K Nandy – Member

CONFERENCE UPDATE CAN BE BROWSED ON:

http://mgmt.iisc.ernet.in/ ~hrda/
http://unix2.iimb.ernet.in/ãhrd>

Conference Schedule

CONFERENCE INAUGURATION: (Sunday, 27th October 2002)	
Registration	5.00 p.m. – 6.00 p.m.
Inauguration Session	6.00 p.m. – 7.30 p.m.
Inaugural Dinner	7.30 p.m. – 9.30 p.m. (courtesy AHRD)
CONFERENCE – DAY 1: (Monday, 28th October 2002)	
Registration	8.00 a.m. – 9.00 a.m.
Plenary Session-1	9.00 a.m. – 10.30 a.m. (Keynote Speaker)
Tea Break	*10.30 a.m.- 11.00 a.m. (courtesy AHRD)*
Parallel Sessions 1	11.00 a.m. – 01.00 p.m. (about 4-6 Presentation Sessions)
Lunch Break	*01.00 p.m.- 02.00 p.m. (courtesy AHRD)*
Plenary-2	02.00 p.m. – 03.30 p.m. (Featured speakers)
Tea Break	*03.30 p.m. – 04.00 p.m. (courtesy AHRD)*
Parallel Sessions 2	04.00 p.m. – 06.00 p.m. (about 4-6 Presentation Sessions)
CONFERENCE – DAY 2: (Tuesday, 29th October 2002)	
Plenary-3	09.00 a.m. – 10.30 a.m. (Keynote speaker)
Tea Break	*10.30 a.m. – 11.00 a.m. (courtesy AHRD)*
Parallel Sessions 3	11.00 a.m. – 01.00 p.m. (about 4-6 presentation sessions)
Lunch Break	*01.00 p.m. – 02.00 p.m. (courtesy AHRD)*
Parallel Sessions 4	02.00 p.m. - 4.00 p.m. (about 4-6 presentation sessions)
Tea Break	*4.00 p.m. – 04.30 p.m. (courtesy AHRD)*
Plenary Session & Awards presentation	04.30 p.m. – 06.00 p.m. (Featured speaker)
Farewell dinner & Cultural Evening	07.30 p.m. – 10.00 p.m. (courtesy AHRD)

(In each of the parallel sessions, about 4/5 papers will be presented by the authors, and will be followed by discussions/questions & answers)

Conference Venue

Conference will be held at the premises of Indian Institute of Management, Bangalore (India). Bangalore is a very picturous garden city. It is known as the IT capital of India, and also known as the Silicon Valley of Asia. It enjoys a very cool climate right through the year. At the time of the conference, the average temperature will be 25 degree C. It is a young city with a lot of pubs and eating places. It is known for its temples. There are a number of educational institutions, including the famous Indian Institute of Science.

Registration and Accommodation

REGISTRATION FEE:

For Conference: For members of AHRD, USA, US $150 – Indian Rupees Rs,7500/ (Rupees Seven thousand five hundred)(covers pre conference dinner on 27th October, conference materials, proceedings, lunch and tea from 28th to 29th October 2002, and the concluding dinner) For non-members US$200(Indian Rs.10000/(Rupees Ten Thousand)

(There will be 25% fee waiver on US$200, only for groups from HRD Network and members of other professional bodies, if a minimum of 10 participants is sponsored by the body)

Fee for Pre-Conference Workshops: U.S.$50/-(Ind.Rs.2500/)(per workshop) for members of AHRD,USA, and for others US$60, (Ind.Rs.3000/)

All registration fees(including pre-conference workshop fee), other than credit-card payments, to be sent to Co-Program Chair, Dr.T.V. Rao. Drafts should be drawn in the name of "Academy of HRD, Asian Regional Conference" payable at Ahmedabad.

Credit card payments in US$ are to be made to AHRD headquarters(USA) through e-mail attachments or through Fax. Please send your completed registration form with credit card details to: office@ahrd.org or Fax: (419) 372-8385(Please type form or print and firmly) Accepted credit cards are:Visa, Mastercard,Discover, American Express). For Credit Card payment, information must include, full name on credit card, type of credit card, credit card account number, and expiration date. On fax, and surface mail, please type name and include signature. On e-mail, please type your full name.

For Surface Mail: Send to: College of Technology, Bowling Green State University, Bowling Green, OH 43403-1301, USA.

(Indian Rupee Equivalent:U.S.$ 1 = Ind.Rs.50/- (Rupees Fifty only)

ACCOMMODATION:
Rooms are available at the Conference Venue (Indian Institute of Management, Bangalore). Their Management Development Centre (MDC) has 45 single and 15 double rooms(spacious, airconditioned with attached bath facilities). Charges are : Single Occupancy:US$50/- per day and for Double $65/ per day which covers room charges, breakfast and dinner. For accommodation at MDC, IIM Bangalore, please book in advance. For details, write to:

Mr.J.R. Saligram, Chief Programs Officer
Indian Institute of Management, Bangalore
Bannerghatta Road, BANGALORE 560076 (India)
Telephones:91-80-699-3203/658 2540(Office)
Fax:91-80-658 4004/658 4050
Email:saligram@iimb.ernet.in

For accommodation at other than IIM Bangalore, MDC, delegates have to approach the hotels directly.

Taj Group of Hotels has been appointed as official host for the conference. They have three hotels in Bangalore and you can get more details by visiting their website:www.tajhotels.com, http://tajhotels.com

Accommodation can be booked by writing to Mr.Ram Pattath of ram.pattath@tajhotels.com. These hotels are about 12 km. from the conference site.

Hotel Nandhini is an economy hotel located about 6 km from the conference site. It has agreed to provide substantial discount for conference participants. Accommodation can be booked at Hotelnandhini@nandhini.com

There are a good number of hotels available in Bangalore for accommodation. Following websites provide information on various hotels at Bangalore:

http://www.bangalorenet.com/hotels/index.asp
http://www.indiainformation.com/bangalore/hotels.htm

Post-Conference Tours Bangalore and Karnataka State are known for its tourist spots. Post-conference tours will be arranged for the participants on payment basis on October 30-31.

How to reach Bangalore There are regular flights between Mumbai and Bangalore, Delhi and Bangalore, Chennai and Bangalore, Calcutta and Bangalore, Hyderabad and Bangalore. It is well connected by air. Indian Airlines and Jet Airways have over 10 flights from Mumbai. It is also an International Airport. If you are coming via Mumbai or Delhi, please note that you have to change over from International Airport to Domestic terminal.

Tours and Accommodation The registration fee for tours and accommodation at IIM, Bangalore Management Development Centre, is to be paid at the venue after arrival.

CALL FOR PAPERS

Academy of Human Resource Development, International
Jointly with the
Academy of Human Resources Development, India

Announces the
First Asian Regional Conference on
Human Resource Development

October 28-29, 2002
(Pre-conference Workshops: October 26-27)

Venue:
Indian Institute of Management, Bangalore, INDIA

Conference Theme:
Human Resource Development in Asia:
Trends and Challenges

- **Activities in National HRD Network Chapters**
  - Hyderabad Chapter
    - Program on "Indian wisdom for management effectiveness" was conducted by Venkata Rao K.K.B.P on 3rd Jan 2002.
    - Program on "Responsibility of corporate India" was conducted by P. Hanumantha Rao, Founder Chairman of Sweekar and Upkaar, Secunderabad on 17th Jan 2002.

References

Bennis, W. G., & Thomas, R. J. (2002). Geeks & geezers: How era, values, and defining moments shape leaders. Boston, Massachusetts: Harvard Business School Press.

Bennis, WG & Thomas, RJ. (2002). Crucibles of leadership. Harvard business review. 80. 39-+.

Pareek, Udai & Rao, Talam. (2008). From a sapling to the forest: the saga of the development of HRD in India. Human Resource Development International. 11. 555–564. 10.1080/13678860802417734. This paper has heavily borrows from "My Institution Building Experiences at IIMA, NHRDN and AHRD (A reflective essay in honor of Prof. Ishwar Dayal) by T V Rao

Pareek, Udai & T.V. Rao (1998). *Pioneering human resources development: The L & T System,* Ahmedabad: Academy of Human Resource Development, 165p.

Rao, T V (2004) *Future of HRD*, New Delhi: Macmillan

Rao, T. V. (2014, 2024) Effective People; New Delhi: Penguin Randomhouse.

PART 4

Abstracts of Papers from First Three Conferences of NHRDN

These abstracts are an illustration of contributions of NHRDN and AHRD to the world of Knowledge. Copies of all the publications of NHRDN and AHRD are available the AHRD Library in Ahmedabad. Abstracts of the following books and conference t papers along with copies are available and can be accessed.

The abstracts presented here are supported by TVRLS (T V Rao Learning Systems Pvt. Ltd., Ahmedabad) and copies made available to various chapter Presidents, NHRDN secretariat and AHRD.

There are 84 papers summarized here by TVRLS team. There are 27 from the book Alternative Strategies of HRD form the conference held at Madras in 1987, and 44 from the Delhi Conference on Towards Organizational Excellence and 13 from the symposium held in 1990. A perusal of these abstracts give lot of insights into the HRD issues as they existed 35 years back. Don't be surprised to conclude that they still remain as issues 35 years after HRD moved. The context has changed. A valuable conclusion may be we have a lot to learn from history and frome ach other.

Abstracts of Papers from Various Books of NHRDN

Abraham, E,;Khandelwal A.K.; Rao, T.V.; Verma, K.K.(editors); Alternative Approaches and Strategies of Human Resource

Development, NHRDN, 1988 Conference Papers for the National HRD Network Madras, September 1987, Published by Rawat Publications, Jaipur

1. Chandra, S; Human Resource Management Policy: A Blue Print in: Abraham, E,;Khandelwal A.K.; Rao, T.V.; Verma, K.K.(editors); Alternative Approaches and Strategies of Human Resource Development, NHRDN, 1988 Conference Papers for the National HRD Network Madras, September 1987, Published by Rawat Publications, Jaipur; pages 1–9

   The workers in our country, in spite of having knowledge and efficiency comparable to those of other countries fall short of corporate expectations when it comes to productivity. Managements bestow more time to policy and systems than to development of human resources. However, compulsions of the modern business environment are forcing a rethink. This has led to careful elucidation, identification and channelizing of the HR policy. This will go a long way in ensuring congruence of individual and organizational values, increasing commitment, engagement, and organizational effectiveness. The management can prepare a policy after discussions with executives and representatives of workers. If need be, it may also appoint a Task Force which will evolve a draft policy based on its discussions. The copies of the resultant policy should be circulated to all employees. For a successful policy, it is important that objectives be framed and there be clarity on goals and action plans for achieving those goals. The author has given a blueprint by framing objectives, elements, goals and action plans for a HR policy

   - JGJ

   Critical Words: HR policy, methodology, elements, objectives, need for policy

2. Rao T.V.; Role of Chief Executives in Human Resources Development in: Abraham, E,;Khandelwal A.K.; Rao, T.V.; Verma, K.K.(editors); Alternative Approaches and Strategies of Human Resource Development, NHRDN, 1988 Conference Papers for the National HRD Network Madras, September 1987, Published by Rawat Publications, Jaipur; pages 10–21

   HRD aims at helping people to acquire competencies required to perform their functions well and make their organizations perform well. Chief Executives, line managers and HRD managers have to make an effort to promote HRD processes as a matter of faith or philosophy as tangible and measurable outcomes may not be easily demonstrable. It is not necessary to have HRD systems or interventions for a good HRD culture. What is required is good leadership and the vision of building a HRD values in the organization. The author has analysed 14 organizations and found trends and strategies of developing human resources. According to Rao, the chief executive can develop the human resources by the following steps: Have a corporate philosophy on Human Resources, Develop a leadership and supervisory style in yourself and senior executives, examine the HRD needs and prepare an action plan, man the HRD department with competent people, examine appraisal systems and initiate needed OD exercises, prepare a training policy with separate budget, develop a HRD climate, encourage managers to share their experiences and develop sensitivity towards incremental changes in human competencies

- JGJ

Critical words: HRD, HRD system, interventions, culture, role of chief executives

3. Joseph, Jerome; Reactivity to Proactivity: IR and HRD in: Abraham, E,;Khandelwal A.K.; Rao, T.V.; Verma, K.K.(editors); Alternative Approaches and Strategies of Human Resource Development, NHRDN, 1988 Conference Papers for the National HRD Network Madras, September 1987, Published by Rawat Publications, Jaipur; pages 21–43

   The paper addresses the questions related to the conceptual basis of changing the praxis of human resources development from reactive to proactive as well as the operational modalities of labour management when influenced by human resource management principles. After a discussion of involved principles, the author presents three ideas for reflection. One, the HRD concept and interventions should be addressed to organized labour and not to individuals or work groups. Second, the theme of development central to HRD has to be focused to shift Industrial Relations from reactive to proactive mode. Third, HRD without the democratization of ownership of an organization will end up alienating the labour force in organizations.

   - JGJ

Critical words: Labour Relations, Industrial relations, Employee relations, Alienation, proactive role

4. Kulkarni S.S.; Future Possibilities in Human Resources Development Area for Banks in: Abraham, E,;Khandelwal A.K.; Rao, T.V.; Verma, K.K.(editors); Alternative Approaches and Strategies of Human Resource Development, NHRDN, 1988 Conference Papers for the National HRD Network Madras, September 1987, Published by Rawat Publications, Jaipur; pages 46–53

The future of HRD in the banking sector is discussed based on the past trends and the desired future trends. Increased service diversity will lead to promotion and recruitment decisions based on competencies of the person rather than the seniority. The performance appraisal system will now be linked with many other decisions like promotion, feedback and training. Assessment centres will be used gradually starting from the executive level. To reduce the incidence of anti-social evils with the rise in salary, more stress on social welfare activities, quality of work and quality of life may be given. The industrial relations scenario will become complex and there may also be the emergence of unions of knowledge workers.

- JGJ

Critical Words: Future Possibilities; Unions; Industrial Relations; Part-time jobs; Social Welfare activities; Training; Assessment Centres; Promotion; Recruitment;

5. Puranik M.B.; HRD in Research and Development Organizations in: Abraham, E,;Khandelwal A.K.; Rao, T.V.; Verma, K.K.(editors); Alternative Approaches and Strategies of Human Resource Development, NHRDN, 1988 Conference Papers for the National HRD Network Madras, September 1987, Published by Rawat Publications, Jaipur; pages 54–61

The HRD policy for Research and Development Organisations will be different as compared to manufacturing organizations. Accordingly, recruitment and management styles have to be different. Excluding the technical, functional and certain areas of specialisation, there are other needs such as creativity, attitude, communication, interpersonal relations, team-building skills, leadership and motivation. In developing these, organizational climate and factors such as delegation, power of responsibility and accountability for results play important roles. Thus it is important that proper diagnosis of the health of the organization be conducted.

- JGJ

Critical words: Leadership; Motivation; Team building; Relationships; Attitudes; Creativity; Communication

6. Varghese, Susan; Potential Development through in-basket exercises: Crompton Greaves Experience in: Abraham, E,;Khandelwal A.K.; Rao, T.V.; Verma, K.K.(editors); Alternative Approaches and Strategies of Human Resource Development, NHRDN, 1988 Conference Papers for the National HRD Network Madras, September 1987, Published by Rawat Publications, Jaipur; pages 62–69

   This author articulates the in-basket approach that was followed at Crompton Greaves for top management selections and appointments. In-Basket is a simulation exercise which enables assessment of capabilities of potential candidates to discharge the responsibility of concerned positions. In this case, five General Managers and three Vice-Presidents were given a scenario to take a decision. The instrument was administered in front of the MD of the company. What followed was a healthy discussion of various ways of action followed by a comment from the MD itself. The whole exercise had many potential learnings for all the participants. The author concludes by commenting on the uses of the approach.

   - JGJ

   Critical Words: In-Basket; Crompton Greaves; Performance Appraisal

7. Chandrashekhar, S; Managing Change through OD in: Abraham, E,;Khandelwal A.K.; Rao, T.V.; Verma, K.K.(editors); Alternative Approaches and Strategies of Human Resource Development, NHRDN, 1988 Conference Papers for the National HRD Network Madras, September 1987, Published by Rawat Publications, Jaipur; pages 70–74

   Realising the need for Organizational Development (OD) in the Construction Group of L&T (LTCG), the management did an organization study in 1979. On the basis of this study, an organization structure was proposed to strengthen structure, systems and people of the organization. Since, most of the interventions were based on HRD, collaborative effort in a climate of mutual trust was required. Initially, an outside consultant was engaged and a senior management team (OD Group) was identified for the whole process. At each stage of the implementation of the OD interventions, senior management involved themselves completely leading to the successful introduction of OD for the first time in 1983. The author notes the positive effects and critical factors necessary in the development.

-JGJ

Critical Words: Organizational Development; Larsen and Tourbo; Construction group of Larsen & Tourbo; LTCG; Productivity Improvement; OD Group; Task Force

8. Shirodkar, Ginil; Human Resource Development at RHL in: Abraham, E,; Khandelwal A.K.; Rao, T.V.; Verma, K.K. (editors); Alternative Approaches and Strategies of Human Resource Development, NHRDN, 1988 Conference Papers for the National HRD Network Madras, September 1987, Published by Rawat Publications, Jaipur; pages 75–83

   The author articulates the process of Human Resource Development at RHL. The process was slow and gradual. The author points out that the critical support of the Chief Executive in the process was very important and contributed to the success of the initiative. Specific measures were taken to restore the balance of power, address issues of anxiety and aspirations of managers with focus on "on-job-training" through live cases. From a slow persuasive stance, the management moved towards creating commitment and ownership among the employees which led to performance and productivity oriented union-management contract. Through this systematic process, the company turned around its performance and showed the way towards "people excellence".

   Critical words: RHL, Gurcharan Das, Culture,

9. Sachdeva, Anil; Arora, A.K;. Improving Employee Relations Climate – HRD shows the way – the Eicher Experience in: Abraham, E,;Khandelwal A.K.; Rao, T.V.; Verma, K.K.(editors);

Alternative Approaches and Strategies of Human Resource Development, NHRDN, 1988 Conference Papers for the National HRD Network Madras, September 1987, Published by Rawat Publications, Jaipur; pages 84–125

The article is a brief summary of the OD process started in Eicher post the market slump and fall in profits that occurred in 1982. In the paper, the authors have elucidated the various steps taken in the organization to give rise to OD interventions which spread over 16 months starting from September 1984. These interventions were in the areas of Appraisal Systems, Employee Communications, Leadership, Team Work, Employee Development, Compensation and Employees' Welfare. The authors conclude that a systemic process of change integrated with effective HRD interventions can go a long way in improving organizational effectiveness.

- JGJ

Critical Words: Eicher; Appraisal Systems; Employee Communications; Leadership; Team Work; Employee Development; Compensation; Employees' Welfare; HRD Interventions

10. Sambamurthy, M.S.; HRD in Sundram Fasteners in: Abraham, E,;Khandelwal A.K.; Rao, T.V.; Verma, K.K.(editors); Alternative Approaches and Strategies of Human Resource Development, NHRDN, 1988 Conference Papers for the National HRD Network Madras, September 1987, Published by Rawat Publications, Jaipur; pages 126–134

Sundaram Fasteners has not lost a single man-hour since its inception around 20 years ago. The Chief Executive of the company decided to formalise the prevalent people oriented processes that has led to this singular achievement to build a greater thrust towards building effective human resources. The article looks critically at the HRD Approach, activities and key processes such as training and development, performance appraisal, manpower planning and job analysis followed at the company that has led to its success in industrial relations. The author concludes that it is important to evolve processes which are relevant and appropriate to the organization. The success in the implementation of these ideas have resulted from the growth and assimilation of ideas from within the cultural and social framework.

- JGJ

Critical Words: TVS, Sundram Fasteners, Performance Appraisal, Manpower Planning, Job Descriptions, Corporate Philosophy, Approach to HRD, HRD Processes

11. Murthy, P.V.R.; Gregory J.X.; Relevance of Japanese HRD Practices in Sundaram-Clayton in: Abraham, E,; Khandelwal A.K.; Rao, T.V.; Verma, K.K.(editors); Alternative Approaches and Strategies of Human Resource Development, NHRDN, 1988 Conference Papers for the National HRD Network Madras, September 1987, Published by Rawat Publications, Jaipur; pages 135–146

The authors have compared the Japanese HRD system with the HRD systems followed at TVS Group with a view to understand the similarities in the principles, the diversity of the approach taken in each of the system and the cultural factors attendant on the differences and the similarities. The article examines the similarities and differences in various processes such as recruitment, induction, training, performance appraisal, career planning, human relations and other managerial processes. The article concludes that both the systems share a common philosophy. The dissimilarities if any, are due to the cultural factors of India. For the same reason, the authors caution against transplanting a process from abroad into India. The authors conclude the article by enumerating some principles from Japanese HRD systems that could be followed in India.

- JGJ

Critical Words: Japanese HRD; Comparison; TVS

12. Sarthi, Parth; Rao S.S.; Human Resource Development in BHEL in : Abraham, E,;Khandelwal A.K.; Rao, T.V.; Verma, K.K.(editors); Alternative Approaches and Strategies of Human Resource Development, NHRDN, 1988 Conference Papers for the National HRD Network Madras, September 1987, Published by Rawat Publications, Jaipur; pages 147–209

The article presents the efforts at HRD undertaken at BHEL. The article covers the structure of the HRD department, the objectives of the department, the process of developing the functional plans for personnel for each part of the department, manpower planning, training and development, performance appraisal and performance evaluation. It also covers in detail the complete set of OD interventions in the organization from September 1976 to 1987. The article concludes by looking at emerging issues in HRD implementation and systems.

- JGJ

Critical Words: HRD systems; BHEL; Manpower Planning; Training and Development; Performance Appraisal; Performance Management; HRD Issues; OD at BHEL

13. Nair M.R.R.; Major HRD Initiatives in SAIL in: Abraham, E,; Khandelwal A.K.; Rao, T.V.; Verma, K.K.(editors); Alternative Approaches and Strategies of Human Resource Development, NHRDN, 1988 Conference Papers for the National HRD Network Madras, September 1987, Published by Rawat Publications, Jaipur; pages 210–226

In this article, the author explains the turnaround strategy adopted at SAIL. In the first phase, there was an organised attempt to collect feedback by interacting with the top management, middle management and the lower management. The feedback was analysed and resulted into a document called "Priorities for Action". The identified areas for improvement were productivity, cost-control and customer service. Interventions were also made in recruitment, training and development. This has led to increasing expectations from the employees regarding the HRD functions. Another finding is that each unit in such a vast company may have its own culture and response pattern. Hence, the effort is to build on the components of local culture and build the concept of unity based on it.

- JGJ

Critical words: SAIL, Organizational Discipline, Work Culture

14. Verma, K.K.; Human Resources Development in Bank of Baroda in: Abraham, E,;Khandelwal A.K.; Rao, T.V.; Verma, K.K.(editors); Alternative Approaches and Strategies of Human Resource Development, NHRDN, 1988 Conference Papers for the National HRD Network Madras, September 1987, Published by Rawat Publications, Jaipur; pages 227–249

The article explains the process of setting up a HRD function in Bank of Baroda. In the initial set-up, the HRD system paid more attention to Performance Appraisal Systems, building and utilising a personnel skills inventory, management development and introducing quality circles. The author found that the enthusiasm of the leader of the quality circle made a difference to the enthusiasm of the participating members. The author concludes by highlighting some impediments that may occur while setting up HRD department in an organization.

- JGJ

Critical Words: Setting up HRD; Bank of Baroda; Quality Circles

15. Kapoot, B; Inside View of HRD Experience of Indian Oil Corporation Ltd. in: Abraham, E,;Khandelwal A.K.; Rao, T.V.; Verma, K.K.(editors); Alternative Approaches and Strategies of Human Resource Development, NHRDN, 1988 Conference Papers for the National HRD Network Madras, September 1987, Published by Rawat Publications, Jaipur; pages 250–263
This article details the planning and implementation of the HRD system in Indian Oil Corporation Ltd. The implementation was divided into six phases starting from formulation of a human resource strategy in 1983 to HRD consolidation and innovation in 1988. In between the first and the sixth phase, the other phases that were Action research projects at selected locations (role analysis), extension of role analysis, implementation of HRD sub-systems and HRD for collectives and trade unions. The article also details the personal experience of the author in the implementation of the HRD system.

- JGJ

Critical words: IOCL, Indian Oil Corporation Limited; Setting up HRD systems;

16. Sarangi, P.K.; A Descriptive Note on Role Analysis: Experience of Indian Oil Corporation Ltd. in: Abraham, E,;Khandelwal A.K.; Rao, T.V.; Verma, K.K.(editors); Alternative Approaches and Strategies of Human Resource Development, NHRDN, 1988 Conference Papers for the National HRD Network Madras, September 1987, Published by Rawat Publications, Jaipur; pages 264–274
Though a role is defined by the expectations from significant persons in the organization, including the person himself, in reality, roles

are given to the employee and never defined by expectations. A large organization requires role analysis to avoid role ambiguity at various levels at the organization. In the article, the author explains the exercise of role analysis undertaken at Indian Oil Corporation Limited. The exercise was first undertaken at select locations and later extended to the whole corporation. While extending to the whole corporation, two approaches were followed – one, replication of the action research effort for similar roles and two, analysis of the new roles at the new locations. The difference in the appreciation level of the exercise has made the difference in impact of the interventions at the organizational level.

- JGJ

17. Bhushan, Y.K.; Training and Human Resources Development – An Experience in Symbiosis in: Abraham, E,; Khandelwal A.K.; Rao, T.V.; Verma, K.K.(editors); Alternative Approaches and Strategies of Human Resource Development, NHRDN, 1988 Conference Papers for the National HRD Network Madras, September 1987, Published by Rawat Publications, Jaipur; pages 275–284
This article attempts to present some experiences on management of training in a public sector bank with reference to the HRD sub-system of Training and Development. The article seeks to go into the structural linkages between Training and HRD and the processes through which it is operationalised. The training was imparted through a college. An attempt was made to effect changes in the Training System and thereby be able to make interventions in Organizational Development, Management Development and Employee Development. The author has used the analogy of the stages of an aircraft on the run-way for explaining the evolution of the Training system. The author concludes by bringing to the fore issues and challenges in the implementation of HRD in the banking sector.

- JGJ

Critical words: Banking Sector; Symbiosis; Training

18. Wadikar, Ashok; Role Making by an HRD Manager – Experiences and Reflections in: Abraham, E,;Khandelwal A.K.; Rao, T.V.; Verma, K.K.(editors); Alternative Approaches and

Strategies of Human Resource Development, NHRDN, 1988 Conference Papers for the National HRD Network Madras, September 1987, Published by Rawat Publications, Jaipur; pages 285–300

The author shares his experience as a HRD Manager in a state bank. The role of HRD Managers are vital, more so in the service industry which is dynamic in nature. The essence of the article is the search by the author to define his own role as HRD Manager in the organization and how he used it to introduce interventions. These interventions took the shape of specific training programmes for the various levels in the company. The author concludes the article with a section devoted to the various issues related to the process of role making. The section discusses the issues with respect to the top management, the role of consultants and evaluation.

- JGJ

Critical words: Role Making; Consultants; HRD Manager

19. Khandelwal, Anil K.; HRD for Workers: Role of the Unions in: Abraham, E,;Khandelwal A.K.; Rao, T.V.; Verma, K.K.(editors); Alternative Approaches and Strategies of Human Resource Development, NHRDN, 1988 Conference Papers for the National HRD Network Madras, September 1987, Published by Rawat Publications, Jaipur; pages 301–315

Most HRD interventions are directed only at the managerial level, not at the worker level. Related with worker affairs is the issue of trade unions and their responses to the area of HRD. HRD for workers has a number of positive impacts. The article then examines the responses given by unions to the introduction of HRD interventions at the worker level and reasons them out. The author also explains the role that is expected to be played by unions post implementation of these interventions. The article concludes by stating that the conduct of management as reflected in the codes, policies and practices of the company would make a difference to the attitudes of the trade unions in accepting or rejecting HRD interventions at workers' level.

- JGJ

Critical words: HRD interventions; trade unions; HRD for workers; HRD roles of unions

20. Shroff, A.G.; HRD in Transpek Industry Ltd. – A Family Owned Business in: Abraham, E,;Khandelwal A.K.; Rao, T.V.; Verma, K.K. (editors); Alternative Approaches and Strategies of Human Resource Development, NHRDN, 1988 Conference Papers for the National HRD Network Madras, September 1987, Published by Rawat Publications, Jaipur; pages 316–322
In this article, the author states the various processes that are followed at Transpek Industry Ltd. During the various interactions of the management with the stakeholders, it was felt that many of the transactions had a lot of subjectivity. To improve the processes, it was decided to formalize the HRD system. The direct result of the implementation of the HRD system was a greater degree of openness within the executive staff. The company decided to de-link performance appraisal from increments and used them as an instrument for improvement. The company has also used FIRO (B) and MAO(B) instruments in its efforts to develop its employees. The article concludes by showing how the interventions in HRD helped bring a professional touch to the company's operational style.

-JGJ

Critical words: Transpek; FIRO (B); Quality Circles

21. Pestonjee, D.M.; Stress Audit as a Mechanism of HRD in: Abraham, E,;Khandelwal A.K.; Rao, T.V.; Verma, K.K.(editors); Alternative Approaches and Strategies of Human Resource Development, NHRDN, 1988 Conference Papers for the National HRD Network Madras, September 1987, Published by Rawat Publications, Jaipur; pages 322–324
Stress is an essential accompaniment to executive work. The author has delineated the types of stress and the occasions where stress becomes a major factor in human transactions. To understand the effect of stress on organizations, stress audit is conducted. This can also be used an organizational development tool and provides valuable insights into functioning of various units, policies, practices and climates. The author concludes the article by explaining how stress audit can be turned into a mechanism of HRD to improve efficiency, effectiveness and health of the human resources.

-JGJ

Critical words: Stress Audit;

22. Srivastava, C.M.; Human Resource Development in Larsen and Tourbo Limited in: Abraham, E,;Khandelwal A.K.; Rao, T.V.; Verma, K.K.(editors); Alternative Approaches and Strategies of Human Resource Development, NHRDN, 1988 Conference Papers for the National HRD Network Madras, September 1987, Published by Rawat Publications, Jaipur; pages 325–333

    The performance appraisal system in 1974 in the company was a non-transparent affair and ineffective. At the company's request, Prof TV Rao and Prof Udai Pareek studied the system and came up with a gamut of recommendations on performance appraisal, potential appraisal, employment counselling, career development and planning, training and organizational development. The article lists out the various steps of implementation of these recommendations and the difficulties faced by the implementation team. The interventions were made in the areas of training, career development, critical attributes, performance appraisal, potential appraisal and personal skills inventory.

    -JGJ

    Critical words: Larsen and Tourbo; Setting up HRD Systems; Performance Appraisal, Potential Appraisal; Employment Counselling; Career Development; Career Planning; Training; Organizational Development

23. Bhatt, I.T.; Dixit, S.A.; Mehta, S.D.; Behavioural Training as a Tool For Development of Employees of Petrofil in: Abraham, E,; Khandelwal A.K.; Rao, T.V.; Verma, K.K. (editors); Alternative Approaches and Strategies of Human Resource Development, NHRDN, 1988 Conference Papers for the National HRD Network Madras, September 1987, Published by Rawat Publications, Jaipur; pages 334–341

    The article talks about the behavioural training programme in Petrofils conducted for non-supervisory staff. The training was imparted in three modules – increasing shop floor effectiveness, creativity and productivity techniques. The article then talks about the improvements that were noted as a result of the programme, the blocks in the implementation and suggestions made by the employees for improvement. The company also decided to rope in the top, middle management and the spouses of the participants to lend more ownership to the training. The article concludes by noting that the training had a positive effect on the shop-floor climate and change in the attitude of the workers towards the organizations.

-JGJ

Critical words: Behavioural Training; Petrofils;

24. Raman, T.P.; HRD Experiences in the State Bank of India in: Abraham, E,;Khandelwal A.K.; Rao, T.V.; Verma, K.K. (editors); <u>Alternative Approaches and Strategies of Human Resource Development,</u> NHRDN, 1988 Conference Papers for the National HRD Network Madras, September 1987, Published by Rawat Publications, Jaipur; pages 342–365
In this article, the author explains the process of planning and implementing the HRD processes at the State Bank of India at a pan-India level. This process was initiated as part of the "Fourth Wave". The first step in the process was to identify people who could be potential HRD Managers, train them in the nuances and inspire them to carry the process forward. In the entire process, the main emphasis was laid on two components – Performance Appraisal and Training. Before launching the system formally, the system was introduced in stages in different circles and critical feedback obtained to improve the process further. The author concludes the article by listing the lessons learnt during implementation. HRD happens to be an area where it is difficult to think of arithmetical parameters of measurement of progress. The results can only be judged by people who have been deeply involved in the process.

-JGJ

Critical words: State Bank of India; Setting up HRD; Performance Appraisal; Training

25. Nair, R.R.; career Development Strategies and HRD in: Abraham, E,;Khandelwal A.K.; Rao, T.V.; Verma, K.K.(editors); <u>Alternative Approaches and Strategies of Human Resource Development,</u> NHRDN, 1988 Conference Papers for the National HRD Network Madras, September 1987, Published by Rawat Publications, Jaipur; pages 366–373

The author starts by stressing that the myriad differences in an organization offer plenty of scope for considerable opportunities for a HRD professional to evolve a suitable career planning strategy. There is however, the requirement of a tracking system to track the high-potential and high-performance managers. The author then discusses the critical elements of such a tracking system viz. performance appraisal, training, reward system and potential assessment. Each organization must decide on check-points, in addition to the mentioned systems, to determine whether the career development plan is working or not. The author concludes the article by listing a few propositions on the basis of the author's experience in career planning.

- JGJ

Critical words: Career Planning; Check-points; Tracking System

26. Athreya, M.B.; Integrated HRD System – Intervention Strategies in: Abraham, E,; Khandelwal A.K.; Rao, T.V.; Verma, K.K. (editors); Alternative Approaches and Strategies of Human Resource Development, NHRDN, 1988 Conference Papers for the National HRD Network Madras, September 1987, Published by Rawat Publications, Jaipur; pages 373–398

The article looks at three kinds of experiences – the forces that trigger HRD interventions in an organization, different leverage points that can be used for introducing HRD in an organization and the interface issues between HRD and other management systems and practices. In the first module discusses triggers such as alienation discomfort, leadership values, insensitivity, and missing links in the structure and user inadequacies. In the second module, individual participation, human resources philosophy, HRD system model and the necessity of skills in the implementation of the system are discussed. In the third module about system levers, the author discusses training, appraisal, career planning, succession planning, role clarity and manpower planning. Each of these are explained and then the author conceptualises certain frameworks which may be used as a guide in future. The author concludes the article by warning about the dangers of formalisation of systems.

- JGJ

Critical words: HRD interventions; HRD interface; Leverage points

27. D'Souza, Keith C; Some Issues Relating to the Structuring of the HRD function in Indian Organizations in: Abraham, E,; Khandelwal A.K.; Rao, T.V.; Verma, K.K. (editors); Alternative Approaches and Strategies of Human Resource Development, NHRDN, 1988 Conference Papers for the National HRD Network Madras, September 1987, Published by Rawat Publications, Jaipur; pages 399–405

    The article examines the structuring of the HRD function in Indian companies. Data was collected about the HRD departments of 29 organizations of Bombay and Delhi. The analysis was done through a qualitative assessment of the data coupled with simple quantitative analysis. The article looks at three aspects – trend towards setting up HRD as a separate function, structural linkages between HRD and the organization and the mechanisms of HRD systems.

    - JGJ

    Critical words: HRD Systems; Structural Linkage; HRD mechanisms

1989 Conference Papers

Abstracts of papers from the book
Nair M.R.R. (editor), Towards Organizational Effectiveness Through HRD, Unedited Papers presented at the 3rd National Conference of the National HRD Network, New Delhi, February 1989, Published by National HRD Network, Jamshedpur

(Reference: Nair, 1989)

1. Naidu M.R., Developing an Appropriate Ethos through Organization Development – A Case Study from the Public Sector in: Nair M.R.R. (editor), Towards Organizational Effectiveness Through HRD, Unedited Papers presented at the 3rd National Conference of the National HRD Network, New Delhi, February 1989, Published by National HRD Network, Jamshedpur, pages 1–6

    A company's shared values and beliefs that drive the way an organization competes, produces and manages are becoming a critical factor in deciding the work ethos of a company. The astonishing success of Japan led many to study the processes employed in Japanese companies and it was found that the various processes employed therein revolved around the Japanese value system. Their corporate value were in sync with the values of the employees thus giving them a sense of belonging and identity to the employees thereby leading to more commitment to work. Indian management has failed in productivity because the corporate values have been imported and hence are not based on the value systems of the employees. Again, because of the many different value systems in the country, it is difficult to have one specific OD intervention that can take care of the differences. In this context, the author cites an OD intervention in HMT which led to the employees' belief in excellence as a value.

- JGJ, TVRLS

Critical Words: Excellence, Japanese systems, Value Systems, Shared Values, HMT, Behavioural Interventions, Organizational Development, OD

2. Aculturisation – An Initiative in Inducting Trainees in: Nair M.R.R. (editor), Towards Organizational Effectiveness Through HRD, Unedited Papers presented at the 3rd National Conference of the National HRD Network, New Delhi, February 1989, Published by National HRD Network, Jamshedpur, pages 6–17
The conventional induction consisted of communicating information about the company and the expectations of the company from the trainee making the entire process passive. This leads to the deterioration of the entrants' corporate citizenship behaviour and does not help in building the psychological contract between the employee and the employer. The article illustrates the changed induction practices, in the light of the above, at Sundaram Calyton Limited. The company conducted an aculturisation workshop for the newly inducted MBA trainees where they were asked to discuss the any issue or concern related to organisational culture or reality. This led to the trainees feeling that the company had gone out of its way to make them feel comfortable and they felt cared for and protected. When exit interviews were conducted of those who left the organization, the reasons lay with the placement in non-preferred function rather than any conflict with policies of the organizations.

- JGJ, TVRLS

Critical Words: Corporate Citizenship, Psychological Contract, Sundaram Clayton, TVS, Organizational Culture, Induction, Aculturisation

3. Mathur Ajeet N., Human Response Development in India By Whom, For Whom in: Nair M.R.R. (editor), Towards Organizational Effectiveness Through HRD, Unedited Papers presented at the 3rd National Conference of the National HRD Network, New Delhi, February 1989, Published by National HRD Network, Jamshedpur, pages 18–25

   There is a lot of hype about the HRD interventions and their benefits without understanding that for a successful system to work, it requires continuous re-appraisal of the assumptions surrounding the existence and growth of organizations. Apart from the differences in the nature of organizations in different regions/industries/services segments, there are fundamental differences in the assumptions made about role holders between government and private sector organizations. The author discusses the implications of de-institutionalising. In this context, the author illustrates the experience of role identification exercise in STP Limited carried by active participation by the Chief Executive. The problem was that no one staked or claimed ownership of the workplace and therefore involvement or ownership was missing. The exercise ended in identifying a central task for the organisation which was broken down department wise. The author concludes by stating HRD practices have to be examined if mutuality in processes cannot be established or assumed.

   - JGJ, TVRLS

   Critical Words: Mutuality, HRD, STP Limited

4. Dixit Anil, Organisational Renewal through HRD Efforts – The BILT Experience in: Nair M.R.R. (editor), Towards Organizational Effectiveness Through HRD, Unedited Papers presented at the 3rd National Conference of the National HRD Network, New Delhi, February 1989, Published by National HRD Network, Jamshedpur, pages 26–40

   This article is a documentation of our efforts towards transforming the organization that BILT was to an Institution – the processes, the method, the achievements, the failures, the realities and the concerns experienced by the various stakeholders. The company constituted a Strategic Planning Group was constituted to study and recommend improvements in the working of the company. The group submitted recommendations in the area of Personnel, Industrial Relations and HRD. A step by step approach was conceived to change the climate at the company. Some hurdles were felt along the way such as employee perceptions, concerns of the employees, communication distortions and the organizational culture. The process is illustrated by the author through the example of the Performance Appraisal System at the company.

- JGJ, TVRLS

Critical Words: BILT, Ballarpur Industries Limited, Performance Appraisal, Organizational Change

5. Nair R.R., Developing an Appropriate Work Ethos – an Indian Experience in: Nair M.R.R. (editor), Towards Organizational Effectiveness Through HRD, Unedited Papers presented at the 3rd National Conference of the National HRD Network, New Delhi, February 1989, Published by National HRD Network, Jamshedpur, pages 41–50

The article addresses few questions in the context of the physical and cultural environment such as the living nature of an organization employing living human beings, the paradox of a bureaucracy mastering the individual thereby fuelling him to achieve technological brilliance and innovation and lastly, whether HRD practices, promotes or hinders organizational building process and if so, what is the impact on the climate of the organization. The author tries to address these questions by presenting and analysing a case from the largest selling branch of a large company. The author analyses this through the paradigms of climate of a company, self-worth and dignity of individuals, recognition, participative problem solving, leadership and effectiveness. The author concludes that long term measures for the development of employees are called for in companies, yet, companies often focus on the short term rather than long term. This is a thinking point for all HRD professionals.

- JGJ, TVRLS

Critical Words: Organizational Environment

6. Aga Anu & Kumar P.M., Creating an Organization Climate – Thermax Experience – An HR Perspective in: Nair M.R.R. (editor), Towards Organizational Effectiveness Through HRD, Unedited Papers presented at the 3rd National Conference of the National HRD Network, New Delhi, February 1989, Published by National HRD Network, Jamshedpur, pages 51–63

   The article attempts to share experiences of creating and maintaining an organization culture that nurtures enterprise, integrity, professional competence and collective endeavour at Thermax Limited. The company focused on individual, team and organizational processes. The HR department faced a challenge in respecting and nurturing different leadership and managerial styles in different divisions and yet, retain corporate values. Therefore, the stance of HR was changed to that of playing as an advocate for the employees, counselling and acting as the devil's advocate for the manager and acting as facilitators for new processes. The authors also list dilemmas faced by the department in this process of change and the failures faced.

   - JGJ, TVRLS

   Critical Words: Thermax Limited, Organizational Change, Organizational Climate

7. Roy S.K., Institution Building through Breathing Life into HRD Processes in: Nair M.R.R. (editor), Towards Organizational Effectiveness Through HRD, Unedited Papers presented at the 3rd National Conference of the National HRD Network, New Delhi, February 1989, Published by National HRD Network, Jamshedpur, pages 64–81

   The author states that the article has evolved out of exploring the possible existential human acts that would be in consonance with the emergence of the phenomenon of an Institution. The author contends that a truly effective organization is an Institution, that an unexceptional and fundamental feature of organizational effectiveness is that it is profitable and that there is a direct relation between the first two contentions. The author has made a number of strategies to address these contentions and these are given in the appendix to the article. The author has also discussed certain issues that surfaced while implementing those strategies principally falling in the realm of facilitating movement from past to present, struggle of unionised employees in harmonising their identity with the changed reality and the need for clarifying roles.

- JGJ, TVRLS

Critical Words: Organizational Effectiveness, Institution Building

8. Rao Kantha V.N., Vijai Electricals – Dimensions of Culture: Its Relevance for Designing HRD Interventions – A Groundwork for the Future of Organisation in: Nair M.R.R. (editor), Towards Organizational Effectiveness Through HRD, Unedited Papers presented at the 3rd National Conference of the National HRD Network, New Delhi, February 1989, Published by National HRD Network, Jamshedpur, pages 82–100

As the stated company grew, the importance of developing and harnessing the potential of Human Resources was increasingly realized. This article is an account of organizational culture and its implication on the process variables of the organization. The paper examines the dysfunctional cultural dimensions of the Organisation and the prospects for HRD interventions. The author stresses that this article has been written from the point of view of an organization that is yet to implement HRD processes. The author has broken down the stages of growth of the organization and interpreted the culture in those stages. To start with, the company did a climate survey. Based on the climate survey, issues have been identified and presented in the article.

- JGJ, TVRLS

Critical Words: Vijay Electricals, Vijai Electricals, HRD Processes, XLRI, Organizational Culture, Individualism, Collectivism, Power Distance

9. Gupta R.R., Authentic Opportunism: A Liberating Strategy for Initiating In-House Organization Development in: Nair M.R.R. (editor), Towards Organizational Effectiveness Through HRD, Unedited Papers presented at the 3rd National Conference of the National HRD Network, New Delhi, February 1989, Published by National HRD Network, Jamshedpur, pages 101–109

Many practitioners of OD have emphasised top-down and organization wide approach of doing organization development. While this may be a workable approach for external consultants, this strategy may turn out to be too constraining for an in-house agent. In this article, the author delineates the philosophy, rationale and operationalization of the strategy which, according to the author, liberates the in-house practitioner from unnecessary structural assumptions of conventional OD. This strategy is called authentic opportunism. The author stresses the need to look at middle and lower management as "mini-Chief Executives" in charge of their own domains, thus increasing the number of clients from one to scores of managers in an organization. The author states that it would be valid to do OD in any part of the organization after fulfilment of certain basic pre-requisites. However, the author cautions that authentic opportunism is riskier than the standard top-down approach and hence due diligence should be exercised.

- JGJ, TVRLS

Critical Words: Organizational Development, Authentic Opportunism

10. Ramanthan S., Organisation Effectiveness through Human Resources Development in: Nair M.R.R. (editor), Towards Organizational Effectiveness Through HRD, Unedited Papers presented at the 3rd National Conference of the National HRD Network, New Delhi, February 1989, Published by National HRD Network, Jamshedpur, pages 110–122

In this article, the author makes a brief review about the HRD efforts made in the Oil and Natural Gas Commission (ONGC) with reference to how these efforts have helped in achievement of corporate objectives, in facilitating technology upgradation, in bringing about attitudinal and cultural changes, in responding to the changing profile of employees and what has been the role of the top, middle and line management in the success of these efforts. HRD interventions in ONGC took place in the areas of mission and vision clarity, information management, research and development, manpower planning and development and personnel information systems. These interventions have been explained in detail by the author followed by an enumerated conclusion where the author lists out the needs for studies or steps in certain key areas.

- JGJ, TVRLS

Critical Words: ONGC, HRD Interventions

11. Khanna Shashi, Bringing about Attitudinal Change in Organizations – An Indian Experience in: Nair M.R.R. (editor), Towards Organizational Effectiveness Through HRD, Unedited Papers presented at the 3rd National Conference of the National HRD Network, New Delhi, February 1989, Published by National HRD Network, Jamshedpur, pages 123–134

    One of the major issues that has been of concern of Indian organizations is finding out a way to motivate people and develop an appropriate work ethos. Due to the number of changes in the business environment, organizations are searching for ways to tackle these challenges dynamically. It is found, increasingly, that the attitude of the workforce is a big hurdle in the way of tackling those challenges. The author's company specialises in mass-training concentrated on bringing about a change in attitudes throughout the organisation level. The author states that though it may not be possible to change the basic attitudes of personnel, it is possible to bring about a change in group attitudes. The author illustrates this through the case study of Bharat Gears Limited. Based on this experience, the author concludes that a holistic approach is required if management training is to have any impact on an organisation. Secondly, the Chief Executive of the organisation has to be deeply involved in the process and work towards removing inconsistencies in communications about the initiatives. However, the new behaviour patterns will take time to establish themselves and need to be nurtured carefully in the initial phases.

    - JGJ, TVRLS

    Critical Words: HRD Interventions, Training, Bharat Gears Limited, Group Attitudes, Individual Attitudes, Attitudinal Change

12. Vidyasagar R., Communication in Business Organization in India in: Nair M.R.R. (editor), Towards Organizational Effectiveness Through HRD, Unedited Papers presented at the 3rd National Conference of the National HRD Network, New Delhi, February 1989, Published by National HRD Network, Jamshedpur, pages 135–151

    Communication is very important in the organizational context. However, it is increasingly found that communication at the macro-level gets mixed up with a number of micro-issues thereby becoming garbled when it is received at the other end of the chain. The author therefore takes a look at the meta-issues of communication in industrial settings in this country. Many large organizations do not address the task of teaching communication skills to the employees who may have speak different languages. This can have many negative implications for organizations if flash-points are not handled properly. The author has stressed the importance of messages, values and beliefs that are coded into systems, structures and processes in order to deal with the unintended consequences of mixed messages and double-binds.

- JGJ, TVRLS

Critical Words: Communication

13. Sampath J.M., Improving Work Ethos Through Value Education in: Nair M.R.R. (editor), <u>Towards Organizational Effectiveness Through HRD</u>, Unedited Papers presented at the 3rd National Conference of the National HRD Network, New Delhi, February 1989, Published by National HRD Network, Jamshedpur, pages 152–163

All HRD efforts are directed towards improving work ethos in an organization. However, most interventions address only the symptoms such as low morale and motivation, but do not address the root cause of these symptoms. At the root of most of these issues, is more often than not, a decline in personal values, a lack of awareness of work ethos which directly brings about a deterioration of work ethos at work. Therefore, there is a need for a rational approach towards improving work ethos through the inculcation of a value system in tomorrow's work-force so that so the future professional values are begun with an ingrained sense of values. To this extent, the author has designed a game for youngsters above the age of 14 which seeks to inculcate the values and work ethos through the medium of the game of snake and ladders and parables. The game is aptly called "Discovery".

- JGJ, TVRLS

Critical Words: Discovery, Games, Work Ethos, Value Systems

14. Khandelwal Gopal, Changing Profile of Young Professionals and Organizational Responses in Managing Them in: Nair M.R.R. (editor), <u>Towards Organizational Effectiveness Through HRD</u>,

Unedited Papers presented at the 3rd National Conference of the National HRD Network, New Delhi, February 1989, Published by National HRD Network, Jamshedpur, pages 164–182

This article is based on the consulting and training experience of the author related to in-company development programmes. The author observed that young professionals were different from the exiting group of employees, most of them were confronted with similar issues regarding changes in personal identities and these issues received only a peripheral/accidental attention. The author has elaborated on these observations along with a critical summary of the existing practices. Based on these, the author comes up with an alternative strategy

- JGJ, TVRLS

Critical Words: HRD Strategy

15. Abrol Sunil, HRD at C-DOT in: Nair M.R.R. (editor), Towards Organizational Effectiveness Through HRD, Unedited Papers presented at the 3rd National Conference of the National HRD Network, New Delhi, February 1989, Published by National HRD Network, Jamshedpur, pages 183–193

    This article is a documentation of the efforts of HRD at C-DOT to recruit and develop young employees. The HRD Group was responsible for their orientation, training, facilities, work environment and well-being. Being a new organization, the department also formulated new policies and introduced them in all areas. Rules were made to encourage efficiency, creativity, innovation and initiative. The author has delineated the systems outlined in the areas of people sensitivity, time and target sensitivity, flexibility and procedures, effective communication and office automation.

    - JGJ, TVRLS

    Critical Words: HRD System, C-DOT, Setting up Systems

16. Avadhani M.H., Institution Building – IFFCO's Experience in: Nair M.R.R. (editor), Towards Organizational Effectiveness Through HRD, Unedited Papers presented at the 3rd National Conference of the National HRD Network, New Delhi, February 1989, Published by National HRD Network, Jamshedpur, pages 194–210

In this article, the author has outlined steps taken to institute a culture of excellence at IFFCO. With the kind of high rate of growth envisaged by the company, a need to tone up the internal environment was felt to achieve the goals set by the top management. In this context, it was imperative to develop a culture of excellence in our Institution. A programme was therefore introduced with the objective of ensuring continued dynamism, developing adaptive and self-renewing capabilities and developing a wholesome institutional culture to achieve the well-being of the institution and its members. The company realised as a result of this programme that an impetus was required in HRD functions and that there was a lack of effectiveness in the existing performance appraisal system. Based on this feedback, the company has developed a future course of action.

- JGJ, TVRLS

Critical Words: IFFCO, Institution Building,

17. Reddy C.M., Reminiscences of a Change Agent in: Nair M.R.R. (editor), Towards Organizational Effectiveness Through HRD, Unedited Papers presented at the 3rd National Conference of the National HRD Network, New Delhi, February 1989, Published by National HRD Network, Jamshedpur, pages 211–225
This article is an attempt by the author to describe the struggles, feelings and learnings from attempts to play the role of a change agent over a period of 3 years in IFFCO. The author hopes that this article may help those who are attempting to be change agents and for those who wish to impart those skills. The author primarily describes the Institution Building exercise carried out by the company. As a direct result of that exercise, a HRD department was set up and a committee set up to spell out the HR philosophy. The author has also reflected deeply on the changes in attitude and personality caused by interaction with other employees and peers. As a conclusion, the author outlines the personal learnings from the entire exercise.

- JGJ, TVRLS

Critical Words: Institutional Building, Self-Reflection, Change Agent

18. Balchandran S., HRD in the L.I.C. in: Nair M.R.R. (editor), Towards Organizational Effectiveness Through HRD, Unedited

Papers presented at the 3rd National Conference of the National HRD Network, New Delhi, February 1989, Published by National HRD Network, Jamshedpur, pages 226–235

This paper is an account of a major restructuring exercise carried out in LIC with the help of an external consultant. This exercise came out due to a need felt to develop strategies that would meet the needs for learning, development, mastery, belonging variety and creativity during task performance as well as possibilities for more individual influence over work arrangements through less restrictive decision rules. The company decided on certain objectives for all its employees and also decided goals therein. Based on these, strategies were developed and a requirement of a comprehensive HRD approach was felt. Interventions were started by way of seminars where zonal officers and association leaders were briefed about the proposed interventions and methodology. The author concludes by taking stock of the situation at the time of writing the article.

- JGJ, TVRLS

Critical Words: Institution Building

19. Dayal Ishwar, HRD in Indian Organizations – Some Approaches in: Nair M.R.R. (editor), Towards Organizational Effectiveness Through HRD, Unedited Papers presented at the 3rd National Conference of the National HRD Network, New Delhi, February 1989, Published by National HRD Network, Jamshedpur, pages 236–249

    This article surveys the HRD approaches in India to draw out the important aspects of these programmes and to highlight the difference between HRD and Manpower Development programmes covered by personnel departments in organizations. The author compares the three models of HRD being followed in the country and critically analyses each of them. The author concludes by stating that the difficulty in HRD is of translating the idea into a concrete plan of action and for this, serious study and a great deal of experimentation is required to evolve an appropriate strategy for action.

    - JGJ, TVRLS

    Critical Words: HRD Approaches, Paternalistic Approach, Reciprocal Approach, Selective Approach

20. Pandhe M.K., Human Resource Development – A Social Approach in: Nair M.R.R. (editor), Towards Organizational Effectiveness Through HRD, Unedited Papers presented at the 3rd National Conference of the National HRD Network, New Delhi, February 1989, Published by National HRD Network, Jamshedpur, pages 253–265

    In this article, the author passionately argues against two issues – discrimination against women workers and the practice of child labour. The question of discrimination against women workers practised in our society is resulting in non-utilisation of a big chunk of labour power for economic development of the country. The author laments that policy framers are now thinking there is too much education deluded by the high number of educated unemployed. The author asserts that true HRD can be achieved only if the needs of the destitute children are taken into account as the success of any such program depends on how we have been able to give succour to the underprivileged children. The author also dwells on the aspects of wastage of human resources, the social aspects of technological change, vocational training and the need for training within the industry.

    - JGJ, TVRLS

    Critical Words: HRD in India, ILO, Child Labour, Women Discrimination, Training, Vocational Training, Wastage of Human Resources

21. Diwadkar A.B., HRD for Workmen in: Nair M.R.R. (editor), Towards Organizational Effectiveness Through HRD, Unedited Papers presented at the 3rd National Conference of the National HRD Network, New Delhi, February 1989, Published by National HRD Network, Jamshedpur, pages 266–274

    There has been an advent of various HRD interventions in many companies. However, most of these interventions have happened at the level of the managers. The author cites an illustration of HRD interventions at the worker level by writing out his experience at an Indian arm of a multinational company. The objectives of these interventions were to create a climate of chanfe, improve trust levels between the management and the workmen, improve team spirit and management staff morale and ultimately improve productivity at all levels. Interventions to this extent were made at the management, union and workman level.

- JGJ, TVRLS

Critical Words: HRD for Workers

22. Mehta Kandarp, Empowering the Powerless through Behavioural Sciences Intervention: An Experiment in the Field of Industrial Relations in: Nair M.R.R. (editor), Towards Organizational Effectiveness Through HRD, Unedited Papers presented at the 3rd National Conference of the National HRD Network, New Delhi, February 1989, Published by National HRD Network, Jamshedpur, pages 275–283
The author believes that there is a certain assumption that behavioural interventions are not applicable in Industrial Relations. Any intervention in this field devoid of the totality of perspective framework and problems ends up dealing with only parts of the problem. There is a lack of acceptance that various functions are actually inter-related and thereby inter-dependant and that this relationship has elements of conflict embedded in it. The author made an attempt at testing and translating these beliefs into practice at an organisational level within a period of 5 years. These led to the acceptance that the assumptions were flawed and to highlight and reinforce this learning, a number of workshops were held at the company.

- JGJ, TVRLS

Critical Words: Industrial Relations, Behavioural Interventions

23. Rangarajan T.S., HRD in Public Sector : A Union View in: Nair M.R.R. (editor), Towards Organizational Effectiveness Through HRD, Unedited Papers presented at the 3rd National Conference of the National HRD Network, New Delhi, February 1989, Published by National HRD Network, Jamshedpur, pages 284–289
In this article, the author writes about the experience of implementing HRD for workers at Indian Oil. The author states that the recent thrust on HRD is a reiteration of the commitment of Public Sector for the development of a growth oriented economy. By virtue of being a young country, the systems and procedures are still in the throes of development. Due to this, unions find themselves confronted with the democratic and socialistic aspirations of its members on one hand

while facing a facing a bureaucratic and process oriented- culture on the other side. The author stresses that trade unions in Indian Oil have committed themselves entirely to the HRD philosophy and is confident that the interventions will bear fruit.

- JGJ, TVRLS

Critical Words: Trade Unions, Indian Oil, HRD for Workers

24. Rao S.S. & Sarathu Parth, Human Resource Development for Non-Supervisory Staff in BHEL in: Nair M.R.R. (editor), Towards Organizational Effectiveness Through HRD, Unedited Papers presented at the 3rd National Conference of the National HRD Network, New Delhi, February 1989, *In this article, the author has described the various HRD interventions at BHEL which are aimed at workers. The author stresses that even when the interventions are made at the executive and top management level, the effect of these interventions on the workers is taken care of. Efforts based on HRD approach are basically in the areas of Job Design, Productivity movement, Quality Circles, employee participation in schemes, organizational development and absenteeism control. Each of these efforts are described in detail in the article. The author concludes that due to taking care of the worker at each level, the workforce of the company has been very loyal and hardworking and the labour environment in the company remains one of peace and quiet compared to the turbulence experienced elsewhere.*

- JGJ, TVRLS

Critical Words: Labour Relations, HRD for Workers

25. Kapse P.K. & Arora A.K., HRD for Workmen at Eicher Motors – An Experience in: Nair M.R.R. (editor), Towards Organizational Effectiveness Through HRD, Unedited Papers presented at the 3rd National Conference of the National HRD Network, New Delhi, February 1989, Published by National HRD Network, Jamshedpur, pages 307–325

In this article, the authors tries to share the experiences in trying to build a new work culture at the company's plant. Due to capital rationing by the RBI, the tractor operations of the company were impacted which impacted the morale of the employees. A survey was conducted to take stock of the situation and the results led to a review of the HR and IR policies of the company. The review led to interventions in the area of training, employee participation, performance appraisal and potential appraisal, collective bargaining and compensation policies. In conclusion, the authors note the future challenges the company faces in the successful implementation of the identified interventions.

- JGJ, TVRLS

Critical Words: Eicher, HRD Interventions, Performance Appraisal, Potential Appraisal, Training, Compensation, Data Analysis

26. Narasimhan K., HRD to Match Technology Progress – Efforts at HAL, Hyderabad Division in: Nair M.R.R. (editor), Towards Organizational Effectiveness Through HRD, Unedited Papers presented at the 3rd National Conference of the National HRD Network, New Delhi, February 1989, Published by National HRD Network, Jamshedpur, pages 329–338

    In this article, the author brings out some strategies and approaches made by the Divisional Management at HAL, Hyderabad to tackle some unique problems faced by the unit due to fast changing technology and large product range. The problems were identified in the area of reskilling skill development and knowledge management. Various steps were taken by the management to address these concerns. Broadly, the steps taken were in the areas of change of trade retraining and subsequent redeployment, conversion of unskilled operators to skilled operators, refresher training to update the skills and knowledge, development of employees on the shop-floor and consolidation of industrial relations. The author states that these interventions and a few others (not mentioned in the article) have resulted in the unit having an employee culture where they are poised to take up new challenges and technologies in the field of avionics.

    - JGJ, TVRLS

    Critical Words: HAL, HRD Interventions, Skill Development

27. Sinha Rajan, HRD in a Sick Public Sector Unit – Bouquets and Brickbats in: Nair M.R.R. (editor), Towards Organizational Effectiveness Through HRD, Unedited Papers presented at the 3rd National Conference of the National HRD Network, New Delhi, February 1989, Published by National HRD Network, Jamshedpur, pages 339–348

In this article, the author has tried to show how lack of top management support can dissipate the benefits gleaned from HRD interventions. The company – Scooters India Limited – suffered from a number of poor decisions right from the genesis of the company and is now resigned to being a loss making company. The author has explained each step followed in designing of the HRD policy of the company beginning from identifying the vision and mission of the company to the various interventions made to empower and develop the employees. The author rues that lack of commitment from the top management and from the Government led to the interventions losing steam and these came to an abrupt end after some time. The author stresses that in a situation where the CEO does not without having adequate power to push through the needed reforms only makes the situation irretrievable.

- JGJ, TVRLS

Critical Words: Scooters India Limited, HRD Interventions

28. Advani H.B., HRD Intervention at Blue Star Ltd. in: Nair M.R.R. (editor), Towards Organizational Effectiveness Through HRD, Unedited Papers presented at the 3rd National Conference of the National HRD Network, New Delhi, February 1989, Published by National HRD Network, Jamshedpur, pages 349–361

The changed economic conditions led to increased competition in the market and this led Blue Star to change their attitudes towards the customers. This entailed the need for HRD intervention that would lead to a change in attitude towards the internal and external customers. As a first step, the company carried out a SWOT analysis to understand the problems in the various departments, took the help of consultants to get a deeper insight and set up Task Forces at the Corporate Level to work out objectives and action plans for the identified problems. The author does admit that implementation of the plans has been uneven and rife with opposition from unions and some sections of the management. Yet, the author is confident that the company is moving in the right direction and that the company will overcome the temporary hurdles and reach the take-off point.

- JGJ, TVRLS

Critical Words: Blue Star, HRD Interventions

29. Chandiramani B.K. & Malhan N.K., HRD: Modi Xerox Experience in: Nair M.R.R. (editor), Towards Organizational Effectiveness Through HRD, Unedited Papers presented at the 3rd National Conference of the National HRD Network, New Delhi, February 1989, Published by National HRD Network, Jamshedpur, pages 362–380

    In this article, the authors have explained the HRD policy and the stages of growth in the policy of Modi Xerox Limited. The approach of the HRD policy has been in proactive and responsive approach, training extended into the field and beyond the classroom, encouraging the role of line managers in taking care of the developmental needs of the subordinates and creating an environment of creativity and excellence. The early phase of implementation of HRD saw identification of organizational and HRD needs while in the second phase these changed to take care of the increased number of employees and the changed profile of the company. At the time of writing the article, the company is in the process of introducing the concept of Total Quality. The article is concluded by the author taking stock of the future needs of the company.

    - JGJ, TVRLS

    Critical Words: Modi Xerox, HRD Interventions, HRD Systems, Total Quality

30. Nandy S.K., Effective Utilisation of Resources : A Burning Issue in: Nair M.R.R. (editor), Towards Organizational Effectiveness Through HRD, Unedited Papers presented at the 3rd National Conference of the National HRD Network, New Delhi, February 1989, Published by National HRD Network, Jamshedpur, pages 381–392

    HRD plays an important role in the current scenario of the Indian Industry especially at a time when there seems to be a big recession across all product lines. A close look into the depression has revealed that two major areas have to be nurtured well – one relates to the effectiveness of human resources and the other relates to the cutting of overhead costs. In this article, the author has analysed how GKW has gone about reducing the costs at various overheads as well as increasing the effectiveness of the human resources at the company.

    - JGJ, TVRLS

Critical Words: GKW, Cost Cutting, Effectiveness of Human Resources

31. Gupta Anil, Turnaround and Transition in Manufacturing – Proctor and Gamble India Limited in: Nair M.R.R. (editor), Towards Organizational Effectiveness Through HRD, Unedited Papers presented at the 3rd National Conference of the National HRD Network, New Delhi, February 1989, Published by National HRD Network, Jamshedpur, pages 393–407

This article is a case history of a series of interventions in the Kalwe manufacturing plant of Proctor and Gamble India Limited. Developments in the market as well as some of the failures of the management at the plant led to the questioning of the viability of operating the plant. The top management decided to diagnose the factors at play and attempt to make the plant cost competitive. The strategy was to help the employees acquire information, skills and communication through involvement. To this extent, specific interventions were made in the areas of communication and information sharing, result orientation of the staff, training and manufacturing systems improvement. Based on the result and the lessons from these interventions, additional interventions were planned to get the employees to a stage where results are consistently achieved and people find a sense of fulfilment in their work.

- JGJ, TVRLS

Critical Words: Proctor & Gamble India Limited, HRD Interventions, Communication, Information sharing, Training, High Commitment Work Systems, Total Quality

32. in: Nair M.R.R. (editor), Towards Organizational Effectiveness Through HRD, Unedited Papers presented at the 3rd National Conference of the National HRD Network, New Delhi, February 1989, Published by National HRD Network, Jamshedpur, pages 408–445

Turnaround management dynamics will be of great use to the country in understanding why companies fall sick and how these can be prevented. The management of turnaround has many players and involves action at multiple levels. The author focuses attention on how the management can revive a sick organization. The author stresses on the humane type of turnaround which features fewer loss of jobs and lesser turnaround time compared to the surgical method applied elsewhere. The author has discussed the mechanics and elements of turnaround management. The author concludes the article by holding forth on the requirement of teaching the basics of turnaround management in management schools in addition to the existing curricula of professional management.

- JGJ, TVRLS

Critical Words: Turnaround Management, Surgical Turnaround, Humane Turnaround

33. Nair M.R.R. & Ramakrishna S.R., The Turnaround in Steel Authority of India Limited : The HRD Strategy in: Nair M.R.R. (editor), Towards Organizational Effectiveness Through HRD, Unedited Papers presented at the 3rd National Conference of the National HRD Network, New Delhi, February 1989, Published by National HRD Network, Jamshedpur, pages 446–465
In this article, the authors explain the HRD interventions in the turnaround process attempted at SAIL. In the beginning, the company conducted a number of interactions between its employees to identify the causes of decline and the results of these interactions were summarised into Priorities for Action. HRD strategies and implementations were chalked out and implemented in the areas of corporate planning, manpower planning, and utilization of existing human resources, communication, team building, motivation, training and development. The authors have also looked into the aspects of resistance faced during the implementation and the future plans of the company.

- JGJ, TVRLS

Critical Words: SAIL, HRD Interventions, Turnaround Management

34. Ghandy, Sarosh J., Remaining Competitive through Human Resource Development (The Telco Case) in: Nair M.R.R. (editor), Towards Organizational Effectiveness Through HRD, Unedited Papers presented at the 3rd National Conference of the National HRD Network, New Delhi, February 1989, Published by National HRD Network, Jamshedpur, pages 466–476
In this article, the author outlines the training programmes at TELCO. The initial training programmes were found insufficient

in gearing the company to the competitive scenario in the industry. It was also found that there was a certain amount of dissonance among the workers regarding the benefits of the existing training programme. The training programme was customised to include short modular skill enhancement courses which would add to the existing repertoire of skills of the workers. Other arrangements were made for the employees to take up higher education by availing degrees and diplomas and to promote training as a gateway to promotion through selection tests. Training for the managerial staff included blanket training on common topics for all with elements of personalized training customised to each manager for complete development. The author applauds the supportive role played by the trade unions in the entire process.

- JGJ, TVRLS

Critical Words: Training, HRD for Workers, TELCO

35. Athreya M.B., Human Resource Development in Government in: Nair M.R.R. (editor), Towards Organizational Effectiveness Through HRD, Unedited Papers presented at the 3rd National Conference of the National HRD Network, New Delhi, February 1989, Published by National HRD Network, Jamshedpur, pages 479–503

The term "HRD in Government" has two dimensions to it - HRD for the government workers in the various departments and the role of the government in HRD for the country. The scope of the latter dwarfs the former in its scale. Yet, it has now dawned that societal HRD would be ineffective until the administrative machinery itself is made more effective through HRD. The author discusses the efforts at implementing HRD at the central and state level government officers. Thereafter the author discusses the ways by which the government can act as a change event for HRD to the people. In this article, the author has looked at the three dimensions of HRD in Administration, for the people and at the societal level.

- JGJ, TVRLS

Critical Words: HRD in Government

36. Vittal N., Human Resources Development in Government in: Nair M.R.R. (editor), Towards Organizational Effectiveness Through HRD, Unedited Papers presented at the 3rd National

Conference of the National HRD Network, New Delhi, February 1989, Published by National HRD Network, Jamshedpur, pages 504–515

In this article, the author has recounted the experiences and ideas the author had as part of the Indian Administrative Services (IAS) and having worked at the state and central level in different ministries. The author states that there are mainly four factors working against HRD in the Government sector. These are red tapism, financial constraints, lack of skill development and adequate training and a culture where positive feedback is hardly given to an employee. The author goes on to deliberate on some of the techniques that were used to combat these negative forces. The author concludes that it is important to pay attention to the creative potential of the people around, it is also equally necessary that we keep abreast of the latest developments in the field.

- JGJ, TVRLS

Critical Words: IAS, HRD for Government, Questionnaire, Delegation, Job Rotation

37. Pestonjee D.M., Role Stress in Government Administration : Suggested HRD Interventions in: Nair M.R.R. (editor), Towards Organizational Effectiveness Through HRD, Unedited Papers presented at the 3rd National Conference of the National HRD Network, New Delhi, February 1989, Published by National HRD Network, Jamshedpur, pages 516–524

In any organization, one of the major areas for HRD interventions is stress in roles. The author has delineated ten dimensions of organizational stress. To analyse the role of stress in government organizations, data was collected from IAS officers and analysed. On the basis of the analysis, the author recommends certain HRD interventions for reducing stress among IAS officers such as role clarity exercises, better performance appraisal systems, a need to formulate training and developmental needs based on the needs of the personnel. The author also recommends that a module on stress management may be added as part of the training of the officers.

- JGJ, TVRLS

Critical Words: IAS, HRD for Government

38. Joseph K.K., Towards Organisational Effectiveness through Human Resources Development in: Nair M.R.R. (editor), Towards Organizational Effectiveness Through HRD, Unedited Papers presented at the 3rd National Conference of the National HRD Network, New Delhi, February 1989, Published by National HRD Network, Jamshedpur, pages 525–530
The company, Bongaigaon Refinery and Petrochemicals Ltd. (BRPL), being located in a backward area faced a lot of problems in recruitment of skilled manpower. Hence, they resorted to recruiting fresh hands in various disciplines and then training them. However, it was felt that the training department was insufficient to cater to the requirement especially at the stage when the company was growing in scale. The company had an external consultant analyse the situation and make recommendations based on analysis of the process engineering, man-power and skill inventory, key performance areas, attitudinal process and anticipated change analysis. Based on the results, the key findings were summarised into a few priorities and these were then formulated into the action plans. The action plans included establishing HRD Department, establishing a full-fledged training centres with the necessary facilities and development of training modules for staff.
- JGJ, TVRLS

Critical Words: Training, BRPL

39. Bami P.S., Human resources Development – NTPC's Experience in: Nair M.R.R. (editor), Towards Organizational Effectiveness Through HRD, Unedited Papers presented at the 3rd National Conference of the National HRD Network, New Delhi, February 1989, Published by National HRD Network, Jamshedpur, pages 531–544
In this article, the author has outlined the experience of NTPC. The development of the human resources has been among the priorities of the company from its very inception. The author states that this has led to the company becoming one of the top performing Public Sector Company in the country with a string of achievements to its credit. The author explains the various components of HRD in NTPC such as Organisation Design, Planning, Training and Development, Performance Appraisal, etc. The author states that HRD has always

been an effective backdrop of the company's corporate philosophy in various process, whether explicit or otherwise.

- JGJ, TVRLS

Critical Words: NTPC, HRD Interventions, Organization Design, Human Resource Planning, Training and Development, Performance Appraisal, Potential Appraisal, Job Design, Reward Systems, Industrial Relations, Participative Culture, Information Systems

40. Chadrasekhar S., Design and Implementation of Need Based Reward System in: Nair M.R.R. (editor), Towards Organizational Effectiveness Through HRD, Unedited Papers presented at the 3rd National Conference of the National HRD Network, New Delhi, February 1989, Published by National HRD Network, Jamshedpur, pages 545–554

    The article documents the design and implementation of new reward systems at the Construction Group of Larsen &Tourbo. An analysis of the organization threw up the need of developing an Appraisal System with a linkage to reward based on fair assessment of performance and least degree of subjectivity. The task force identified for the exercise reviewed the existing performance appraisal system, drew up the weaknesses, identified the elements of a desirable system and came up with some recommendations. The task force suggested improvements in range and choice of rewards, need of recognising and promoting extra-ordinary performance and need of consistency in giving out rewards.

    - JGJ, TVRLS

    Critical Words: Performance Appraisal System, Reward System, Larsen & Tourbo

41. Padaki Rupande& Padaki Vijay, Towards Effective Organizational Diagnosis in: Nair M.R.R. (editor), Towards Organizational Effectiveness Through HRD, Unedited Papers presented at the 3rd National Conference of the National HRD Network, New Delhi, February 1989, Published by National HRD Network, Jamshedpur, pages 555–564

    In this article, the author tries to understand whether it is within the jurisdiction of HRD to identify organizational conditions that require intervention and if yes, does the human resource function]on have the sufficient base to be able to predict change in human behaviour from changes in organizational conditions. The author argues that both the questions can be answered in the affirmative. Further, the author makes a case that the HRD function should look increasingly towards requirements of interventions in organizational factors. As per the findings of the research conducted by the author, there is a direct correlation between the prevailing climate in an organization and a standardized measure of operational efficiency. This is consistent across industries, sectors and sizes of industries. The author outlines that in the future, organizational diagnosis through organizational climate will fall into two broad spectrums – of increasing the accuracy and reliability of the climate measurement and maximizing the benefits from behavioural science inputs.

- JGJ, TVRLS

Critical Words: Organizational Diagnosis, Organizational Climate

42. Screwvalla Zarire S., Human Resources Development at Standard Chartered Bank in: Nair M.R.R. (editor), Towards Organizational Effectiveness Through HRD, Unedited Papers presented at the 3rd National Conference of the National HRD Network, New Delhi, February 1989, Published by National HRD Network, Jamshedpur, pages 565–589

The author documents the process of change that Standard Chartered Bank went through in India. The company found that the degree of success of actions initiated in various areas was decreasing as days passed by. To get over this, the company adopted a multi-pronged strategy for a number of areas to be acted upon simultaneously. Efforts were primarily made in the areas of role clarity, goal direction of function, manpower development, need oriented approach to training and an emphasis on communications improvement. Specific interventions were made in the areas of career planning, job rotation and counselling skills. The author concludes by stating that constantly changing circumstances are an occupational hazard in any industry and therefore the ability to identify corrective measures and implement them are prerequisites in the management of managerial excellence.

- JGJ, TVRLS

Critical Words: HRD Interventions, Standard Chartered bank

43. Khandelwal Anil K., HRD in Banks – Some Critical Issues in: Nair M.R.R. (editor), Towards Organizational Effectiveness Through HRD, Unedited Papers presented at the 3rd National Conference of the National HRD Network, New Delhi, February 1989, Published by National HRD Network, Jamshedpur, pages 590–612

The article raises some critical issues related to the Banking Industry. The article is divided into four parts. The first part defines the context of HRD in the industry. In the second part, the author has presented case studies of four major banks with special focus on the impediments faced by them in the implementation of the HRD systems in the respective organization. The third part focuses on the limitations of the present efforts and the last part deals with the problems in the designing and implementing HRD and the possible action mechanisms to get over the problems. The observations made in the paper are based on the interaction of the author with professional bankers and employees with substantial experience. In the concluding remarks, the author stresses that for effective HRD implementation, interventions are required at the board and top level management, government level and at the level of the trade unions. There is also a need to develop an industry level forum where these issues may be discussed with the involvement of the trade unions.

- JGJ, TVRLS

Critical Words: Trade Unions, Banking Sector, Bank of Baroda, Canara Bank, State Bank of India, State Bank of Hyderabad

44. Gandidoss, Guntipilli Francis, Rosario Rupert & Vadudevan A.S., HRD Experiments in Aneka; : Case Study in Rural Development in: Nair M.R.R. (editor), Towards Organizational Effectiveness Through HRD, Unedited Papers presented at the 3rd National Conference of the National HRD Network, New Delhi, February 1989, Published by National HRD Network, Jamshedpur, pages 613–626

This article makes an attempt to describe the process of application of HRD in human service organizations and its resultant effect on work, personnel and the organizations involved. Though the concepts of Process Development or internal resources development is not new, the application of these concepts in the give context have not been attempted or measured. The authors state the classical hierarchical model did not work well leading to slower decision making, lack of role clarity, functional misdirection and improper deployment of skill and expertise. Therefore, a team model of implementation was proposed and implemented. In the concluding remarks, the authors point out that there is enough scope for development of the HRD function at the government level and in the sector of social organizations.

- JGJ, TVRLS

Critical Words: Social Organizations, Anekal, Process Designers

Excellence Through HRD

Abstracts of Papers from the book

Nair, M. R. R and Rao, T. V. (editors), Excellence Through Human Resource Development: Improving Productivity And Competitiveness, NHRDN, 1990 Conference papers for the National HRD network Symposium Madras, February, 1990, Published by Tata McGraw-Hill, new Delhi

(Reference: Nair and Rao, 1990)

1. Krishnamurthy, V; Towards Excellence in Productivity through HRD, in: Nair, M. R. R and Rao, T. V. (editors), Excellence Through Human Resource Development: Improving Productivity And Competitiveness, NHRDN, 1990 Conference papers for the National HRD network Symposium Madras, February, 1990, Published by Tata McGraw-Hill, new Delhi; pages 3–15.
   In this article, the author presents his experiences and insights from BHEL, Maruthi, SAIL, TISCO and Japanese organizations to support his conviction that productivity can be achieved mainly through people. The author conveys through this article that HRD is integrated into every aspect of Organizational life. Maruti promoted HRD by minimizing employee distinctions, focusing on their development and creating a family culture through communications and teamwork. SAIL turn around was achieved through priorities for action. The

article concludes that the HRD manager's commitment to the philosophy of HRD is imperative to the success of HRD.

Key words: HRD Manager; SAIL; Maruti; TISCO; Japanese management; Future of HRD Excellence in HRD

2. Krishna S.; HRD Issues/Opportunities-Top Management's Views, in: Excellence Through Human Resource Development: Improving Productivity and Competitiveness, NHRDN, Conference papers for National HRD Network Symposium Madras, February, 1990, Published by Tata McGraw-Hill, New Delhi; pages 16–24.

   It is tempting to look for a ready-made way of organizing and structuring the HRD system in organizations. We can draw examples from some industrial successes of some of the advanced countries like Japan which has built a formidable economic strength by emphasizing on shared values, collective achievement and continuous development of human resources. But it is important to realize that these strategies have been successful since they were structured so as to suit their society and not by simply implanting them in entirety. If we adopt a strategy we need to ensure that it is modified to match the Indian society. We need to rediscover the unique Indian forms of "Man-Management" as they could easily offer a more enduring base because they are indigenous. It is the human resource that holds the key to sustained profitability and growth.

   Key words: Man-Management techniques, HRD Issues/ Opportunities in view of Top Management

3. Nohria K.K.; Expectations of a Chief Executive from HRD, in: Excellence Through Human Resource Development: Improving Productivity and Competitiveness, NHRDN, Conference papers for National HRD Network Symposium Madras, February, 1990, Published by Tata McGraw-Hill, New Delhi; pages 25–30.

   To be an effective HRD one must be evolutionary in approach, is a catalyst for change, must have ability to honor a human being and trust their capabilities and have reflective insights. While being a primary facilitator an HRD can make direct contribution in the transformational process of an organization. HRD must be efficient at anticipating changes and readying the organization to respond appropriately for continued competitiveness. HRD can create the right environment through ensuring role clarity, goal orientation, effective appraisal, development etc of employees; developing organizational leaders, ensuring the enhancement of synergy through team development etc, being creative. HRD needs to work closely with the chief executives to influence the value systems of an organization and thus must develop organizational values such as openness, trust, expert-based-power, autonomy, justice, truthfulness, etc. HRD is an initiative based role.

4. Athreya M.B.; Line Manager Expectations from HRD on Productivity and Competitiveness, in: Excellence Through Human Resource Development: Improving Productivity and Competitiveness, NHRDN, Conference papers for National HRD Network Symposium Madras, February, 1990, Published by Tata McGraw-Hill, New Delhi; pages 33–52.

   HRD professional should raise managerial competence, strengthening managerial system discipline, deepening worker involvement and earning union partnership. Training and other HRD interventions, improve the knowledge, attitude and skills of maintenance labour, so as to increase both equipment availability, equipment reliability and capability for a sustained rate of output. Managerial interests in competitiveness has increased in two stages like defensive interests (to ensure survival in a growing competitive environment) and positive interest (to exploit opportunities that deregulation, autonomy and competition provide). HRD can respond to both these interests. There are several dimensions in competitiveness namely Quality, cost effectiveness, speed and innovation. HRD inputs are needed on Framework (which gives different time span, different function and different levels), Skills (providing initial inputs and updating managerial skills for planning, implementation and control), Appraisal and Rotation.

   Key Words: HRD Action, Cost Effectiveness, Managerial Productivity, Capital Productivity, Cost Benefit Management Skills.

5. Ramaswamy. E. A; HRD Viewed from the Other End, in: Excellence Through Human Resource Development: Improving Productivity and Competitiveness, NHRDN, Conference papers for National HRD Network Symposium Madras, February, 1990, Published by Tata McGraw-Hill, New Delhi; pages 53–59.

Managers would hasten to add the problem with permanent labour is not just its cost but also its attitude. *Speaking more objectively much is happening to lend weight to labours appreciation. No impartial observer can fail to notice the all-out effort being made by industry to reduce the labour force. It is more important task is to ensure that managers from line functions take greater responsibility for the management of the human resources from day to day.*
Key Words: Permanent Labour, Cost of labour, HRD Functions, Management Levels

6. Nair M.R.R; Dynamics of HRD Process and Role of HRD Manager, in: Excellence Through Human Resource Development: Improving Productivity and Competitiveness, NHRDN, Conference papers for National HRD Network Symposium Madras, February, 1990, Published by Tata McGraw-Hill, New Delhi; pages 63–79.
HRD has a significant role to play in establishing and maintaining a healthy productive work culture. Good Industrial Relations and effective systems of participation and a good collective bargaining framework is key to success of all HRD activities. In the organization contest, HRD is a means for improving effectiveness (in terms of better productivity, reduction if costs, better generation of internal resources, better profits and better customer service) and not an end in itself. Communication is the key to ensure the involvement of the employees. Generally organizations suffer from two weaknesses (A) Weakness in correctly identifying the problem. Once the problems are correctly identified, solutions are relatively easier to find. The problems in most cases are within the organization, but people tend that all is well with them. (B) There is considerable gap between generation of ideas and their implementation. Weakness of Indian Organizations is we tend to draw up action plans which look good but lag behind in their implementation. Training should be derived from the company's objective. It should be need based, line-led. Training and Development should be staffed with right kind of people. There is a need to ensure a judicious use of internal and external training programmes.
Key words: Involvement, Team Building, Organization Effectiveness, Commitment, Moral Competence, Productivity

7. Rao T.V.; HRD Manager and their Role, in: Excellence Through Human Resource Development: Improving Productivity and Competitiveness, NHRDN, Conference papers for National HRD Network Symposium Madras, February, 1990, Published by Tata McGraw-Hill, New Delhi; pages 80–89.
   Most frequently used HRD Instruments are Role Analysis, Performance Planning, Performance Analysis and review, Performance Counselling, Induction Training, Training, Job Rotation, Quality Circles, Task Forces, Managerial Learning Networks, etc. HRD Department and their Tasks are Developing A human resources, Keep Inspiring the Line Manager, Contently Plan, be aware of the business, work with unions, Influence personal policies. HRD Department has high inter-dependencies with the Personal Department. Personal Policies affect to a great extent the motivation and development of the employees as well as organizational health.
   Key Words: Spiritual Development, Power Trap, Empire Building Trap, Insulation Trap, O&M Department
8. Ramanujam G.; The Role of HRD Manager, in: Excellence Through Human Resource Development: Improving Productivity and Competitiveness, NHRDN, Conference papers for National HRD Network Symposium Madras, February, 1990, Published by Tata McGraw-Hill, New Delhi; pages 90–95.
   HRD will have to be individualized, personalized and humanized. Each employee, whether blue or white collared is a world by himself. He has his own particulars and prejudices too. He has already developed certain attitudes towards discipline, towards productivity, quality and generally towards his work. HRD manager must respect the human personality of the employees at all levels. Nature of the worker is to resist change.
   Key Words: Labour, Dis-Employment, Labour Welfare Officer, Personal Officer, Personal Department, Natural Justice
9. Gupta R.; Agenda for Professional Development, in: Excellence Through Human Resource Development: Improving Productivity and Competitiveness, NHRDN, Conference papers for National HRD Network Symposium Madras, February, 1990, Published by Tata McGraw-Hill, New Delhi; pages 99–107.

Some of the areas where there is an even lesser competence available in HRD function are Designing of reward systems for HRD, Potential appraisal, career planning and development systems, OD and Development Process.

Key Words: Role Analysis, Reward Management, Comprehensive educational programme, Self-Directed development, Learning Projects

10. Pareek U.; The Making of HRD Facilitator, in: Excellence Through Human Resource Development: Improving Productivity and Competitiveness, NHRDN, Conference papers for National HRD Network Symposium Madras, February, 1990, Published by Tata McGraw-Hill, New Delhi; pages 108–115.

    Development of concern for excellence and self –actualisation would contribute to the development of individual identity. Career planning and succession planning helps the process of identity formation. An organization gets its identity by developing a distinct culture value and norms (including rituals) leading to traditions by which the organization is known. HRD manager Collaborates with other managers to develop common understanding of the mission in the organization. Competencies can be developed by helping experience the value process.

    Key Words: Competency, Structural Arrangement, Training, HRD Facilitator, HRD Process

11. Dayal I.; Designing an HRD Programme, in: Excellence Through Human Resource Development: Improving Productivity and Competitiveness, NHRDN, Conference papers for National HRD Network Symposium Madras, February, 1990, Published by Tata McGraw-Hill, New Delhi; pages 116–125.

    Some basic considerations required to design and operate an HRD programmer are Learning Process, Cultural Factors, Managerial Orientation, and Administrative Strategy. Consideration for growth and development requires an individual must be involved personally in the process of development and know what new learning could lead to his growth, the organization would have to provide a variety of experiences to an individuals to learn from these experiences. Experience is also important for an individual to learn values, attitude, meaning of work. In the social environment of many Indian organizations, the concept of growth assumes by presenting a role modal the supervisor officer expects his subordinates to become like himself and by constant inducement and direction the supervisor officer expects his subordinate to become an ideal person, as per his modal.

Key words: Administrative Strategy, Rational Factors, Psychological Growth, Managerial values, Review Systems

12. Kumar. P. M; HRD Transitions: An Experiential Snapshot, in: Excellence Through Human Resource Development: Improving Productivity and Competitiveness, NHRDN, Conference papers for National HRD Network Symposium Madras, February, 1990, Published by Tata McGraw-Hill, New Delhi; pages 126–136.

    Enlightened self-interest has pushed senior management to take HRD seriously in the face of social, Psychological and cultural changes in the society. Management education has played a critical role in underlining the potentials and possibilities of HRD. HRD does not fail because of lack of top or line management support only- more organizations are into HRD because senior executives support who is willing to persist with in the senior line executive who may prefer to concentrate on the "expedient" rather than the "important process issues.

    Key Words: Self-Doubt, HRD Manager, Line Manager, Hierarchical Authority

13. Mahesh. V.S; India in the 90's: A Great Opportunity and Challenge for Human Resource Management Professional, in: Excellence Through Human Resource Development: Improving Productivity and Competitiveness, NHRDN, Conference papers for National HRD Network Symposium Madras, February, 1990, Published by Tata McGraw-Hill, New Delhi; pages 137–147.

    Over the past decade, a few chief executives have rightly begun to place a greater emphasis on the proactive, development aspects of HRM. Unfortunately, many organizations have suffered due to the inadequacy of our fellow professionals some have lost their credibility due to mistaken attachments to specific tools and approaches such as Sensitive training, T.A., Gestalt therapy etc. Majority of jobs being created in India and elsewhere are in the front-line of service Industry, calling for a major exercise of empowerment of the lowest echelons of organizational hierarchies. To balance worker- representatives on the

Board of Directors, the HRM professionals are going to be invited to join the Board: Wrong reason but right Opportunity. Accelerating rates of changes and obsolescence have led to organizations viewing themselves as learning Communities, Agents, the HRM professional's role is paramount.

Key Words: Flexitime, Physical Decentralization, HRM professional, HRM Practices

History of HRD:
Select Photos of Early Years

T. V. Rao Learning Systems Private Limited
Talent Management and Organization Development

Center for HRD at XLRI

Birth of NHRDN

Birth of NHRDN

Founding Trustees of NHRDN

First AHRD-XLRI Fellow Program at IIMA Campus

NHRDN and AHRD

NHRDN First Conferences

Conferences at Delhi and Bangalore NHRDN